CURIOUS
SCOTLAND

CURIOUS
SCOTLAND

TALES FROM A HIDDEN
HISTORY

GEORGE ROSIE

THOMAS DUNNE BOOKS / ST. MARTIN'S PRESS

NEW YORK

THOMAS DUNNE BOOKS.
An imprint of St. Martin's Press.

Photographs are reprinted with kind permission of the following: Mary Evans
Picture Library, Hulton Archive/Getty Images, Topham Picturepoint, British
Film Institute, *The Herald* and *Evening Times* Picture Archive.

www.thomasdunnebooks.com

www.stmartins.com

Library of Congress Cataloging-in-Publication Data

Rosie, George.
    Curious Scotland : tales from a hidden history / George Rosie.—1st ed.
        p. cm.
    Originally published: London : Granta Books, c2004.
    ISBN-13: 978-0-312-35416-9
    ISBN-10: 0-312-35416-9
    1. Scotland—History. 2. Scotland—Social life and customes. I. Title.

DA760.R67 2006
941.1—dc22

                                                            2006040194

First published in Great Britain by Granta Books

First U.S. Edition: August 2006

10 9 8 7 6 5 4 3 2 1

For James

CONTENTS

CONTENTS

ACKNOWLEDGEMENTS

THIS BOOK IS THE RESULT of years of sporadic research and fact-gathering. It's a process that has owed much to the assistance, advice and encouragement of people all over Britain, Europe and the USA. Some of them are friends and colleagues with whom I have worked closely: others are strangers whose names I never knew but who went out of their way to satisfy my curiosity.

Thanks first of all to Ian Jack, editor of Granta, who had the idea of collecting my various stories into a book and then deciding to publish them. Also to my agent David Godwin, who was as encouraging as ever. As many of these stories have spun off, as they say, from television work I'm grateful to various colleagues in the industry: Alistair Moffat, Les Wilson, Seona Robertson, Ross Wilson, Rhoda Macdonald, Sandy Ross and Agnes Wilkie.

And, of course, to the staff of any number of museums, libraries, art collections, churches, cathedrals and cultural centres. In particular I would like to thank the curators and officials at the Cherokee Nation in Tahlequah, Oklahoma and their counterparts at the Cherokee Nation East in Cherokee, North Carolina. I was particularly grateful to the insights of Bruce Ross and John Ross, then Chief of the United Keetoowah Band of the Cherokee. For light on the state of pre-Gaelic Scotland I owe a lot to that accomplished Welsh historian John Davies.

Every writer of history owes a substantial debt to record keepers and librarians. So my thanks to the staffs of Britain's national archives at Kew in London and at Charlotte Square in Edinburgh. And to librarians in New York, Tulsa, Chattanooga, Washington, Cheltenham, and Cardiff. In particular, I'd like to thank the endlessly helpful men and women of the British Library in London and the National Library of Scotland in Edinburgh.

Finally, and as usual, a large thank you to my wife Liz for putting up with the writing of yet another book.

George Rosie
Edinburgh
February 2004

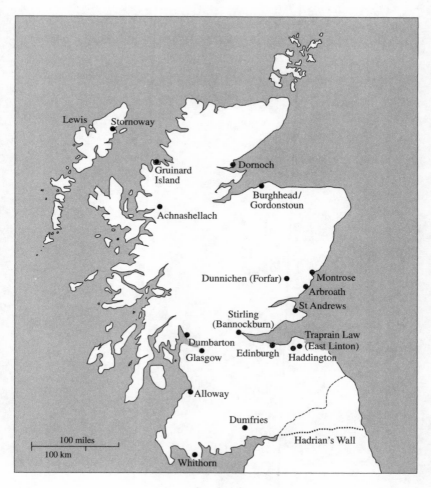

Scotland

CURIOUS
SCOTLAND

George Rosie, aged nine

INTRODUCTION

THERE ARE TWO SMALL black and white photographs in the family archive that I particularly cherish. Both were taken around 1950, at sea aboard an Edinburgh trawler somewhere in the North Atlantic west of Shetland. One of them shows me as a grubby nine-year-old with sticking-out ears, dressed in a dirty white polo-neck jersey, dark shorts, and wellington boots with the tops turned down. I am sitting on a pile of rope and canvas and grinning through one of the ship's lifebelts, which bears the legend *Eileen Paton Glasgow*. In the other I am standing in a 'pond' on the trawler's deck with another boy, the skipper's son, Billy Alexander. We are both holding up big, diamond-shaped flatfish by their tails. Judging from the size they must be halibut. I am grinning like mad, delighted with the trawler's catch.

These little snaps are mementoes of an episode that, I suppose, had a curious significance for me. To claim that it was some kind of watershed might be too much. But the three weeks that I spent aboard that trawler make up my most vivid childhood memories. In retrospect they seemed to set in motion a train of thought, a restless, sometimes unfocused curiosity and a way of seeing things that has remained with me ever since.

The routine aboard the *Eileen Paton* was simple, but relentless. The nets went down for two or three hours and then were brought to the surface for the catch to be gutted, boxed, iced and stored in the ship's hold. In between shooting the nets the crew tried to snatch a couple of hours' sleep, unless they were on watch in the wheelhouse. It was a routine that went on twenty-four hours a day every day for the two or three weeks when the ship was fishing.

At night the men worked under arc lights, their yellow oilskins gleaming in the brightness. Their bloodied fingers flew as they slit open the bellies of the fish with their wooden-handled gutting knives. At the end of the carnage – which usually took about an hour – the mess of fish entrails was hosed off the deck into the scuppers and over the side.

I can still recall that startling moment when one of the deckhands would cut open the 'cod end' of the net and a silver mountain of fish would collapse and slither and thrash onto the deck. Most of the catch was what we were hunting for: cod, haddock, whiting, ling, hake. There were also prized flatfish such as lemon sole, halibut, flounder and skate, all of which could fetch good prices in the market. These fish were our reason to be out there.

But among the catch were also grotesques, odd creatures plucked from the deep water. They fascinated me. There were monkfish and angler-fish, all heads and gaping jaws. There were squid and cuttlefish that could – and often did – squirt ink at us in their death throes. There were pinkish octopuses that seemed able to live out of water longer than other sea creatures and which, according to the crew, had been known to walk up the ship's funnel. I tried to encourage one on such a venture but it refused and died at my feet. There were the iron-jawed monsters which in Scotland are known as catfish and which elsewhere are wolf-fish.

One of the deckhands, a little dark man nicknamed Piebald, took me under his wing. Maybe he had been instructed by the skipper to make sure that I came to no harm. Maybe the novelty of having a curious nine-year-old aboard appealed to him. Maybe he just liked me. And just as the skipper enjoyed explaining to me the workings of the radar, the log-line, the radio-telephone and the rest of the trawler's equipment, so Piebald took pleasure in introducing me to the mysteries of the catch and the creatures that came up every two or three hours from the seabed.

Fishermen are cruel and Piebald was no exception. The idea that fish are sentient creatures capable of suffering never entered his mind. They were a commodity to be iced and stored or dumped over the side. But Piebald did seem to know the peculiarities of the various species in a way that the other men did not. He took it on himself to instruct me in which fish were the biters and which had enough poison in their fins to make a man's hand balloon. 'And that might see off a wee fellae like yersel' . . .' were his words. 'And then what wid the skipper say?'

I remember him flipping a big skate onto its back and with his gutting knife slicing open its chest to reveal its beating heart. I watched as he made another small cut and grinned as the fish's heart, still pumping vigorously, spurted blood in his face. It was callous but it was interesting. When the cook asked him to kill a big conger eel, Piebald clubbed the thrashing beast to death, all the time marvelling at how long the eel took to die. He liked to drag dogfish out of the 'ponds', heave them over the side, and watch them as they recovered their wits on the surface before slowly circling down into the dark.

The sea beast that intrigued me more than any other was the angler-fish. Whenever the net was opened I would scan the heaps of fish to see whether there were any anglers among them. About two feet long and brownish-grey in colour, the angler-fish bristled with spines. It was mostly head with a gaping mouth that revealed rows of teeth curving inward like so many scimitars. Between its eyes grew a long spine tipped with a luminescent chemical that glowed in the dark and attracted other creatures into that fearsome mouth. Piebald told me that he had once slit open the belly of a big angler that contained a sizeable lobster, still mostly intact.

'Ugly bugger, isn't it?' I remember Piebald saying when he found me staring down at an angler. 'Even worse looking than mah wife, and that's sayin' something. An' wi' a mooth that's just aboot as big.' And he stuck the toe of his seaboot into the creature's open mouth to see if it would react. It did. The jaws snapped and the curved teeth sank into the heavy rubber. Extracting the boot from the angler's jaws cost Piebald a bloody finger.

The angler seemed to have its own way of dying. While the other fish heaved and thrashed the angler just seemed to lie there, with only an occasional twitch of its paddle-shaped pectoral fins or its short tail. The eyes on the top of the beast's head seemed to glare defiance. Which was nonsense, of course. Like all the other fish on the trawler's deck, the creature was suffocating to death. And pointlessly too, because it would eventually be dumped overboard. But I was too fearful of those needle-sharp teeth to risk grabbing it by the tail and throwing it over the side while there was still life in that strange body.

I have many memories of that summer voyage. One in particular can still raise the hairs on the back of my neck. It was a flat-calm evening, the sea was like glass, and both sea and sky were a peculiar shade of green. The sun had almost set and was low in a cloudless sky. I was in the wheelhouse sipping cocoa with the skipper who was explaining the meaning of the ink traces produced by the trawler's echo sounder. Suddenly the little ship gave a curious shudder, quite a strong one.

'Whales,' Frank said with a smile, seeing my alarm. 'They're rubbing themselves against the keel. I think they do that to rub the barnacles off their backs. They'll jump now. Watch.'

Seconds after he spoke two black and white killer whales leapt out of the water off the starboard side, hung in the air for a second or two, then collapsed back into the sea in a huge explosion of water. Then there was another shudder and this time the beasts emerged on the port side to soar into the air and fall back with another mighty splash. For the next ten minutes or so they continued diving under the ship, scraping themselves along the keel and then surfacing to leap before going back into the sea in clouds of spray.

I was beside myself with excitement. I rushed from one side of the wheelhouse to the other to keep track of the great creatures. I thought then – and I still think – that those leaping whales were among the most beautiful things I have ever seen. And I remember the strange sense of loss I felt when they disappeared into the sea. That night in my bunk in the skipper's cabin I could hardly sleep. In my mind's eye I kept seeing these great black and white creatures rising out of the green sea in a torrent of white water, and then turning in the sunset.

One way or another it was a remarkable experience for a nine-year-old boy, and well worth the initial two or three days of seasickness. I don't think anything in my childhood was quite so vivid as those summer weeks aboard a Granton trawler. Certainly, nothing had made me so curious. When the long summer holidays were over and I returned to my primary school in what was then the fishing village of Newhaven I began to quiz my teacher about obscure sea beasts. She had no idea what I was talking about but she did point me in the direction of the public library along the shore in Leith.

The custodians of the children's section steered me into the reference library with a warning to 'mind and behave'. The lady there refused to believe that I'd seen such fish on a trawler. 'You shouldn't fib,' I remember her telling me. 'Boys your age are not allowed on the trawlers. It's illegal.' (She was quite right. It *was* illegal.)

Still, she found me a big old book about sea fishes, illustrated not with photographs but with engravings. She also gave me a pencil and paper so that I could copy them. To my amazement, they were all there, my acquaintances from the deck of the *Eileen Paton*: the dogfish, the octopus, the cuttlefish, the John Dorys, the conger eels, the rays, the monkfish, the wolf-fish. In the book they were not thrashing about in their death throes, but darting across the seabed, or lurking in seaweed, or coiling in their rocky dens, or swimming in vast shoals. There was a fine drawing of an angler-fish. It was doing exactly what Piebald had told me it did. It was lying on the seabed, its jaws gaping, its curved teeth glistening, its luminous 'rod' glowing as a couple of small fish swam unsuspecting towards their doom. From the text I learned that only the female angler was equipped with the luminous fishing rod, and that in some varieties the males are only one-tenth the size of the female and latch onto her like parasites.

For a few months I became an amateur icthyologist. Having discovered this mine of information about sea creatures, I plundered it relentlessly. I enjoyed putting together what I'd seen on the trawler with what I'd learned in the library and then passing it on to my friends. I remember sitting in a storm drain that emptied onto the grubby stretch of north Edinburgh foreshore that was a favourite playground and regaling two of my classmates with tales from the deck of the *Eileen Paton*. No doubt I exaggerated, particularly when describing the size and ferocity of the angler-fish.

What fixed the experience in my mind was reading about what I'd seen. I can hear the acoustics in that library almost as vividly as I can see the leaping whales. My memory of that engraving of the angler-fish is as acute as my recollection of the real animal dying on the deck of the *Eileen Paton*. Connecting what I saw and heard with knowledge of the experience filled me with real satisfaction. The one seemed to validate the other.

I'd like to say that I never lost the library-going habit, but I did. My enthusiasm for acquiring knowledge soon passed. For years I never set foot in a library unless I absolutely had to. Edinburgh had too many other attractions. Most of my spare time was spent in the city's billiard halls, cinemas, dance halls, jazz clubs, pubs, concert halls, and football grounds. But every now and again I would see something or hear something that would engage my imagination or my curiosity, and I would be off, rummaging around in the book stacks.

Finding out: in adulthood it became my main urge and suited me to a working life as a reporter and writer. I am not a professional historian. Professional historians build their reputations by scraping away layers of confusion, reportage, myth and error until they have arrived at some kind of truth, however approximate. Journalists are different. Journalists are gadflies. They hop from one tasty episode to another. Quite often we become genuine experts on a subject for a week or two – and then forget most of it when we move on to another story.

This, then, is a book of random histories: an autodidact's anthology of neglected episodes in Scottish history, episodes that sometimes happened in places beyond Scotland. Many of them – maybe even most – are stories that I have stumbled across by chance. Many are the result of late-night conversations with press and television colleagues, a surprising number of whom share my enthusiasm for the obscure and forgotten. Some are the result of encounters in pubs, motorway cafés or airport lounges. A few come from the footnotes in other people's books. At least one emerged from a snatch of conversation overheard on the train between Edinburgh and Glasgow.

They have been assembled over a number of years. One or two appeared in programmes made for Channel Four and Scottish Television, particularly in two series called *Secret Scotland*. Several of them emerged from the Public Record Office in Kew, or the Scottish Record Office in Edinburgh, and then never found their way onto the screen. Television has its drawbacks and unless it can find interesting locations and/or decent 'talking heads' to tell the story, that story tends not to be told. Documents alone are never enough.

Television also has its advantages – budgets big enough to pay for travel and research. It can buy time, airline tickets and hotel rooms.

Some of these stories have taken me into corners of the world that I never thought to see. My fascination with the life of John Ross, the son of immigrant Scots and the man who led the Cherokee Nation at its most crucial time, took me to Georgia, Tennessee, the Smoky Mountains of North Carolina, and eventually to Oklahoma, where most Cherokees now live. There, in the strange little city called Tahlequah, I met Ross's descendants, who looked no more Cherokee than I did.

My pursuit of the *Gwyr Y Gogledd*, the 'Men of the North' of Welsh-speaking Scotland, had me examining stained glass in Glasgow Cathedral one day and then scrambling up to ancient hill forts or into lochside *crannogs* the next. Tracking down the sons of Robert Burns found me rummaging through the archives of the Honourable East India Company in the British Library in London, and then wandering around the Regency terraces of Cheltenham. The bizarre wartime tale of 'Operation Vegetarian' – Britain's plan to destroy the German cattle herds with anthrax – stretches from Porton Down in Wiltshire to the notorious 'plague island' of Gruinard in Wester Ross.

Places loom large in these accounts. I was an unexceptional pupil at my Edinburgh secondary school but I had a brilliant if eccentric history teacher named John Scott-Allan who did what he could to encourage me. I still remember one of his homilies: 'All history happens *somewhere*. Decisions were made, things happened. That place is usually still interesting. Sometimes it is important.'

There was a time when the history of my country was understood – at least at school and popularly – in simpler ways. The Battle of Bannockburn (1314); the Union of the Crowns (1603) and of Parliaments (1707); Bonnie Prince Charlie (the 1745 rebellion); lists of the great Scottish inventors (James Watt to John Logie Baird); and then it became subsumed into the more general flow of British (which was usually English) history. Today our understanding is – or should be – more sophisticated. Scotland may be a small country but it has a complex story. I taught myself this, serendipitously and unsentimentally. In that sense this book is the story of my enlightenment, written on no greater principle than the one that says, 'Really? How interesting! I never knew.'

George Rosie
Edinburgh, 2004

KING ARTHUR'S
SCOTLAND

EVERY NOW AND AGAIN I LIKE to drive down from my home in Edinburgh to East Lothian, and there scramble my way to the top of the whaleback hill known as Traprain Law. As Scottish hills go it is not very high, about 650 feet. But there is enough sheer rock on the south side to offer local enthusiasts some decent rock climbing, and on a clear day the views from the top are stunning: to the north the Bass Rock and the coastline of Fife; to the east the coastal town of Dunbar and the North Sea; to the south the undulations of the heather-clad Lammermuir Hills; to the west the city of Edinburgh. Traprain Law is one of the joys of south-east Scotland.

What fascinates me about Traprain is that 1,400 years ago a vigorous little city was perched on the few acres of its summit plateau. If evidence from similar sites is anything to go by, the Traprain community comprised clusters of round timber houses probably grouped around a big council hall. There may also have been some kind of rudimentary royal residence for whichever kinglet ruled the tribe at the time. One of them may have been Lot, the man who gave his name to the surrounding countryside – Lothian. At the foot of the hill the people would have grown their wheat and barley, tended their flocks of sheep and goats, raised their cattle.

Traprain Law's strategic value is plain for anyone to see. From its summit no hostile force of any size would have been able to get close without being spotted. Enemy vessels would have been seen far out to sea unless the haar (cold sea-fog) from the North Sea was heavy. The steep flanks of the hill are eminently defensible. A freshwater spring on the hilltop would have made a long siege bearable. Archaeologists digging on the hill in 1919 uncovered a hoard of more than twenty kilos of Roman silver: cups, plates, spoons, dishes, brooches, belt buckles, earrings, wine cups, flagons, ladles, coins. Most of it can be seen at the Museum of Scotland in Edinburgh. There are two explanations for this hoard. One is that it was plundered from the Romans or the Romanized Britons who lived south of Hadrian's Wall. The other is that the silver was a bribe, paid to stop these northern folk harassing the peaceable citizens of Roman Britain on the other side of the wall. Most archaeologists and historians favour the bribe theory. But if the Roman authorities were prepared to pay such a high price then the folk from Traprain must have been a formidable enemy.

They were, of course, Celts. But they were not Gaels. It was not Gaelic that was spoken on Traprain but a northern dialect of Brythonic, the language that evolved into Welsh. Traprain Law was one of the strongholds of the Celtic people whom the Romans knew as the Votadinni, and who knew themselves as the Gododdin. Gododdin was one of three kingdoms of the Britons that dominated what are now southern Scotland and northern England. They were: Gododdin in the south-east; Rheged in the south-west, based on Carlisle; Strathclyde (or Strath Clutha) which stretched into the Central Highlands as far as Crianlarich. The people who inhabited them were known to their fellow Britons as *Gwyr Y Gogledd*, the Men of the North.

There is a decent chance that the legendary Arthur was an Edinburgh man. Because Din Eidyn – to give Edinburgh its Brythonic name – was the capital of the Gododdin. And the very first mention of Arthur is contained in the seventh-century epic poem *Y Gododdin*, which is written in archaic Welsh. Camelot may well have perched on the same volcanic rock as Edinburgh Castle. Arthur may have been king of the Gododdin and high king of the northern kingdoms. Certainly a number of modern scholars and writers are convinced that Arthur (and his druid Merlin or Myrddin) were legends of the Celtic north imported into Wales and Cornwall at a much later date, and from there hijacked by the Norman French.

Writing about the North Britons is rather like pursuing Arthur himself. So much of their story is, as the popular Americanism goes, 'smoke and mirrors'. Written archives are scarce. Literacy was minimal. The Christian church was in its infancy. The archaeological record is incomplete. Hugely important sites – such as the old Roxburgh Castle near Selkirk – have never been excavated. The histories that do exist have been assembled from scattered fragments. Fantasies, legends and myths abound. As a result, all writing about the Britons of the north is peppered with qualifying words such as 'seems', 'perhaps', 'likely' and 'probable'. This writing will be no exception, but for all that it is hard to understand why the Welsh-speaking kingdoms of southern Scotland have been so overlooked. They were crucial to the formation of Scotland. They dominated the area north of Hadrian's Wall for more than a thousand years. Without the stubborn resistance of the *Gwyr Y Gogledd*, the Men of the North, it seems likely that southern Scotland would have become part of the Anglian kingdom of Northumbria and would eventually have been absorbed into England. But somehow the Gododdin and the other Britons of the north have been written out of Scottish history.

I suppose the history of Celtic Scotland has been hijacked by the Gaels. Modern Scotland took its name from the Gaels of Ireland, the people whom the Romans knew as the Scotti. Gaelic is spoken of as Scotland's 'original' language, something that I find irritating. The Gaels were, in fact, relative latecomers. They began to appear in Scotland in the fifth century, around the same time as the Angles from what is now Denmark and northern Germany. But long before the Gaels set foot in the land north of the Roman walls, the land had been occupied by Brythonic-speaking Celts from the European mainland. And an early version of the language we now know as Welsh was spoken all the way from the Orkneys down to Cornwall.

The two Celtic languages are related but distinct. The Gaelic now spoken in parts of Ireland, Scotland and (until recently) the Isle of Man contains no letter P. The Welsh spoken in Wales, Cornwall and Brittany contains no letter Q. So to linguists Gaelic is known as 'Q-Celtic' and Welsh as 'P-Celtic'. To the Romans the P-Celtic British tribes between Hadrian's Wall and the Antonine Wall (which stretched from the Clyde to the Forth) were known as the Votadini, the Damnonii, the Selgovae and the Novantae. The people north of the Antonine Wall were the Picts, which is possibly a Roman nickname meaning 'painted people'. The Gaels knew the Picts as 'Cruithne'.

But traces of Welsh-speaking Scotland are not hard to find. The southern parts of the country are littered with place names that sound familiar to Welsh ears. They mark out those parts of Scotland that were once the kingdoms of Gododdin, Rheged, Strathclyde, and, to a lesser extent, Pictland. The prefix 'aber', for example, which is the Welsh word for 'mouth of a river', is extremely common in Scotland: Aberlady, Aberfeldy, Abernyte, Abernethy are a few examples. Also common is the prefix Penn, meaning 'head': Pennygant, Pencaitland, Penkill, Penicuik. Then there is the prefix 'caer', the Welsh word for 'hill' or 'fort', which gives us Caeralmond (Cramond), Caerfrae, Caerlaverock. The names Lanark, Lanrick and Lendrick are from the Old Welsh 'llanerch' meaning 'open space' or 'clearing'.

The Celtic society that developed in Scotland in the first five centuries AD seems to have been stable and relatively sophisticated. Its economy has been described as comprising 'mixed farming, cottage industries, some trading but no currency'. It supported metalworking smiths, potters, woodcarvers, carpenters, thatchers, stonemasons, wheelwrights and armourers. In the fertile valleys of southern Scotland and northern England, the Britons grew wheat, barley and vegetables and grazed their cattle, pigs and goats. The rolling, grass-covered hills like the Lammermuirs, Moorfoots and Cheviots were ideal country for sheep.

I find the artistic culture of the northern Britons harder to fathom. They do not seem to have lavished as much effort on, say, jewellery as did the Gaels. And their sculptures do not compare with the intricate crosses crafted by the Angles or the elaborately incised cross slabs of the Picts. There is a collection of North British sculptures in the parish church in Govan in Glasgow and they are poor things compared to the stonecraft of Pictland and Northumbria. But every culture has its different emphasis and it may be that of the North Britons was on music and storytelling. The epic poems of the P-Celtic bards Aneirin and Taliesin are among the earliest we have in any North European language. From their Latin neighbours (overlords?) the Men of the North acquired Roman military technology. Their weaponry was of a high quality: breastplates, helmets, and chain mail were common. They were skilled horsemen and (possibly) crossbowmen – the earliest form of crossbow dates from around 400 BC. They learned Roman combat discipline – how to fight in formation, form shield walls, withstand cavalry assaults, and make fighting retreats. Their warlord Arthur, the *dux bellorum* of the Britons, was probably skilled in the Roman arts of war. Certainly the *Gwyr Y Gogledd* enjoyed a large military reputation. Other Britons spoke of them with awe. In the year AD 450 or thereabouts, the Gododdin warlord Cunedda (Kenneth) was 'invited' to take his war bands down to what is now North Wales to clear out the Irish Gaels who were then settling in large numbers. Cunedda accepted the invitation to indulge in some 'ethnic cleansing'. From a hill fort at Castell Dyganwy near Lllandudno he rid north Wales of Irish settlers. It was done, say the chroniclers, 'with great slaughter'. Cunedda's offspring went on to found the kingdom of Gwynedd which at its peak covered almost a third of Wales.

The Britons of the north seem to have turned to Christianity remarkably early. According to the historian Gordon Donaldson this was crucial. 'Political institutions were then rudimentary,' he writes in *Scotland: Church and Nation*, 'and government a matter of strong kings and chiefs rather than of administrative machinery. The church, however, was an institution long before the state was and there are indications that the church made a real contribution to . . . the making of one kingdom out of those warring Angles, Britons, Picts and Scots . . .'

Donaldson has no doubt that it was the Britons who brought the church to what is now Scotland. According to him, 'It was in the Romano-British civilization of southern Scotland that Scottish Christianity began.' Out of that civilization emerged two religious figures who were to become renowned missionaries and, eventually, Christian saints – Ninian and Kentigern. The last-named is better known as Mungo, the patron saint of the city of Glasgow. Both are Britons, and both are crucial to the spread of Christianity in what is now Scotland.

Of the two, Ninian (whose real name seems to have been Uinniau) is the more important. His presence still haunts southern Scotland. A few years ago I walked the mile or two along the beach at Glasserton on the shore of Luce Bay, just a few miles from the town of Whithorn. Set back from the beach I found the niche in the rocks known as St Ninian's Cave. According to the legend this is where Ninian came to meditate. I am no Christian, but I found it moving that 1,600 years after Ninian died Christian folk are still making pilgrimages to his cave. They leave little tributes: a cross made out of twigs; another made of spears of grass; one scratched in a stone; another carved on the walls of the cave.

What do we know of Ninian? Not much for certain. He seems to have been born around the year AD 360, probably a son of the Rheged aristocracy. At the age of eighteen he made the journey to Rome, was received by Pope Damasus I, made a bishop, studied under Saint Jerome and Saint Martin, and in AD 392 was sent back to Britain to evangelize the Celts. The first biography of Ninian was written in 1165 by Aelred, abbot of Rievaulx in Yorkshire. Aelred's life of Ninian is short on fact but long on miracles. He describes the saint as a man '. . . sparing in food, reticent in speech, assiduous in study, agreeable in manner, averse from jesting; and in everything he subjected the flesh to the spirit'.

From his base at 'Candida Casa' (the White House) at Whithorn in Galloway, Ninian struggled to bring Christianity to the Britons and Picts of the north. He founded churches, abbeys, monasteries and nunneries all over southern Scotland. According to Aelred he also tried to Christianize the Picts of the north, travelling through Angus and Aberdeenshire as far north as the Cromarty Firth. Ninian died in AD 431, the same year that Patrick (another Briton) began his mission among the Gaels of Ireland.

For a thousand years the cult of Ninian thrived. The town of Whithorn became one of Europe's centres of pilgrimage. Ninian-worshippers from all over Britain and Ireland came to pray at or to the saint's relics. Worshipping at the Candida Casa became a political act. Nearly every Scots monarch made the journey down to Whithorn to make obeisance to the fifth-century saint from the kingdom of Rheged. James IV – probably the most successful and popular of the Stuart monarchs – was a particularly enthusiastic devotee of Ninian. Even after the Reformation of 1560, pilgrims continued to turn up at Whithorn until the Presbyterian authorities stepped in and in 1581 banned the practice as 'idolatrous'.

Even more fables surround that other pious Welsh-speaking Man of the North, Kentigern, better known by his nickname Mungo. The legend of Mungo takes us back to Traprain Law in East Lothian. According to the legend Kentigern/Mungo was the bastard son of a Gododdin princess called Thenan whose father ruled on Traprain Law. When she fell pregnant by a local shepherd her father condemned her to death. After she survived being thrown down the rocky side of Traprain she was cast adrift in a coracle in the Firth of Forth. But instead of drowning Thenan landed safely at Culross in Fife where Kentigern was born in the year AD 520. The infant was raised and educated by Saint Servanus (or Serf), a Briton working among the southern Picts.

When Kentigern was eventually ordained his mission was to spread the word among the people of Strathclyde. His first community was set up at the confluence of the rivers Clyde and Molendinar and was known as Glas Gu, the P-Celtic words for 'dear family'. (I have always thought this a more likely derivation of the name Glasgow rather than 'dear green place' in Gaelic.) The Molendinar has since been driven underground, but it still flows into the Clyde, a few hundred yards from the cathedral around which Glasgow was built. Kentigern's biographer (a twelfth-century monk called Jocelyne) claims that Kentigern quite quickly fell foul of Morken, King of Strathclyde and was forced to flee down into Wales where he came under the influence of Bishop (later Saint) David.

Jocelyne would have us believe that Kentigern deepened his faith by making no fewer than seven trips to Rome after which he was invited back to Strathclyde by the new king, Rhydderch Pen. The pious Rhydderch gave Kentigern *carte blanche* to spread the Christian gospel the length and breadth of Strathclyde. This Kentigern duly did, with the assistance of the 'Angel of the Lord' and a whole series of miracles.

Glasgow's 'salmon and ring' symbol – which can be seen all over the city on most pieces of council-owned wrought iron – is taken from another Kentigern legend. King Rhydderch had given his adulterous wife a valuable ring, which she had given to her lover. The king found it on the lover's hand, removed it when the man was sleeping, and pitched it into the River Clyde where it was swallowed by a salmon. Rhydderch then challenged his wife to produce it. The distressed queen sought help from Kentigern who sent one of his monks to the river to start fishing. Miraculously the monk caught the very salmon that had swallowed the queen's ring, thus saving the woman's life. After her narrow escape the queen became distinctly more pious.

This strange and far from Christian fable is depicted in twentieth-century stained glass on three windows in the south wall of the choir of Glasgow Cathedral, while Kentigern himself is supposed to lie under an altar-like tomb in the crypt. The tomb is carefully spotlit and draped in elaborate cloth. I have seen people on their knees praying at it, though there is not the slightest evidence that Kentigern/Mungo's bones lie under the stone flags.

By the time Kentigern died around the year AD 600, the Britons of the north had been under heavy pressure for almost a hundred years. At the beginning of the fifth century, the Roman legions were withdrawn from Britain to help defend the crumbling empire. The Britons of the now largely Christianized and partly Romanized P-Celtic kingdoms found themselves facing three increasingly powerful and aggressive enemies. To the north were the Picts, fellow P-Celts, but mainly pagan and largely untouched by Roman culture. To the north-west were the Scots, Gaelic-speaking Q-Celts, Irish immigrants who had carved a kingdom, Dalriada, out of what is now Argyll. The greatest threat, however, came from the Teutonic-speaking Angles who had sailed across the North Sea and were now settling in Britain in increasing numbers. By the middle of the sixth century the Angles had set up the kingdom of Bernicia in what is now the north-east of England and were pressing north and west into the lands of Gododdin and Rheged. The Anglian invasion was part of the great confrontation between Celt and Teuton that racked Britain for several centuries.

Celtic propagandists have always painted the Angles as dim and brutal sea pirates, but in most ways they were as sophisticated as the

Britons. They built fine, fast ships. Their stonecarving – examples of which can be found at Jedburgh Abbey and Ruthwell – is better than anything the Britons managed. Their weapons and armour were good and they knew how to use them. They were disciplined and well organized, open to new ideas and quick to see the political advantages of Roman Christianity. They were resourceful, aggressive and hard to repel. The first of the old kingdoms to suffer from the Angles was Rheged; by AD 570 the Angles were locked in constant warfare with Urien of Rheged, one of the hero-kings of the North Britons, described by the bard Taliesin as 'King of the Golden North'. Some historians believe that he was the figure from whose life grew the legend of Arthur. In the year AD 590 he died in a skirmish with another Briton, one Morcant (who may have been a minor Gododdin chieftain; the similarity between the name of Morcant and that of Arthur's nemesis Mordred adds some slight credibility to the Urien/Arthur theory). Without his leadership, the kingdom of Rheged collapsed and fell into the hands of the Angles, who made it the western part of their kingdom of Northumbria and installed an Anglian bishop at Ninian's Candida Casa at Whithorn.

Ten years after Urien's death the Angles inflicted an even greater calamity on the Men of the North. The epic poem *Y Gododdin* – the most famous of the early Welsh poems – chronicles the disaster. Although it was composed in the early seventh century and not committed to paper until the ninth century, it is a vivid piece of work, even in translation. *Y Gododdin* is to the Britons what the *Odyssey* is to the Greeks or *Beowulf* is to the Saxons: their great epic. It tells how three hundred of the finest warriors of the Goddodin and their allies from Rheged, Strathclyde, Powys and Gwynedd spent a year feasting at the fortress of Mynyddawg Mwynfawr (Mynyddawg the Wealthy) at Din Eidyn (Edinburgh) before leading their war bands in an attack on the Angles at Catraeth (probably Catterick Bridge) in what is now Yorkshire. It was a suicidal mission. The odds were overwhelming – 300 against

100,000, according to the bard – and the Britons were slaughtered. According to the legend only one man, the bard Aneirin, returned from Catraeth to tell the story.

The earliest manuscript of *Y Gododdin* is now in the National Library of Wales and for generations Welsh scholars have been poring over it for the clues it offers to the history and culture of the Britons of the north. It gives a glimpse into the great timber halls erected by the north British chieftains. 'Never was a hall built so durable' the bard says of the one perched on the rock at Din Eidyn and goes on to describe 'the well-fed fire, the pine logs blazing from dusk to dusk'. Mead and wine drunk from beakers of gold, silver, glass and horn are mentioned. In his *History of Wales to the Edwardian Conquest* the Welsh scholar Sir John Edward Lloyd described *Y Gododdin* as 'a genuine relic of a long-forgotten strife, a massive boulder left high on its rocky perch by an icy stream which has long since melted away'. The suicidal ride of the Gododdin against the Angles could be compared to the stand of the Spartans at Thermopylae against the Persians. The legend is more important than the outcome. Five lines sum up the carnage and its impact. The translation is by A. O. H. Jarman in his book *Y GODODDIN – Britain's Oldest Heroic Poem*:

> *Three hundred men hastened forth,*
> *Wearing gold torques, defending the land,*
> *And there was slaughter.*
> *Though they were slain they slew*
> *And they shall be honoured till the end of the world.*

The defeat at Catterick Bridge fatally weakened the Gododdin's resistance to the encroaching Angles. Within forty years, Din Baer (Dunbar), Traprain Law and then Din Eidyn had fallen to the Angles, followed only a few years later by the western Gododdin stronghold at Manau (Stirling).

For most of the seventh century the Angles slowly pushed north and west, into Strathclyde and across the southern Pictish lands of Fife. By the year AD 650 even the Scots of Dalriada were paying tribute to the Angles. It seemed that nothing could stop their advance – until, in the spring of AD 685, the Angles overreached themselves and were destroyed by an army of Picts at Dunnichen in the countryside of Angus, twenty miles north of the River Tay. Dunnichen is a watershed in British history. The defeat checked the advance of the Angles and pushed them back south of the Firth of Forth. It also killed a hyper-aggressive Anglian king who was replaced by his peaceable half-brother, who did much to bring about the 'golden age' of Northumbrian culture. And it gave the remaining Celtic kingdoms of the north – British, Pictish and Gaelic – the time they needed to develop the societies that grew into Scotland.

For all that, by the beginning of the eighth century the Northumbrian Angles had done enormous damage to the Britons of the north. First Rheged and then Gododdin had been more or less wiped out. Those Britons not content to live under the rule of the Angles made their way south into the Celtic kingdoms in what is now Wales, or fled into Strathclyde. By the eighth century Strathclyde was the only northern P-Celtic kingdom left intact, with its chief centre at Dumbarton (Dunn-Brittein, the 'fort of the 'Britons') on the north bank of the Clyde, and territory that stretched from Galloway to Loch Lomond and the start of the Central Highlands. Strathclyde was surrounded by enemies and potential enemies – the Scots of Dalriada to the west, the Picts to the north, the Angles to the east and the south – but by a combination of careful diplomacy and well-organized defences the Britons of Strathclyde managed to survive, and indeed to flourish, for another 170 years.

Then came the Vikings. Norse longships began appearing off the coast of Britain towards the end of the eighth century. The Scots of Dalriada were the first to suffer their raids, then it was the turn of the Picts and the Angles. By the middle of the ninth century the

Norsemen were now raiding down the coast of Britain and establishing their settlements. One of the most important of these was at Dublin. In the year AD 870 Olaf the White, the Norse king of Dublin, struck an alliance with the Norse king of York and launched an assault on Dumbarton Rock, the very heart of the Kingdom of Strathclyde. That summer a huge fleet of Viking ships sailed up the Clyde to attack the last kingdom of the North Britons. Dumbarton proved a hard nut to crack; every Viking attempt to scale the rock and the ramparts came to nothing, and hundreds died in the attempt. In the end the Norsemen settled in for a long siege. After four months the 'black strangers', as the Norsemen were known to the Celts, succeeded in starving the Britons into surrender.

The consequences of that surrender were dire. Hundreds of Strathclyde Britons were butchered on the spot. Hundreds more – perhaps even thousands – were shipped back to Dublin as slaves, while every item of value was plundered from their homes. It is said that more than two hundred longships were needed to ship the booty and the slaves back to Dublin. Everything that could not be carried back was destroyed by fire. The survivors formed a new wave of Celtic refugees on their way down to Wales.

According to the Welsh historian John Davies, these refugees took with them the culture and legends of the Men of the North. He argues that the first written version of *Y Gododdin* was brought down to Gwynedd in north Wales only after the downfall of Strathclyde. He also thinks it likely that the legend of Arthur and his druid Merlin or Myrddin made its first appearance among the Britons of Wales around that same time, probably as as import from Strathclyde.

But against all the odds Strathclyde did survive. Somehow its king, Artgal, seems to have escaped the general slaughter, only to be assassinated a few years later on the orders of Constantine, ruler of the newly formed Picto-Scottish kingdom known as Alba (which is still the Gaelic name for Scotland). It has been suggested that

Constantine had Artgal killed because the Briton refused to accept Constantine as his overlord. Artgal's successors, however, did agree to Picto-Scottish overlordship – as the only alternative to allying themselves with the Angles of Northumbria.

But the Brythonic-speaking Celts of Strathclyde hung on. Some new work suggests that they staged something of a comeback in the late ninth and tenth centuries. Another historian, Tom Clancy of Glasgow University, argues that there are so many legends of Kentigern/Mungo in the west of Scotland because the Britons used the saint as a symbol when they were fighting to reclaim territory that they had lost to the Angles. By the end of the tenth century the Britons had driven the Angles out of the south-west and had reoccupied land that was once part of Rheged. For a few hundred years thereafter the area, which is still known by the P-Celtic name of Cumbria, was hotly disputed between the Scottish and English crowns.

It may have been to secure this territory that the remaining Britons threw in their lot with their fellow Celts, the Picto-Scots of Alba. In the year 1018 Owen the Bald, the King of Strathclyde, led the *Gwyr Y Gogledd* south to join Malcolm II's army to settle scores with the Angles of Northumbria. Near the village of Carham on the south bank of the River Tweed another crucial but mostly forgotten battle was fought between the warring Celts and Teutons of Britain. The Celts were victorious and the Northumbrian army was crushed. From 1018 the River Tweed defined the eastern border between the countries that eventually became known as Scotland and England, a border that has survived almost a thousand years.

The battle at Carham was the beginning of the end of the *Gwyr Y Gogledd* as a distinct polity. Owen the Bald, the last Welsh-speaking king of the northern Britons, was killed in the mayhem. After Owen's death Malcolm III made his nephew Duncan ruler of Strathclyde. When Duncan succeeded his uncle in 1034 the ancient realm of Strathclyde – the last of the North British kingdoms –

became part of the Kingdom of Alba. And the *Gwyr Y Gogledd* – the Men of the North, Welsh-speaking Scotland – passed into history.

Gone but not quite forgotten. On the cobbled approach to the battlements of Edinburgh Castle stands a cluster of nine black-painted, gilt-edged poles on which are fixed boards that describe the castle's long history. One of them offers a brief account of King Mynyddawg and the Gododdin and how 'in the taper-lit hall the war band pledged themselves in strong drink to die for their king, and almost all did die, on a raid into the territory of the Angles at Catterick in Yorkshire'.

Much more satisfying is a poem by the modern Welsh poet Hari Webb. He writes about Edinburgh Castle by night:

> *Floodlit the rock of the Gododdin floats*
> *Above the shops and bars. Valhalla? No,*
> *More like the island of Laputa, incompatible*
> *With the real world . . .*

Webb goes on to make a sour comment on the fragility of ancient, half forgotten cultures:

> *Our language was spoken here once, and here*
> *Our literature began, chanted on these ramparts*
> *Whose magic is dependent on a switch*
> *That can be turned off at any time.*

SCOTLAND
ON THE MAP

THERE'S AN OLD PIECE OF DOGGEREL which first appeared in the *Scottish Mountaineering Club Journal* in 1897 and which is still quoted now and again by aficionados of the Scottish hills. It runs:

> *A mountain's a mountain in England, but when*
> *The climber's in Scotland, it may be a Beinn,*
> *A Creag or a Meall, a Spidean, a Sgor,*
> *A Carn or a Monadh, a Stac or a Torr.*

Just as the Eskimos are popularly supposed to have dozens of words for different kinds of snow and ice, so the Gaels of Scotland evolved an extraordinary number of nouns and adjectives for the rocky topography of the Highlands. As Gaelic orthography is complex – and usually bears no relation to pronunciation – map-reading in Scotland can be a baffling business. The following are some of the most common Gaelic names that feature on the Ordnance Survey's maps.

Aonoch	A mountain ridge
Ban	White
Beag	Little, small
Bealach	Mountain pass
Beinn/Ben	Any mountain or high hill
Binnein	Peak, or top of the hill
Braigh	Steep slope or 'brae'
Breac	Speckled, dappled
Buidhe	Yellow or dun-coloured
Caisteal	Castle (usually an outcrop that looks like a castle)
Carn	A cairn, or conical hill
Ceann	Head, as head of a loch
Corr	Pointed
Creag	A cliff or a steep precipice
Dearg	Red
Donn	Brown
Druim	Ridge or spine
Dubh	Black or dark
Dun/Dyn/Dum	Fortress or hill fort
Fionn	Fair, pale-coloured
Garbh	Rough
Glas	Grey
Gorm	Blue, blue-green
Liath	Grey
Mam	Breast (usually a round hill)
Maol	Bald, bleak
Meall	Round hill
Monadh	Mountain, sometimes moorland
Mor/Mhor	Big, high
Odhar	Dun-coloured
Or	Gold
Ruadh	Reddish-brown
Sail	Heel

Sgurr	Steep, rocky, sheer
Sidhean/Sithean	Fairy or enchanted hill
Sron	Nose
Stac	Sheer, steep (usually applied to columns of rock)
Suidhe	Seat
Torr	Low, mound-like hill

Not all names on maps of Scotland are of Gaelic origin. South of the Highland line most place names are Scots (i.e. Middle English) or the proto-Welsh spoken by the Britons and the Picts.

Cock	Cap, hat
Comb	Crest
Dodd	Round hill
Heugh	Steep-sided hill
Kip	Pointed hill
Knock	An isolated hill
Law	A hill or mountain (often an extinct volcano)
Mount/Mounth	High moorland
Pap	Breast, rounded hill
Pen	Head, hilltop
Rigg	Ridge

Very few of Scotland's mountain and hill names are Norse. But maps of the Scottish coastline – and particularly those of the far north – are peppered with Norse names that mostly date back to the six hundred or so years when Caithness, Sutherland, Orkney, Shetland and the Hebrides were part of the King of Norway's empire.

Geo	Inlet
Gloup	Sea spout

Holm	Island
Ness	Headland
Skerry	Reef, rock
Stack	Column of rock
Voe	Sheltered anchorage, sea loch
Wick	Bay

THE SOULES
CONSPIRACY

JUST OUTSIDE THE CITY OF Stirling, a few hundred yards east of the M9 motorway, there is a statue of Robert I, King of Scots, usually known as Robert the Bruce. Erected in 1964, it is a huge bronze sculpture mounted on a granite plinth and it sits on a hill at Bannockburn, where Bruce's army decisively defeated the army of Edward II in 1314. Bruce is perched on his great charger, his battle-axe in his right hand, scowling out to the east, as if watching the English army limp away. With the mountains of the Highlands behind him and the plain of the Forth before him, Bruce looks the very essence of a man in charge. He is the master of all he surveys.

I suppose the image is appropriate to the myth. The statue's sculptor, Pilkington Jackson, has caught the popular notion that the battle at Bannockburn settled everything. Once Bruce and his band of heroes had chased off Edward's army and the Declaration of Arbroath was issued in 1320, an independent Scotland was secured and the land enjoyed decades of stability and prosperity under Robert I. In this widely held version of history only persistent meddling by the dastardly English prevented Scotland from becoming a medieval nirvana on the north-western edge of Europe.

The truth, as usual, is different. For a start Robert the Bruce was far from universally popular. He was widely seen as a usurper. The brutal way in which he had disposed of the supporters of his rival John Baliol had not been forgotten. And, just like the Jacobites four hundred years later, the Baliol faction did not disappear. They were lurking in exile. In the years following Bannockburn, the supporters of John Baliol's son Edward plotted incessantly to overthrow Bruce and install Edward Baliol as the 'rightful king'. The grip of the Baliols was particularly strong in the south-west of Scotland in Galloway, Dumfries and Ayrshire – and in parts of Argyll among the Macdougalls, and among powerful border families such as the Maxwells, the McDowalls, the Mowbrays and the McCans.

It was discontent that the English were happy to cultivate, but in Europe, too, Bruce had his enemies. When the Scots drove the English out of Berwick-upon-Tweed in 1318 the Vatican viewed it as a breach of the post-Bannockburn peace that the Vatican itself had engineered. Pope John XXII promptly excommunicated Bruce and three of his bishops. These grave censures were repeated in 1319 and 1320. Such excommunications were politically important. They released the Scottish people from any loyalty they might have pledged to 'Robert Bruce', who was now officially a sacrilegious murderer. The Pope's plan (or at least hope) was to undermine Bruce's power and encourage his enemies.

It almost worked. For two years, between 1318 and 1320, pro-Baliol forces in the south-west plotted a *coup d'état* against Robert the Bruce. They were led by a clutch of landowners: William Soules, Sir Roger Mowbray, Sir David Brechin, and Agnes, Countess of Strathearn. These big-time conspirators were supported by smaller fry (knights and esquires) who included John Logie, Patrick Graham, Eustace Maxwell, Walter Barclay, Gilbert Malherbe, Richard Broun, Hamelin de Troup and Eustace Rattray.

These men were serious players. Most of them could drum up a few hundred heavily armed and battle-hardened soldiers.

Just how Bruce got to hear of the Soules conspiracy is uncertain. Some say that the Baliol faction had a traitor in their ranks, a 'lesser knight' by the name of Murdoch of Monteith. Other historians suggest that word of the conspiracy was picked up in France by the Earl of March who was with the Scottish delegation that was making its way to Avignon to present the Pope with the Declaration of Arbroath. What is known is that, for some reason, March turned round and hurried back to Scotland.

However Bruce learned of the plot, he reacted with characteristic speed and dispatched his army to round up the conspirators. Some of them managed to flee to safety in England but many were hauled in chains to Scone (then the Scottish capital) to face the king's wrath. They were tried for treason in August 1320. Six of the men charged had been signatories to the Declaration of Arbroath, the ringing statement of Scottish independence that still resonates around nationalist circles (and which some of its admirers claim is the basis for the American Declaration of Independence).

In the end, Bruce's pragmatism made him lenient. He knew large swathes of the country remained ardent for the Baliol cause and that mass executions and large-scale reprisals could ignite a civil war, with all the consequent expenditure of blood and treasure. Also, it would create a crisis, which the English would inevitably exploit.

So the leaders of the conspiracy – William Soules and the Countess of Strathearn – were sentenced to be imprisoned for life, a sentence which both of them seem to have evaded. Other members of the renegade Scottish gentry were 'forfeited', i.e. stripped of their lands and possessions. More were quietly forced into exile in England and France

But examples had to be made. Somebody had to die a traitor's death. That dire fate fell upon four men: John Logie (from Perthshire), Gilbert Malherbe (from Stirlingshire), Richard Broun (from Ayrshire) and Sir David Brechin (from Angus). Brechin was not an active plotter, but it was said that he knew about the conspiracy and had failed to alert the king. All four were hanged, drawn (i.e. disembowelled while still alive) and then beheaded.

It was the same cruel death that the English had handed out to the 'traitor' William Wallace on 24 August 1305. But there are no known memorials to the leaders of the Soules conspiracy. Bruce's Scottish enemies have been written out of history.

WHAT KNOX DID FOR US

SOME YEARS AGO HOLLYWOOD (or its little English brother) had a go at making a film about the life of Mary Stuart, better known as Mary Queen of Scots. The title role was played by Vanessa Redgrave, a tall, handsome, red-headed woman who more or less fits the contemporary descriptions of Mary. I recall it as a routine, cliché-studded biopic, full of sub-Shakespearean dialogue. Just about the only scene I can remember is Mary's first encounter with the religious reformer, John Knox. Mary/Redgrave sat prettily on her horse, the very picture of a sixteenth-century queen, while this ragged old party sporting a long beard and carrying an Old Testament kind of staff shouted doom at her from an open hillside. He ranted and railed and fumed and threatened. A madman, and plainly up to no good. You could tell that because Mary's faithful courtiers frowned and looked worried in an actorly way.

This perception of Knox as a half-demented moorland preacher (or as an Orangeman in a bowler hat, as he is depicted in Liz Lochhead's play *Mary Queen of Scots Got Her Head Chopped Off*) says much about the way Scotland sees its great Protestant reformer. The Sentimental Left is strong in Scotland. It has done much to shape popular notions of history. And just as it has made the quintessentially right-wing figure of Charles Edward Stuart into some kind of eighteenth-century Che Guevara, so it has transformed the radical, left-wing figure of John Knox into a reactionary, ecclesiastical bully whose first victim was poor dear Mary Stuart.

Historical movies are, of course, popular history. According to popular history, once Knox had succeeded in running Mary Stuart out of Scotland he created a society that was peculiarly harsh, brutal and intolerant, even for the sixteenth century. In this version of events Knox and his disciples rampaged across the land, pulling down cathedrals and monasteries, stripping them of their stained glass, tapestries and statues. Music was banned. Art and beauty were suppressed. Joy was banished from Scotland. And in their place Knox installed a gloomy Calvinism that lingers to this day.

Like much popular history, this is nonsense with a dash of truth. There is no doubt that Knox was a very determined man. There is no doubt that he loathed Roman Catholicism; no doubt that he set out to extirpate Popery from Scotland; no doubt that, while very few lives were lost in the process (certainly compared to elsewhere in Europe, where thousands died), many beautiful religious artefacts were destroyed. Knox and the Reformers drove the Roman Catholic hierarchy into an exile from which it did not return until the end of the nineteenth century.

But I have always felt that Scotland gained more than it lost. Knox may have 'cast down' the interior of many a kirk, but he also fostered democracy, debate and an enthusiasm for learning that once made the Scots among the best-educated people in Europe. Knox and his colleagues crafted a system of church government that still – more than four hundred years later – defines the relationship between Scotland, the monarchy and the British state. I would also argue that it was John Knox – an Anglophile who had reason to be grateful to the English – who made possible the United Kingdom by steering Scotland away from Roman Catholic France and towards Protestant England.

Knox and the men who came after him created a sceptical, intellectual milieu in Scotland, one that was eventually to produce a stream of philosophical, scientific and artistic talent that no country of comparable size could match. When Thomas Carlyle tried to work out just why Scotland had produced such a proliferation of genius he credited Knox. 'Scotch literature and thought; Scotch industry; James Watt, David Hume, Walter Scott, Robert Burns; I find Knox and the Reformation acting in the heart's core of every one of these persona and phenomena; I find that without the Reformation they would not have been.' ('The Hero as Priest', *On Heroes, Hero-Worship and the Heroic in History*, 1840)

In other words, no one man did more to create modern Scotland than John Knox. I can never read his *Book of Discipline* without feeling that it is one of the key documents of the Reformation, at least in Britain. True, it is suffused with some very unpleasant anti-Catholic polemic, but it also contains ideas on democracy, church government, universal education and social welfare that are many years – some would say centuries – ahead of their time. Knox's *Book of Discipline* is the political manifesto of the Protestant movement. For all his faults – pride, intellectual arrogance, an excess of zeal – it could reasonably be argued that John Knox was the greatest man Scotland ever produced.

Not too much is known about Knox's early life. The best evidence is that he was born in 1505 or 1515 in the East Lothian town of Haddington, in a small house in the Giffordgait, just across the River Tyne from the beautiful collegiate church of St Mary's. We know that his father was one William Knox and that his mother's name was Sinclair. He was educated at St Andrew's University where he was instructed by the Scots philosopher/theologian John Major (who also taught Ignatius Loyola in Paris). Knox was ordained a priest in 1530 and returned to East Lothian where he preached at St Mary's and served as chaplain and tutor to various gentry families.

John Knox preaching before the congregation

Like most Scots, the picture I have of Knox is taken from one or two sixteenth-century engravings that show a gaunt figure with a long beard and wearing a strange flat cap. It is a stern and off-putting image. But none of his contemporaries describe Knox as particularly forbidding. One description comes from Sir Peter Young, tutor to King James VI, and a man who was no friend of the reformer. He portrays Knox as 'slightly under middle height, of well-knit and graceful figure, with shoulders somewhat broad, longish fingers, head of moderate size, hair black, complexion somewhat dark and general appearance not unpleasing'.

Young goes on to describe Knox's blue-grey eyes set in a long-nosed face with a big mouth, 'his beard black mingled with grey a span and a half long and moderately thick'. Other observers say that Knox was quietly spoken with a pronounced English accent, about which he was often teased and sometimes mocked.

Like the rest of northern Europe, the Scotland that Knox grew up in was changing. The banned writings of the German reformer Martin Luther were being smuggled across the North Sea. Between 1528 and 1558 a series of Scots intellectuals (most of them friars and priests) were burned for the 'heresy' of complaining about the state of the church and/or spreading the ideas of Luther. Knox's own mentor, George Wishart, was burned to death at St Andrews in 1546 at the behest of Cardinal David Beaton, the town's bishop (Wishart's death is still remembered in St Andrews: there is a brass plaque in the street where he met his end and a rather gruesome reconstruction of the burning in the town's tourist centre.)

Wishart's execution hardened the attitude of the Reformers and made Knox an implacable enemy of Rome. In 1547, Protestant activists took revenge for the martyrdom of George Wishart by murdering Cardinal Beaton, and then fled into the castle at St Andrews where Knox joined them as their chaplain. After a French fleet bombarded the castle into surrender Knox was taken prisoner and spent a miserable nineteen months as a galley slave aboard a French merchant ship, the *Notre Dame*. It was an experience of Roman Catholic France and the French that he would never forget or forgive.

Released thanks to the intervention of England's Protestant regime, Knox did not return to Scotland but became an Anglican clergyman in Berwick-upon-Tweed, where he met his first wife Marjorie Bowes (daughter of Richard Bowes, the Captain of Norham Castle in Northumberland). Knox then found a living at St Nicholas's church in Newcastle and later became one of King Edward VI's royal chaplains. Knox was so effective as an advocate of Protestantism that he was offered the bishopric of Rochester and the living at All Hallows in London. Knox declined both, and when Mary Tudor, a zealous Roman Catholic, became Queen of England in 1553, he fled to Europe where for the next five years he ministered to Protestant refugees, mainly those who had escaped 'Bloody Mary' in England. Eventually he found his way to Jean

Calvin's Geneva which he regarded as the 'very school of Christ' and the nearest place to heaven on earth.

On my first visit to Geneva I was surprised to find that John Knox is well remembered in that city. A large and impressive bas-relief of the Scots reformer stands on the *Mur des Reformateurs* alongside the figures of Jean Calvin, Guillaume Farel and Theodore Beze. It was in Geneva that Knox 'regularized' his marriage to Marjorie Bowes and where his sons Nathanael and Eleazer were born. Then, on a fleeting *sub rosa* visit to Scotland in 1555, he found that Protestantism there was growing fast along with hostility to the French regime of Mary of Guise. Encouraged by the fact, John Knox returned to Scotland in May 1559 at the request of the Protestant aristocracy who called themselves 'The Lords of the Congregation'.

Knox might well have returned to England rather than Scotland had he not written the notorious pamphlet entitled *The First Blast of the Trumpet Against the Monstrous Regiment of Women*. Although the work was targeted at Mary of Guise in Scotland, Mary Tudor in England, and Mary of Medici in France, the English Mary had been succeeded by her half-sister Elizabeth by the time it was published. Elizabeth let it be known that the man who described her gender as 'weak, frail, impatient, feeble and foolish creatures' was not welcome in her England and refused him permission even to travel through it on his way to Scotland.

The first attempt by the Scots lords to oust the French was a dismal shambles. The little Scots army was no match for the French professionals. Knox quickly realized that Scotland could only be rid of the French with the help of the English. It was Knox (through an emissary) who persuaded Elizabeth's adviser William Cecil that the French forces in Scotland were a threat to England. In turn, it was Cecil who persuaded Queen Elizabeth's privy council to send troops into Scotland to help the Lords of the Congregation drive out the French, an operation that was successfully completed by the summer of 1560. In August that year the Scottish parliament 'abrogated' the authority of the Pope in Scotland. In less than a year, Scotland had become one of the most completely reformed Protestant nations in Europe.

There is a tiny building in the Cowgate in Edinburgh that sits in the shadow of George IV Bridge. It is known as the Magdalen Chapel and was begun in 1541 by a wealthy merchant and moneylender called Michael Maquhen as an almshouse and hospital. When he died the work was finished by his wife Janet Rynd. For many years the Magdalen Chapel was the headquarters of the city's 'hammermen' (that is, metalworkers) whose coat of arms is still above the doorway. Although the chapel has been partially restored by the Scottish Reformation Society, it still looks rather neglected, which it most certainly is by Edinburgh's tourist trade. This small building has a central role in the history of Scotland. It was in the Magdalen Chapel that the very first General Assembly of the Church of Scotland was held in the autumn of 1560. It was also in the Magdalen Chapel in the same year that John Knox and five of his colleagues (John Douglas, John Winram, John Row, John Spottiswoode and John Willock) hammered out the document by which the Scottish people would be governed. It became known as Knox's *Book of Discipline* and was produced at high speed: commissioned at the end of April, a draft was put to the Privy Council by the end of May. A revised version by the 'Six Johns' was then laid before the Parliament in September.

Although it was never formally ratified by Crown or Parliament, the *Book of Discipline* laid down the foundations of new Scottish ways of thinking and living. Some of it is taken up with anti-Papist rhetoric, but other sections – it was arranged under nine 'heads' or chapters – are genuinely far-sighted, many years ahead of their time. Knox built democracy into his system. For example, Head IV gave every congregation in Scotland the right to *elect* its own minister, after the congregation had been satisfied with his morals, qualifications and performance as a preacher. This may not seem hugely important to the twenty-first-century secular eye, but in the sixteenth century, when the minister's word was both gospel and law, it was a huge leap forward. It gave to the people a power that is still denied them by the hierarchies of Roman Catholicism and the Church of England, and which also vanished in Scotland for a time when the British parliament created by the Acts of Union in 1707 attempted to bring Scotland into line with England, where Anglican vicars traditionally were appointed by the aristocracy and the gentry.

Head VIII set out rules for electing the church's elders and deacons, the people who would supervise the life and work of the minister. 'If he [the minister] be worthy of admonishment, they must admonish him; of correction, they must correct him; and if he be worthy of deposition, then with consent of the Kirk and Superintendents, they may depose him . . .' These elected officials were also tasked with preparing an annual report on the minister's 'life, manners, study and diligence', which had to be passed on to the church authorities.

The church historian Gordon Donaldson (who as a confirmed Anglican was no admirer of Presbyterianism) points out that Knox's ideas for the Kirk were, in modern parlance, 'inclusive'. In Knox's scheme of things authority 'ascended' from the congregation and did not 'descend' from the bishop. 'They [the people] were to be raised through education,' Donaldson writes. 'Learning was to be no monopoly of a priestly caste, and an instructed people were to have a part in church affairs from which they were previously excluded . . . The vernacular was substituted for Latin, metrical psalms were introduced and service books were put in the hands of the people so that all could take part.'

Along with democracy came education. Schooling was vital, Knox and the Reformers argued, 'seeing that God hath determined that his Kirk here in [sic] earth shall be taught not by angels but by men, and seeing that men are born ignorant of God and of all Godliness'. A clear distinction was made between the rich and the poor. The rich were to pay for the education of their own children but 'The children of the poor must be supported and sustained by the charge of the Kirk.'

Knox expanded on his educational ideas in his own *History of the Reformation*. Every parish church was to have its school and schoolmaster able to 'teach grammar and the Latin tongue'. In remote areas the minister himself or his 'reader' had to do the teaching. 'Further, we think it expedient that in every notable town there be erected a college, in which the arts, at least logic and rhetoric, together with the tongues, be read by sufficient masters for whom honest stipends must be appointed.'

A school in every parish and a college in every town was one of the great dreams of the Reformation. It was never quite realized and Knox conveniently ignored the fact that the Roman Catholic church had already put in place its own network of schools. But it was a serious aspiration that put Scotland among the best-educated societies in Europe. 'This must be carefully provided,' Knox wrote of the need for decent schools 'that no father, of what estate or condition that ever he be, use his children at his own fantasy . . . But all must be compelled to bring up their children in learning and virtue.'

'Everlasting honour to brave old Knox, one of the truest of the true' was the verdict of Thomas Carlyle. 'That in the moment while he and his cause, amid civil broils, in convulsion and confusion, were still struggling for life, he sent the schoolmaster forth to all corners and said "Let the people be taught!"'

Knox was writing in the sixteenth century and not all of his measures would appeal to the modern liberal. For instance, only adult male members of the congregation had the right to vote in Kirk elections. The *Book of Discipline* also laid emphasis on what are now called family values. Sex was to be kept for the married state and 'If any commit fornication with that woman he requires in marriage, they both do lose . . . benefit as well of the Kirk as of the Magistrates.' The father of a deflowered virgin 'hath power by the law of God to compel the man that did that iniquity to marry his daughter'. As for adultery: 'And because whoredom, fornication, adultery are sins most common in this realm, we require of your honours [i.e. the parliament] . . . that severe punishment according as God hath commanded be executed against such wicked contemners.' This was a plea for the death penalty for adulterers, as laid down in Leviticus, chapter 20, verse 10. The Scots parliament did pass such a law in 1563, but it seems that only one or possibly two convicted men were ever executed.

Knox and the reformers are often accused of trying to create a theocracy in Scotland, where every miscreant in the land would quake at the power of the Kirk. But the *Book of Discipline* states quite clearly that the trial and punishment of all major crimes and offences should be left to the civil power. Only relatively minor offences such as drunkenness, excess, fornication, 'oppressing of the poor . . . and licentious living tending to slander' were to be the province of the Kirk's own courts.

Knox's radical Protestantism set him on a collision course with Mary Stuart when she returned from France in 1561 to claim the Scottish throne. Mary was only nineteen at the time, but already widowed and from all accounts a sophisticated and intelligent young woman. What her modern admirers forget (or ignore) is that Mary was fiercely committed to Roman Catholicism; the Guise family, who brought her up, engineered the infamous St Bartholomew's Day massacre in Paris in 1572, when thousands of French Protestants died. While Mary's public policy was to recognize Scotland as a Protestant country it was no secret that she preferred the hierarchical splendours of her own church.

The collision between Knox and Mary was not long in coming. In a series of three interviews (all held at Mary's behest at the Palace of Holyrood House and her hunting lodge at Falkland in Fife) she engaged Knox in debate. Their confrontations were as much about political power as they were about religion. They were often acrimonious. Like her grandson Charles I, Mary Stuart was deeply affronted by the notion, popular among Protestants, that a people had the right to remove their sovereign if he or she stepped out of line. In Scotland this was an old belief, having been written into the Declaration of Arbroath of 1320. Knox recorded the conversation with Mary in his book *The History of the Reformation of Religion Within the Realm of Scotland*.

'Think ye that subjects, having the power, may resist their princes?' she demanded of Knox.

Knox's reply was firm. 'If their princes exceed their bounds, Madam, no doubt they must be resisted, even by power.'

'Well, then, I perceive that my subjects shall obey you and not me. They shall do what they list, and not what I command; and I must be subject to them, and not they to me.'

Knox declined to step into that trap. 'God forbid that I ever take upon me to command any to obey me,' he told Mary 'or yet to set subjects at liberty to do what pleaseth them! My travail is that both princes and subjects obey God.'

In another exchange Mary announced her determination to 'defend the Kirk of Rome for it is, I think, the true Kirk of God'.

Knox's reply was uncompromising. 'Your will, Madam, is no reason; neither doth your thought make that Roman harlot to be the true and immaculate spouse of Jesus Christ.'

The two ended up detesting one another. More than once Knox reduced Mary to tears of exasperation. To Mary, brought up in France in the tradition of Roman Catholic absolutism, John Knox was an impudent and over-mighty subject. To Knox his new sovereign was a danger to everything he had tried to build. 'If there be not in her a proud mind, a crafty wit and an indurate heart against God and His truth' he wrote 'my judgement faileth me.'

In December 1563, Mary tried to have Knox tried for treason; a dangerous moment for Knox and the Reformation, because if she had succeeded Knox could well have been executed and the Reformation in Scotland might have faltered. 'Yon man gart me greet [made me cry] and grat never a tear himself,' Mary announced just before Knox's trial. 'I will see if I can gar him greet.' The trial took place in Holyrood Palace and was presided over by Mary herself. But every time she asked for a verdict, the jury of Scottish nobles acquitted Knox of any treason. They knew, even if Mary did not, that convicting Knox might have sparked a civil war. Time after time, Mary asked them to reconsider: each time they found Knox not guilty. Eventually Mary flounced out of the chamber, humiliated by the support for Knox.

Bit by bit, Knox's vision of the 'Godly Commonwealth' seemed to be falling into place. The Papal Jurisdiction Act of 1562 abolished Roman Catholicism in Scotland, along with the saying of the Mass. The Church Act of 1567 provided for the legal establishment of Protestantism 'to be the only true and holy church of Jesus Christ within this realm'. In the same year that the Church Act was made law Mary Stuart's supporters were routed at a (relatively) bloodless battle at Langside near Glasgow and the young queen fled Scotland into exile in England (where she and her co-religionist supporters plotted the overthrow of her cousin Elizabeth).

I've never been able to understand why the Reformation in Scotland is usually perceived as a harsh and bloody business. Compared to the deluge of blood that was shed elsewhere in Europe it was a mild affair. There were few religious martyrs in Scotland, and nothing to compare with the mass executions of Mary Tudor's regime in England in which an estimated three hundred Protestants were burned at the stake, or even with Queen Elizabeth's counter-enthusiasm for burning Roman Catholics (she killed two hundred of them). 'In this era,' writes the historian Gordon Donaldson, 'every form of persecution, bloodshed and cruelty was less conspicuous in Scotland than in England.'

Indeed, the Protestant regime in Scotland was remarkably accommodating by the standards of the time. Any Roman Catholic clergyman who was prepared to renounce Rome – as many of them did – was welcomed into the Church of Scotland. Even the clergy who refused to abandon the Pope and were consequently 'deposed' were paid two-thirds of their stipends for life. Former Roman Catholic bishops continued to sit in the high councils of the Scottish state. Monks and friars were allowed to live off the money that they had earned from their industries.

Nor was there anything like the destruction wrought in England by Henry VIII when he decided to 'dissolve' the monasteries. In Scotland when a church was 'cast down' that did not mean it was razed to the ground. Usually it was only stripped of its 'idols' – its statuary, stained glass and ornamentation. Scotland was far too poor a land to go in for wholesale destruction. Most existing church buildings – many of which had been badly neglected by the Catholic hierarchy – were pressed into use by the new Kirk. Indeed, Knox's *Book of Discipline* insists that every useful church building in the land should be made windproof and watertight.

It is even hard to blame Knox and Calvinism for the formal rigours of the Scottish Sunday. Strict Sabbatarianism was introduced into Scotland as far back as the eleventh century by Queen Margaret (who was English) who ruled that on Sunday 'we apply ourselves only to prayers'. In the decade before the Reformation took root in Scotland, John Hamilton, the Roman Catholic Archbishop of St Andrews, published his *Catechism*, which laid down severe rules for Sabbath observance. And it was the Roman Catholic regime of Mary of Guise that tried to suppress Scotland's traditional May Day festivities. The joyless note that has sometimes sounded so loud in Scotland predates Knox by several centuries.

Knox's own life was not without turbulence or scandal. In 1563 his wife Marjorie died and Knox's mother-in-law Elizabeth Bowes moved in with him to look after his two young sons. For months Edinburgh was swept with rumour that Knox was 'fornicating' with his own 'good mother'. It might have been to kill these rumours that in 1564 the fifty-year-old Knox took a second wife. She was Margaret Stewart, the seventeen-year-old daughter of Lord Ochiltree, and a distant cousin of the Queen (who was incensed that Knox had the temerity to marry one of her relatives). Despite the thirty-three-year difference in their ages, their marriage seems to have been happy enough. Nathaniel and Eleazer, Knox's two sons by Marjorie Bowes, were dispatched to England to be educated. Both became Anglican clergymen and fellows of St John's College, Cambridge. Knox went on to have three daughters by his young wife. One married a minor aristocrat while the other two became the wives of Kirk ministers.

Knox died in Edinburgh on Monday, 24 November 1572, at the age of sixty-six. At his funeral in the kirkyard of St Giles, where Knox had been the senior minister, the Regent of Scotland, the Earl of Morton, paid fulsome tribute to the great reformer and declared that 'There lies he who never feared the face of man.'

Knox's ideas lived on long after his death. His notion of ecclesiastical independence from the state fuelled the great politico-religious debates of the eighteenth and nineteenth centuries. It led to the disruption of the Church of Scotland in 1843 and the setting up of the Free Church. It is why the Westminster parliament has no say over the internal workings of the Kirk, and why the Queen has no rightful place at the Kirk's General Assembly (all she can do is send a 'commissioner' who is there at the Kirk's invitation).

Given Knox's legacy – education, democracy – why is the man himself so uncelebrated? My own view is that the Anglo-Royalist cast of popular history is to blame, the same cast that turns Oliver Cromwell into one of history's villains. Also, Knox's reputation began to suffer during the Scottish Enlightenment when the *philosophes* of Edinburgh and Glasgow found that his ideas did not sit well in their rational, moderate – and increasingly Anglicized – universe. That was certainly the opinion of that brilliant Victorian writer Hugh Miller, who wrote: 'Robertson, Smollett, Kaimes, Adam Smith, Gilbert Stuart, Tytler, and Moore had all caught the English mode and the English spirit and were, in at least as marked a degree as any of their English contemporaries, tinctured with infidelity. Hence, in part, the disrespect shown by almost all these writers to the memory of Knox.'

Today, whenever Knox is portrayed on the screen or on the stage it is as a figure of fun – or of hate. In a widely publicized lecture in 1999, the Scots composer James Macmillan ludicrously bracketed him with twentieth-century tyrants and mass murderers such as Hitler and Pol Pot, men who caused the deaths of millions of people. Knox made Mary Stuart cry.

For a man who did so much to shape his country, John Knox is ill commemorated in Scotland. There are only two major statues of the great reformer, one outside New College in Edinburgh and the other perched on a column in the Eastern Necropolis in Glasgow. Neither of them compares with the bas-relief of Knox in Geneva.

John Knox's remains lie in what used to be the kirkyard at the rear of St Giles in Edinburgh. It is now the High Court's car park. Knox's bones are believed to lie beneath parking space number 44. I've seen tourists peering under some lawyer's BMW to catch a glimpse of the place where those bones might be.

Virtual Psalms

PRESBYTERIANISM HAS HAD A bad press for two hundred years and more, a byword for sanctimony and hypocrisy. Kirk ministers are routinely portrayed as small-town wet blankets, ever anxious to stifle the flames of pleasure. I think this is unfair and I partly blame Robert Burns. Like the gentry he longed to join, Burns enjoyed jeering at the populist ministers of Ayrshire. As a result, evangelicals like 'Daddy' Auld and 'Holy Willie' Fisher (both of whom were brilliantly depicted by Burns) have become the archetypes of Scottish Presbyterianism: humourless killjoys suffused with overweening piety.

There are such folk in the Kirk and the Free Kirk, of course, but they also exist in every other denomination of Christianity: among Anglicans, Catholics, Methodists, Baptists, you name it. Some of the Plymouth Brethren who still flourish in Scotland's fishing towns make Free Kirk elders look like Woodstock hippies. Presbyterianism has no monopoly of dismal Godliness, and it has always had its brighter side.

Proof of this comes from an unlikely source, a book called *Four Centuries of Scottish Psalmody* by Millar Patrick DD, published by the Oxford University Press in 1949. Doctor Patrick offers an intriguing account of the development of the rich musical form we call metric psalms, and an equally intriguing account of Scotland's ecclesiastical history. My favourite chapter concerns 'Practice-Verses'. For centuries Presbyterians refused to sing hymns. They were seen as quasi-secular confections, fit only for Episcopalians and suchlike folk. Only the words of the Holy Bible were good enough, so the songsters of the Kirk confined themselves to 'metric' versions of the Psalms of David set to music. However, because the words of the psalms were drawn from the Bible they were regarded as sacred. They were to be used only in divine services, never in choir rehearsals. As a result, words had to be invented for whatever psalm tune was being rehearsed. There grew up an intriguing subculture of 'practice verses', ranging from the bland and pious to the jaunty and satirical. Many were shot through with the sardonic humour common in lowland Scotland. Sometimes the practice verses incorporated the name of the tune:

> *The name o' this tune is called York,*
> *The reason I don't know:*
> *They micht as weel have called it Cork,*
> *Carmarthen or Raphoe.*

Some of the practice verses had a satirical edge. If it suited the choir, the minister himself was not spared:

> *Keep silence, all ye sons of men,*
> *And hear with reverence due;*
> *The minister he's gane oot tae smoke,*
> *But he'll be back the noo.*

According to Doctor Patrick, the tune *O Mother Dear, Jerusalem* seemed to lend itself to any number of ingenious and irreverent words:

O mither dear, Tod Lowrie's lum,
Whan sweepit will it be?
For a' the soot's come tummlin' doon,
An' spilet ma grannie's tea.

I wish I were a brewer's horse
Yoked tae a cairt o' yill,
And that my heid was at my tail,
Then I could drink my fill.

While many of the psalms are beautiful and moving in their simplicity, the quality of the singing could never be guaranteed. That great 'improver' of Scottish manners, the Reverend Hugh Blair, complained in 1829 about those 'unmerciful bawlers, whose roarings are generally loud in proportion as they are untuneable'. But most bawlers were undeterred. When the congregation at Paisley Abbey tried to shut up one particularly 'untuneable' old woman she flatly refused to pipe down. She would 'praise the Lord wi' a' her micht, whether she kent the tune or no'. For many years, every psalm was sung to one of only twelve tunes. New melodies were deplored – even those tunes that are now regarded as 'classic'. Doctor Patrick tells the story of an incident at a church at the Bridge of Teith near Stirling. When the precentor – the man who led the singing – broke into the new tune *Bangor*, the minister was so appalled by the sound that he knocked the unfortunate fellow unconscious with the pulpit Bible.

NEIL MACLEOD OF LEWIS

IN SCOTLAND'S DIVERSE AND ragged landscape there are many strange little roads that lead nowhere. To my mind, one of the strangest is the ten miles or so of the B8059 on the west side of the Hebridean island of Lewis. It runs north-west across a sodden landscape of low rocky hills, peat bogs and hundreds of little lochs, and then up the peninsula of Great Bernera until it ends in a car park beside an Atlantic bay called Camas Bosta. The view seaward is of a tangle of tiny islands, some of them no more than rocks, all of them uninhabited: Little Bernera, Floday, Fleasgear, Harsgeir, Sgeir na Galla, Braigh nan Stacannan. The only land that stands between them and the coast of North America is St Kilda.

One of the larger islands is Bearasay which lies about a mile and a half north-west of Camas Bosta and it looks higher, rockier and more inaccessible than the others. This remote and unlikely place was the last refuge of Scotland's most obdurate rebel, Neil Macleod of Lewis. According to the folk history of the Hebrides, Macleod held out on Bearasay for almost two years, eventually surrendering to his Mackenzie enemies after they threatened to drown all the women and children of his clan. Macleod was then hauled down to Edinburgh in chains, tried at the High Court of Justiciar, sentenced to death, hanged until he was half dead, and beheaded. The Edinburgh crowd turned out in force to see him go. If contemporary accounts are to be believed, he gave a good account of himself on the scaffold, meeting his end with the same snarling defiance with which he had confronted the power of James Stuart, King of Scots and the first king of Great Britain and Ireland.

Neil Macleod is one of Scotland's forgotten figures. His life and death say much about the suspicion and loathing that characterized relations between Lowland and Highland Scotland for centuries. Half hero, half villain, he was both charismatic and treacherous. For fifteen years he waged war on James VI, the Stuart monarch who was determined to 'civilize' Gaelic Scotland by settling it with English-speaking Lowlanders – a policy he later employed on a much wider scale in Ireland when he became King James I of Britain, with results that still resonate.

The Gaels of the Highlands and Islands had always been a problem for the Kings of Scots. A law unto themselves, they sometimes fought with the King and sometimes against him. Clan Donald, for example, were among Robert the Bruce's most loyal supporters; Clan Dougall were his implacable foes. Every now and again, ambitious Highland politicians struck secret deals with the English. The powerful Macdonalds posed a serious threat to the stability of Scotland until 1411 when their huge clan army was fought to a standstill by a small but heavily armed Lowland force at Harlaw in Aberdeenshire. In the sixteenth century there were so many Gaelic incursions across the Highland line that the Gaelic bards used to sing of the 'age of the forays'. Some of the farming communities of the Angus lowlands still have an unreasonable dislike of Highlanders that can only be folk memories from the days of the Gaelic cattle thieves.

In the years straddling the sixteenth and seventeenth centuries, the King of Scots had another reason to worry about his Gaelic subjects: they threatened to drag Scotland into England's wars with the Irish. For generations Highland Scots had been fighting as heavily armed mercenaries (known as 'gallowglasses') for the Irish kinglets. In England's 'Nine Years' War' in Ireland (1594–1603) the Scottish clans provided a steady flow of swordsmen to fight for their fellow Gaels. The English were leaning on the Scottish authorities to stem this flow of military aid. The prospect of an English counter-strike into Scotland was a constant concern.

The Macleods of Lewis had always been one of the most troublesome of the Highland clans. More Norse than Celtic, they were descendants of the Vikings who had ruled over the bleak 'long island' of Lewis and Harris since the time when the Outer Hebrides had belonged to the King of Norway. Like their Norse ancestors, they were skilled seamen, pirates and raiders. Even among their fellow Gaels they were viewed with suspicion. A Gaelic poet once wrote of the Macleods:

> *It is my opinion of Clan Leod, that they are like pikes in water.*
> *The oldest of them, if the larger, eats the younger.*

By the end of the sixteenth century James VI had decided that something needed to be done about his Gaelic subjects. He was open in his dislike of them, particularly the Hebrideans. 'As for the Highlands', he wrote in one of his many pamphlets, 'I shortly comprehend them into two sorts of people: the one that dwelleth on the mainland, that are barbarous for the most part, yet mixed with some show of civility; the other that dwelleth in the isles are all utterly barbarous.' Inevitably, the king's distaste for his 'utterly barbarous' subjects found its way into law. A Scottish statute of 1581 characterized the Gaels as 'companies of wicked men coupled in fellowship by occasion of their surnames or near dwellings together'.

Other eyes were also turning north. Like the rest of northern Europe, early modern Scotland was becoming increasingly mercantile, with a 'civil state' of merchants, manufacturers, lawyers, and administrators who were looking for new ways to invest their money. They had little trouble in persuading King James that the economy of Scotland (and the royal exchequer) would greatly benefit if the natural assets of the Highlands and Islands could be exploited. They presented the north as a modest Eldorado. Not stuffed with gold and silver (although there was some of that) but a place where fine black cattle could be reared, good grain cropped, and slate, granite and marble quarried. Above all there was fish. The merchants of Edinburgh pointed out that Dutch fishing fleets were making fortunes from the herring-rich waters around Scotland, and that it was high time some of this profit lined the pockets of Scots. It was an argument that James Stuart, who prided himself on his modernizing ways, found impressive. And so began the first of James Stuart's ventures in internal colonization, by which he planned to pacify Gaeldom and enrich his realm and himself. He wrote that it would be to the benefit of Scotland's Gaels to '. . . reform and civilize the best inclined among them, rooting out or transporting the barbarous and stubborn sort and planting civility in their rooms [places] . . .'

At the end of 1597, with the backing of the King, the Scottish parliament passed an act to build three 'royal burghs' in the Highlands – one on the Mull of Kintyre, one in Lochaber and the other on the island of Lewis. These new towns were seen as nodal points from which English-speaking 'civilization' would spread out until it conquered the native 'barbarism' of the Gaels. In the end the Kintyre and Lochaber projects were pursued half-heartedly or dropped altogether. Only the one on Lewis – which seemed to have the best commercial prospects – went ahead. There the job of pacifying and civilizing the Gaels – in this case, the Macleods – was given to a company of businessmen and aristocrats who called themselves *Gentlemen Adventurers for Conquering of the Isles of Lewis*. Most of them came from Fife and their leaders included Ludovic the Duke of Lennox, Sir James Anstruther, and James Learmonth of Balcomie. (The nineteenth-century Russian soldier-poet Mikhail Lermontov was a descendant of the Learmonths of Fife.)

A deal was struck in the Privy Council and then ratified by the Parliament, which gave the Fife adventurers a seven-year, tax-free lease on the whole island of Lewis. The Fifers were delighted with the arrangement but it set alarm bells ringing all over the Highlands and Islands. As the Gaelic chiefs saw it, what was happening to the Macleods of Lewis could happen to them. Secretly, they plotted to undermine the Fife entrepreneurs. One of the most astute of the plotters was Mackenzie of Kintail, the King's lieutenant in the north-west, and a man who had long claimed the Macleod lands on Lewis for himself.

There was nothing secret, however, about the hostility of Clan Leod. The Fife Adventurers had hardly set foot on Lewis in October 1599 when Macleod warriors led by Neil and his brother Murdo began raiding and harrying the settlement. The Lowlanders were well prepared for conflict – they knew that the natives would be hostile. They had brought with them about five hundred mercenaries, including engineers and labourers – and a stockade was speedily thrown up around the settlement of what is now Stornoway. Behind its walls the Lowlanders began building their 'Royal Burgh'. In this way, they were behaving like early colonialists in North America, just as Neil and his clansmen had much in common with the North American Indians who were struggling to defend their ways of living against the encroaching whites. The shock of Lowland settlement on the Gaels of Lewis may not have been quite so traumatic as it was to the Iroquois or the Cherokee, but it was severe enough. As Neil Macleod's story demonstrates, the Macleods were certainly prepared to fight and die for their land.

Many things went wrong for the Fife adventurers. Their landing coincided with the onset of winter. The provisions that had been brought from the south soon began to run out; there was nothing to be had from the hostile locals and it was far too late to plant crops or vegetables. The weather was harsh. Before the winter was over dozens of the Lowland settlers had died from exposure, starvation and typhoid. Others who ventured beyond their stockade were stabbed to death by the dirks of Macleod war parties. Then, in the early months of 1600, one of their most capable leaders, James Learmonth of Balcomie (described as 'the Frenchest, Italianest, jolly gentleman'), was intercepted at sea off the Orkneys by a fleet of galleys and birlinns commanded by Neil's half-brother Murdo. The crew of the Fife ship were butchered and thrown over the side and Learmonth was taken hostage and brought back to Lewis. A ransom of 3,000 merks was demanded, but Learmonth died in captivity before it could be paid.

At which juncture Neil displayed the treachery for which the Macleods were renowned. For some reason he fell out with his half-brother Murdo, ambushed him and handed him over to the King's men. Murdo was shipped south and charged with the 'Treasonable capture and detention of the late James Learmonth of Balcomie . . . and the cruel murders of Arthur Hamilton, Joseph Learmonth and David Short and various other persons.' Because Learmonth was a gentryman from Fife, Murdo Macleod was tried and executed at St Andrews.

Before he died Murdo Macleod claimed (rightly) that Mackenzie of Kintail had been working to undermine the Fife Adventurers. His accusation was taken seriously. Mackenzie was arrested and jailed in Edinburgh Castle. But Mackenzie had friends in high places and one of them, the Earl of Dunfermline, the Lord Chancellor of Scotland, arranged Mackenzie's escape from the castle. Returning to his Highland fastness in Kintail, Mackenzie added a severe distaste for the Macleods to his enmity towards their enemy, the King.

In Lewis, Neil Macleod's betrayal of his half-brother made him no more trusted by the Fife settlers, who still saw him as their most dangerous enemy. They decided that he had to be taken and killed. Two hundred armed Lowland men were assembled, and on a 'very dark night' they ventured out of their Stornoway stockade to hunt him down: a desperate foray – it is easy to imagine the Lowland men struggling in their body armour through the peat bogs – which ended no more than a few miles from Stornoway when they were ambushed by the Macleods. Sixty of them were killed in the running battle that accompanied their retreat to the stockade. The business of 'civilizing' the Macleods of Lewis was proving far more costly than James VI and the Fife Adventurers had ever imagined. By 1601 there was open warfare between the colonialists and the natives. Time after time Neil's clansmen raided the Lowland settlements, burning houses, driving off cattle, picking off individual stragglers. Meanwhile, Mackenzie of Kintail played one side off against the other, to devastating effect.

At the end of 1601, Mackenzie's wiles brought the Fife settlement to its knees. He promised the Lowlanders a ship full of provisions – and at the same time told Neil's men where the supply ship would anchor. The supplies were duly captured by the Macleods while the settlers starved. Neil Macleod got the blame, while Mackenzie was credited with trying to help the King. Then, when the settlers were weak with hunger, Neil and his clansmen swept over the walls of the stockade, burning and killing. The Fifers surrendered, but had their lives spared after their leaders signed a document making several promises. They promised never to return to Lewis. They promised to seek a pardon from King James for the Macleods, and to return the title to the lands of Lewis to the Macleod chieftains. They also left Sir James Spens and his son-in-law behind as hostages. It was a complete capitulation, and King James was furious. As he saw it, one of the most enlightened and ambitious kings in Europe was being held at bay by a handful of northern savages.

Plans were laid to reinvade Lewis in 1602 and then in 1603. They came to nothing. In fact, the Lowlanders did not return to the 'long island' until 1605, two years after James Stuart had inherited the English throne to become the first monarch of Britain and Ireland. This time the venture had the support of the King's (mainly

English) ships, and the second wave of Lowland settlers was better armed and better prepared. Still, the Macleods refused to give up. Between 1605 and 1607 they harried the settlers so effectively that once again they were pinned into the heavily-defended area around Stornoway. In 1607 they abandoned even that small territory and sailed away.

Then the shrewd Mackenzie of Kintail made one of his few mistakes. He openly claimed title to all the Macleod lands on Lewis. King James was incensed, removed the title from Mackenzie and assigned it instead to Lord Balmerino, Sir George Hay of Nethercliffe and Sir James Spens of Wormiston, the three remaining members of the original Fife consortium. But when Balmerino was tried and convicted for treason in 1609 his share in the Lewis venture was inherited by Mackenzie of Kintail. That same year Hay and Spens made a third attempt to 'settle' the island of Lewis. With help from Mackenzie a few shiploads of Lowland settlers sailed into Stornoway harbour to try to rebuild the colony. Once again they met the relentless hostility of the Macleods. Once again it became dangerous for the Lowland settlers to wander far from the Stornoway stockade. Once again the Lowland folk lived in fear of their lives while they struggled to build a town and put in place a profitable fishery and a few modern industries like textile-weaving and boat-building.

At the end of 1609 the Fife Adventurers finally gave up. Too much blood had been spilled, too much treasure had been wasted. The prospect of any profit looked remote. They decided to abandon the project for good. The settlers sailed away, leaving behind them the nucleus of the town that became Stornoway (which is now the administrative capital of the Western Isles). Neil Macleod may have looked on this signal as a victory. In fact, it contained the seeds of his defeat. Mackenzie of Kintail acquired the Fifers' interest in Lewis in exchange for their right to extract timber and iron ore from the Mackenzie lands at Letterewe in Wester Ross. He and his younger brother Roderick (an educated man known as the Tutor) were to prove far more dangerous to their fellow Gaels, the Macleods, than the Lowland settlers had ever been. In 1610 the Scottish Privy Council granted Mackenzie a 'commission of fire and sword' with which to 'search, seek, hunt, follow and pursue the said Neil, his complices, assisters, and partakers, by sea and by land, wherever they may be apprehended.'

Four hundred years on, the Privy Council's document makes grisly reading – the kind of instruction that might have come from a cruel, twentieth-century dictatorship. The commission gave the Mackenzies a free hand to kill and destroy in their pursuit of Neil Macleod: 'And if in pursuit of this commission there shall happen slaughter, mutilation, fire raising or any other inconvenience to follow, the said Lords discern and declare that the same shall not be imputed as crime or offence.' The Mackenzies struck with a ferocity that the Crown had never managed to muster. Roderick the Tutor landed on Lewis with more than seven hundred armed men and swept across the island, burning and killing. (In Lewis, until recent times, his name and deeds were remembered in the saying that the three worst evils that could afflict a crofter were a May frost, July rains and the Tutor of Kintail.)

Neil Macleod fled to the little island of Bearasay, where he had laid up enough supplies to defy Roderick the Tutor for almost two years. According to Lewis legend, the siege ended when the Tutor rounded up all the Macleod women and children whom he could find, and put them onto a rock in the sea where they would be drowned by the incoming tide unless Neil surrendered. Unwilling to sacrifice the innocents, Neil offered to surrender to his kinsman Macleod of Harris. Mackenzie accepted the deal and Neil was duly handed over to his relation. But the treachery that seemed to bedevil the Macleods asserted itself yet again. Macleod of Harris was made of the same stuff as Neil himself. As soon as he had Neil in his care he promptly marched him under guard to Edinburgh where Neil was indicted and tried in April 1613 for 'all manner of barbarous cruelty and wickedness, and following the pernicious example of your Godless parents, kinsfolk and country people, having committed innumerable oppressive hardships and violent facts . . . within the country of Lewis and other Highland isles thereabout, to the high offence of Almighty God, displeasure of the King's Majesty, contempt of his royal authority and violation of his Highness's laws.'

Neil Macleod's trial in Edinburgh was in front of a jury of Lowland Scots, none of whom spoke Gaelic and most of whom would have been instinctively hostile to Gaels. Neil had little English; to make him understood the court employed three Gaelic-speaking Scots as translators (the first such case on record). The jury's guilty verdict came as no surprise when it was delivered on 30 March 1613, but the court's sentence was harsh, even by seventeenth-century standards. Neil Macleod was to be '. . . taken to the Mercat Cross of Edinburgh, and there to be hanged upon a gibbet until he be dead: and thereafter his head to be stricken from his body and affixed and set upon a priket (spike) above the Netherbow Port of the said burgh. And his whole lands, heritage, dykes, steadings, rooms, possessions, goods and gear pertaining to him, to be forfeit and escheat to His Majesty's use.'

Neil Macleod did not go quietly. The story is that when he got to the gallows one of the men who were to hang him addressed him as 'old man' and told him to hurry up. Macleod shouted at him in Gaelic, 'If this were a ship's deck where it was hard to stand and the sea was heaving, you would not call me "old man", laddie.' And then he felled him with one blow.

Gradually the Crown took a grip on Gaeldom. Four years before Neil Macleod was hanged the 'Statutes of Iona' had forced most of the Gaelic chiefs to pledge allegiance to the British Crown, as well as allegiance to the established (that is, Anglican) church and the promise that they would reduce their armed retinues to no more than one hundred men. They also promised to give their children a Lowland (that is, Anglophone) education and to banish the wandering bards who were an important element in Gaelic culture.

In 1616 the Statutes of Iona were reinforced. Highland grandees now had to restrict themselves to one sea-going vessel per chief and to reside in a 'designated' residence. They also agreed to have their rents fixed by the Crown. Although many of these pledges and promises were ignored, the Gaelic culture and society of the Highlands and Islands was slowly eroded – a process that has gone on for centuries. At the last count in 2001 only 50,000 Scots (less than one per cent of the population) were native Gaelic speakers.

After Neil's death the Macleods of Lewis never regained their title to the lands of the long island. A grateful King James assigned the title to Neil's nemesis Mackenzie of Kintail who was made Earl of Seaforth. Lewis remained part of the Mackenzie empire in the far north until 1844 when it was sold for £190,000 by Mrs Stewart Mackenzie. The buyer was Sir James Matheson, the Sutherland-born drug dealer and entrepreneur who had made his huge fortune selling Indian opium to Chinese addicts and who was a far greater brigand and killer than Neil Macleod.

THE BLASPHEMER

THERE IS AN EDINBURGH tradition that most visitors find both inexplicable and repellent. A few yards from the doorway of the High Kirk of St Giles, the granite cobbles in the pavement are patterned in the shape of a heart. Many local people – mainly the older ones – spit into this heart when they pass by. By the end of a busy weekday there can be enough mucus and saliva on the pavement to make it worth avoiding. As traditions go, it is mildly disgusting. But it is one that I never fail to observe, although nowadays I am inclined to go easy on the spit.

This is no ancient Celtic rite. We are not talking witchcraft here. There is nothing mystical about that granite spittoon beside St Giles. That neat configuration of cobbles marks the spot where the condemned cell of the city's Tolbooth prison once stood. It was known to Edinburgh folk as the 'black heart of Midlothian'. For hundreds of years, men and women had huddled in its straw until they were hauled out to be hanged, beheaded or burned. Many of them must have been innocent. It is a place that deserves to be spat upon. When I spit, I recall one particular tenant of the condemned cell: Thomas Aikenhead. Aikenhead was a twenty-one-year-old student at Edinburgh University when, in the year 1697, he was taken from here and marched north to the place known as Shrubhill where he was hanged. He was the last person in Scotland to be executed for the crime of blasphemy. His trial was a mockery, his execution was a piece of judicial murder. The English historian Thomas Babington Macaulay described the affair as 'a crime such as has never since polluted the island'.

I came across the story of young Aikenhead in the early 1990s at the time of the Iranian *fatwah* on the writer Salman Rushdie for his alleged blasphemy against Islam in his novel *The Satanic Verses*. That murder threat came as a genuine shock to Western intellectuals, with its revelation that there were people who were still prepared to kill to preserve, as they saw it, their idea of God. I remember it as a bad time. Liberals who had always seen themselves as champions of ethnic and religious minorities in Britain suddenly found themselves face to face with an elemental religiosity that threatened one of their own. Less liberal commentators, meanwhile, seized the opportunity to paint Islam (and by extension Arabs, Iranians and Pakistanis) as primitive and 'medieval' and all Muslim states as uniquely brutal.

It was in this disconcerting and confusing atmosphere that I found myself reading the legal papers on Thomas Aikenhead's trial for blasphemy. The parallels with the Ayatollah Khomeni's strictures against Rushdie were striking. Iran in the late twentieth century seemed eerily similar to late-seventeenth-century Scotland. The economies of both were in serious trouble, there were enemies at home and abroad and the recent revolutions (Islamic in one case, Presbyterian in the other) were far from secure. In effect, Scotland's law officers and religious leaders had conspired to lay a Presbyterian *fatwah* on young Aikenhead that led him to the gallows in Edinburgh in January 1697.

One of the remarkable things about the Aikenhead affair is that so many of the trial documents have survived. The indictment, proceedings, witness statements, Aikenhead's justification of his philosophical opinions are all to be found in the Scottish Record Office (now known as the National Archive) in Edinburgh. As the historian Michael Hunter remarked in his thorough and brilliant account of the Aikenhead affair (published in *Atheism from the Reformation to the Enlightenment*, Clarendon Press, 1992): 'Not only do we have a full account of the aggressively anti-Christian views that Aikenhead was accused of publicly expressing, which indicate their unusual range and ingenuity, but we also have a written account by Aikenhead of the rationale of his apostasy.'

Thomas Aikenhead was born into a respectable Edinburgh family in 1676. His father, James, was a city apothecary who fell foul of the law when one of his customers was poisoned by one of his aphrodisiac potions. Aikenhead's mother, Helen, was the daughter of a Kirk minister. Thomas Aikenhead matriculated at Edinburgh University in May 1693, by which time both his parents were dead.

He had grown up in a country of religious oppression and counter-oppression. The 1680s are still remembered in Scotland as 'the killing times' when Graham of Claverhouse and his dragoons hunted Dissenters – the Covenanters – across the moors of the south-west and dozens of Presbyterian ministers were hanged in the Grassmarket in Edinburgh. Their bodies were prepared for burial in the little Magdalen Chapel in the Cowgate, where John Knox and his colleagues had drawn up their *Book of Discipline*.

After the Glorious Revolution of 1688, the Presbyterians took their revenge. It was not bloody but it was relentless. The Episcopal Church in Scotland was driven underground; Episcopalian priests were 'rabbled' out of their churches and homes and Episcopalian services were held in secret, always at risk from the Presbyterian authorities. The events that followed 1688 were blows from which the Scottish version of Anglicanism never recovered. (The Episcopal church used to embrace forty per cent of the Scottish population: its Sunday services are now lucky to get one per cent.)

The Stuarts were an ever-present danger. The Williamite regime had been rattled by the Jacobite insurrection of 1690, which had been brilliantly led by John Graham of Claverhouse, popularly known as 'Bonnie Dundee'. Graham had been killed at the battle of Killiecrankie and his army was later fought to a standstill at Dunkeld by a determined force of Covenanters, but Presbyterian Scotland in the 1690s felt far from secure. Both Kirk and State saw themselves threatened by foreign and domestic enemies, the Kirk being particularly fretful about the spread from England of what it regarded as Godless atheism in the shape of sceptical, free-thinking philosophers such as Lord Herbert of Cherbury, Charles Blount, Thomas Burnet, Walter Grotius and John Toland. The Privy Council pursued Edinburgh booksellers for material deemed to be 'atheistical, erroneous or profane and vicious' and in 1696 one young merchant, John Frazer, was jailed for publicly denying the existence of God, the soul and Satan.

Into this intellectually turbulent and politically hazardous milieu stepped the outspoken student Aikenhead. According to a pamphlet written by his fellow student Mungo Craig (who became a prosecution witness) Aikenhead told anyone who would listen that Christianity was nothing but a 'rhapsody of feigned and ill-invented nonsense, patched up partly of the moral doctrine of philosophers, and partly of poetical fictions and extravagant chimeras'. The New Testament was nothing but 'the history of the impostor Christ', a man who had learned to work magic from the Egyptians and who had 'picked up a few blockish fisher fellows' upon whom 'he played his pranks, as you blasphemously term the working of his miracles'. He thought it high time that religion in general – and Christianity in particular – was swept away and replaced by a belief in human progress. Redemption, he argued, lay in ourselves. He believed that 'man's imagination duly exalted by art and industry can do anything, even in the infinite power of God.' Human ingenuity, he predicted, would see to it that people would one day fly in the air and travel to the moon.

Rashly, Aikenhead made no secret of his views. He rehearsed them on the steps of the Tron Church and spoke them openly in front of Kirk ministers, until he was reported to the Lord Advocate of the day, Sir James Stewart of Goodtrees. At the end of 1696 Stewart drew up a long indictment that charged Aikenhead with the crime of blasphemy under the Blasphemy Act of 1661 (which had been passed in the reign of the despised Charles II). That act carried the death penalty for anyone who 'not being distracted in his wits, shall rail upon or curse God, or any of the persons of the blessed Trinity'. Stewart also invoked the act of 1695 which made it a grave offence for anyone to 'deny, impugn or quarrel, argue or reason, against the being of God, or any of the persons of the Holy Trinity, or the Authority of the Holy Scriptures of the old and new testaments, or the providence of God in the Government of the World'.

On 10 November 1696, Aikenhead was hauled up before the Privy Council to hear the indictment against him and was then handed over to the High Court of Justice 'to be tried for his life' before a jury of fifteen Edinburgh citizens. The outcome of the trial was a foregone conclusion. The most important witness against Aikenhead seems to have been his one-time friend Mungo Craig, whose evidence bears all the marks of a man who has been manipulated or pressured into incriminating the accused. Even before the trial began, Craig had published a pamphlet entitled *A Satyr Against Atheistical Deism* which rubbished Aikenhead's opinions. It was a dismal piece of work, written in rhyming couplets. But in it Craig went so far as to urge the court to 'atone with blood, the affronts of heaven's offended throne'. Afterwards Aikenhead wrote of the 'abominable aspersions' heaped on him by Mungo Craig whom he left to 'reckon with God and his own conscience, if he was not as deeply concerned in those hellish notions (for which I am sentenced) as ever I was'.

Not surprisingly, young Aikenhead lost his swagger. Even before his trial he had petitioned the authorities for leniency, pleading his belief in Christianity and the 'principles of our holy Protestant religion', stressing his youth, and expressing remorse for opinions which he had acquired from the 'most villainous and atheistical' books and pamphlets, which he now saw should never have been published. Sentenced to death, he wrote an even more desperate petition, which acknowledged the justice of his sentence but asked that it might be postponed so that 'I may have the opportunity of conversing with godly ministers in the place, and by their assistance be more prepared for an eternal rest.'

Was Aikenhead's repentance genuine? Some contemporary reports claim that the Privy Council offered Aikenhead a reprieve in exchange for repentance, 'which he refused to do'. Michael Hunter points out in his study of the case that if this were true, it suggests that the formal petitions were not written by Aikenhead himself but composed on his behalf by ministers or lawyers.

Many thoughtful Scots were appalled at the harshness of the sentence. The fact that only a few months before John Frazer had been punished by a few weeks in gaol and a few Sundays on the repentance stool for the same offence made Aikenhead's sentence particularly cruel. William Lorimer, a Scots clergyman working in London, and George Meldrum, the minister at the Tron Church, both pleaded Aikenhead's case with the authorities. In a pamphlet (entitled *Two Discourses* and published in 1713) Lorimer claimed that 'the Ministers could not prevail with the Civil Government to pardon him' and that the aristocratic politicians of the Privy Council were determined that Aikenhead should hang 'that there might be a stop put to the spreading of that contagion of blasphemy'.

A very different version of events is given by Lord Anstruther, one of the members of the Privy Council. In a letter dated 26 January 1697 Anstruther wrote to one of his friends that the government would have granted clemency if the Kirk had intervened on Aikenhead's behalf. But it did not. In Anstruther's view the clergy 'in their ignorant zeal spoke and preached for cutting him off'. Scotland's ministers, he declared 'are of a narrow set of thoughts and confined principles and not able to bear things of this nature'.

In the week or so before he was hanged Aikenhead wrote a long, rambling and somewhat confused document which has gone into the record as *Thomas Aikenhead, his Cygnea Cantio* (swansong). One of the copies is now in the Bodleian Library in Oxford. In Michael Hunter's opinion the *Cygnea Cantio* oscillates between 'lucidity and virtual incoherence' and between repentance and defiance 'in a manner that bears witness to the tortured state that the young man's mind must have been in by this time'.

After ruminating on his intellectual and philosophical progress, Aikenhead concludes: 'These things I have puzzled and vexed myself in, and all that I could learn therefrom is, that I cannot have such certainty, either in natural or supernatural things as I would have. And so I desire all men, especially ingenious young men, to beware and take notice of these things upon which I have split.'

They hanged Thomas Aikenhead on the afternoon of Friday, 8 January 1697. Dressed in his shroud, and with a Bible in his hand, he was taken from the condemned cell in the Tolbooth and walked through the streets of the city to the 'gallowlee' (now called Shrubhill) between Edinburgh and the Port of Leith. One report says that he walked his last mile between 'a strong guard of fusiliers, drawn up in two lines'. His body hung in chains for many weeks, as a warning to other blasphemers.

There is an oddly modern postscript to his execution. A few months later the Reverend Robert Wylie, a leading Presbyterian churchman, wrote a long letter to his friend William Hamilton, the laird of Wishaw. In it he defends the prosecution of Aikenhead against what he called the 'pious & charitable wits' who accused the Government of being too harsh. 'And when these witty critics consider that reason, common sense and good manners (their own Trinity) do require that no man should in the face of a people spitefully revile & insult the object of their adoration, and that a Christian could not be innocent who should rail at or curse Mahomet at Constantinople, and consequently that their pleadings against Aikenhead's condemnation were most unjust . . .'

That seems to me to be the kind of reasoning that the late Ayatollah would understand.

THE WITCH-HUNTERS

SCOTLAND BEGAN TO TRACK down and kill witches in the late fifteenth century and continued the habit into the first few decades of the eighteenth century. Women identified as witches were likely to find themselves in front of an assize (court) after a spell in the local torture chamber. The lucky ones would strangle at the end of a hangman's rope. The unlucky would be roasted alive on a pile of timber that was often dampened so that the victim wouldn't burn too quickly. There was nothing a crowd liked better than listening to a witch scream and then watch what was left of her or him (though male witches were rare) being scattered to the winds.

There is a dismal irony here. This cruel business peaked under one of the most well-read and enlightened monarchs that Scotland ever had – James VI, later James I of Great Britain. Sometime in the early 1590s James Stuart became preoccupied with witches – obsessed enough to publish in 1597 his own *Daemonologie* in which he wrote that: 'Witches ought to be put to death, according to the law of God, the civil and imperial law, and the municipal law of all

Christian nations.' To spare witches and warlocks, James wrote, was 'a treason against God'.

Usually witch-hunters cited the Bible as their authority, particularly the verse in the Book of Exodus (22:18) which declares: 'Thou shalt not suffer a witch to live.' The New Testament is much less adamant about witches, although one of Paul's Letters to the Galatians (5: 19–21) cites idolatry and witchcraft among the 'works of the flesh' whose sins also included adultery and fornication. The early Christian church, however, seems to have paid scant attention to witches, seeing them as no great threat compared to, say, the cult of Mithras or the Roman army.

That changed when the idea took root that the Devil was almost as powerful as God. Satan's acolytes – witches – were people to be dreaded. By the fifteenth century the 'witch craze' was so rampant that in 1484 a pair of Dominican friars called Heinrich Kramer and Johan Sprenger persuaded Pope Innocent VIII to issue a fierce anti-witch papal bull. Two years later Kramer and Sprenger produced a text called *Malleus Maleficarum* (*Hammer of the Witches*) that became the witch-finders' handbook. With its careful instructions on how to track down, torture and kill witches it must be among the most inhuman documents ever published – a truly wicked piece of work.

The religious and social earthquake of the Reformation did nothing to shake Europe's enthusiasm for killing witches. The Reformers took up where the Popes and the Inquisition left off. Lutherans and Calvinists were just as ready to torture, hang and burn distracted old women as were Jesuits and Dominicans. In his account of the Reformation in Scotland, John Knox notes (in 1563, the time of Mary Queen of Scots): 'Two witches were burned – the eldest was so blinded with the Devil that she affirmed "no judge had power over her".' Many of the sixteenth-century trial records end with the words *Convicta et Combusta* – convicted and burned.

While it is true that many more witches were hounded to death in France, Germany and Italy than in Scotland, the Scots did enter into the spirit of the business with enthusiasm. The spate of killings presided over by James VI in the 1590s was followed by others in the 1620s, 1640s, and 1660s. Men known as 'common prickers' roamed the land, identifying women as witches by stabbing them with needles. The theory was that if their subjects felt no pain or didn't bleed they were witches. In Paisley in 1697 seven women and a man were hanged and burned on Paisley Green on the word of the eleven-year-old Christiana Shaw, the hysterical daughter of a local laird.

No one is sure how many witches died in Scotland. One estimate is that in the forty years between the first Scottish anti-witchcraft Act being passed and the accession of James VI to the throne of England as James I in 1603, around 4,000 Scots died as witches, an average of one hundred a year. Hundreds more died in the bitter religious feuds and wars of the seventeenth century. Only the short-lived regime of Oliver Cromwell put a stop to the work of the witch-finders. The witch-hunting resumed after the restoration of the monarchy in 1660.

The last witch legally killed in Britain was put to death in Scotland – at Dornoch, Sutherland – in 1727. An addled old woman and her daughter were accused of casting spells on their neighbours' livestock. The old woman was also charged with turning her daughter into a pony and riding her at night. In the eyes of the magistrate who heard the case, the proof was that the girl had injured her hands and feet. The daughter escaped but the mother died. Witnesses said the old woman clapped her hands with delight when she saw the 'bonnie fire' on which she was to die.

DANIEL DEFOE,
SECRET AGENT

JUST ACROSS THE ROAD FROM the High Kirk of St Giles in Edinburgh there is an alleyway (or 'close' in Scots parlance) known as Old Stamp Office Close. It sits under a six-storey nineteenth-century tenement, squeezed between a liquor store and a café. The narrow entrance opens out into a courtyard that on most days serves as a playground for a local nursery school. At the entrance to the close a brass plaque fixed to the wall carries the information that in the seventeenth century in this close sat the town house of Susannah, the handsome and sociable Countess of Eglinton, 'and her seven beautiful daughters'.

By the beginning of the eighteenth century the Eglinton family had abandoned the house and it had become one of Edinburgh's many hostelries. It was officially called 'Fortune's Coffee House' but was usually known as 'Sue's', a tribute to the previous aristocratic owner. As it was within a short walk of the Scottish Parliament, the law courts and the High Kirk, business at Sue's was brisk. Edinburgh was in an uproar as Scotland moved closer to a Parliamentary union with England.

One of Sue's regular customers in 1706 and 1707 was an affable, rather foppish middle-aged Englishman who told anyone who cared to listen that he was a great admirer of Scotland and the Scots, and that he intended to settle north of the border as and when the Union had been achieved. He was Daniel Defoe, later the author of that great literary prototype *Robinson Crusoe*. He was at this time, however, also the English government's secret agent in Scotland. Sue's was where he wined and dined his contacts and picked up the information that he passed on to his masters in London.

These are facts that always make me cringe slightly. At my Edinburgh secondary school we were taught a poem that used to bring a blush of pride and patriotism to the faces of my sixteen-year-old classmates. It was called *Caledonia etc., a Poem in Honour of Scotland and the Scots*, and it was by Daniel Defoe: a sustained hymn of praise to the courage, ingenuity, genius (and, of course, beauty) of our native land, all the more satisfying because it had been written by an Englishman.

The poem, I now know, was a fraud, a fake, part of a spy's 'cover'. 'I am writing a poem in praise of Scotland,' Defoe wrote to his boss in London at the beginning of November 1706. 'You will say that is an odd subject to bear a panegyric but my end will be answered. I make them believe I am come away from England and resolved if the Union goes on to settle in Scotland and all conduces to persuade them I am friend to their country.'

Defoe was 'undercover' for England at one of the most crucial periods in British history – the months leading up to the Union of the Parliaments in 1707 – and it was dangerous work. As one of his Scots acquaintances of the time remarked, 'He was a spy among us, but not known to be such, otherwise the mob of Edinburgh had pulled him to pieces.'

Defoe's spying days in Scotland are chronicled in his own words and those of his masters. The correspondence that passed between Defoe and the English Secretary of State, Robert Harley, can be found in *The Letters of Daniel Defoe* (edited by George Harris Healey, Oxford University Press, 1955). Defoe may not have been the bravest secret agent who ever lived (he had a tendency to panic) but he was certainly one of the most literate. Most of his reports to Harley were shrewd, some were far sighted, and a few have a peculiar resonance in the present, when the Union of 1707 between Scotland and England is being examined and tested as never before.

Like most Englishmen from a Puritan background Defoe was a dyed-in-the-wool Whig, an ardent Williamite. A union of the Scottish and English parliaments had been a Whig project ever since William III himself had suggested it in 1689. King William's idea was not taken up by the English parliament, but he never abandoned it. A few days before his death in 1702 he argued again for a 'firm and entire union' between Scotland and England.

Many Englishmen – particularly Tories – hated the notion of a union with their ancient enemy. In 1700 the Tory leader Sir Edward Seymour told the English parliament that a union with Scotland would be the political equivalent of wedding a beggar and that 'whoever married a beggar could only expect a louse for her portion.' The view was widely held throughout England, but by the early 1700s powerful men in both countries were beginning to see the benefits of such a union. For all their old enmities, the two nations shared the same island, the same monarch, the same language and a similar (but not identical) Protestant ethos. King William's enthusiasm for the project had been inherited by his daughter Anne, the last of the Stuart monarchs. Politicians on both sides of the border, however, knew that such a huge step would require careful handling, and that overcoming resistance to it in England and Scotland would need political intelligence of high quality. In 1705, Defoe wrote to the new Whig government's Secretary of State (or Prime Minister), Robert Harley: 'Intelligence is the soul of all public business. I have heard that our Secretary's office is allowed £12,000 per annum for this weighty article, and I

Daniel Defoe

am credibly informed the King of France has paid eleven millions in one year for the same article, and 'tis allowed he never spares his money on that head, and thereby outdoes all the world in the knowledge of his neighbours.'

In Defoe's opinion what England needed was an intelligence system that was both large and well funded. And nowhere would those secret funds be better spent than in Scotland. 'A settled intelligence in Scotland, a thing strangely neglected there, is without doubt the principal occasion of the present misunderstandings between the two kingdoms; in the last reign it caused the King to have many ill things put upon him, and worse are very likely to follow. I beg leave to give a longer scheme of thoughts on that head than is proper here, and a method of how the Scots may be brought to reason.'

Defoe's memorandum to Harley is an odd document, an impertinence which offers advice on politics and statecraft to one of England's most able practitioners from a man whose own life was a shambles of debt and bankruptcy. Harley may not have taken it too seriously; he never took Defoe as seriously as Defoe wanted – he was always begging for an official position or sinecure. But he took it seriously enough to try Defoe out as a government agent, commissioning him in the summer of 1705 to wander through the West of England and the Home Counties gathering political intelligence.

From the middle of July to the beginning of November in that year, Defoe rode from town to town, village to village, chatting to clergymen, merchants, local gentry, shopkeepers and small tradesmen. He conducted lengthy interviews, listened to gossip, collected political tracts and generally swept up all the intelligence that came his way. Just how useful Robert Harley found this political information from Middle England is hard to tell. Three hundred years on, much of it seems trivial in the extreme. But Harley must have been reasonably impressed by Defoe's intelligence-gathering skills because in the summer of 1706 he offered Defoe the much bigger job of acting as the English government's secret agent in Scotland.

Harley certainly needed all the intelligence from Scotland that he could get. The union negotiations were moving quickly. Queen Anne had appointed a sixty-two-strong commission – thirty-one Englishmen and thirty-one Scots – to thrash out a Treaty of Union that would be ratified by the respective national parliaments. Through a London-based Scots merchant called Scott he met and dined with some of the most influential of the pro-union Scots commissioners: Lord Stair, Sir David Dalrymple, Lord Rosebery, John Clerk of Edlin. He became particularly friendly with the able and amiable John Clerk.

It was at the suggestion of these pro-union Scots that Defoe wrote a pamphlet entitled *An Essay at Removing National Prejudices Against a Union with Scotland* which set out to lift 'the mists and vapours from the eyes of the people'. Defoe argued that a Union would make the Scots more prosperous and keep them at home instead of joining the legion of Scots mercenaries 'which now fill the armies, and spread the colonies of all the nations in Europe'. And for England, 'here are lands and people added to the English empire.' That the Scots might not like the idea of being 'added to the English empire' does not seem to have occurred to him.

Before Defoe left for Edinburgh he and Robert Harley set up a system whereby the spy's reports would find their way to the spymaster. It was agreed that Defoe would send his messages to John Bell, the postmaster in Newcastle-upon-Tyne, who would then relay the messages to a Mrs Collins at the Middle Temple in London, or to Michael Read at York Buildings. Read was one of Harley's factotums who was described by Swift as 'an old Scotch fanatick and the damnedest liar in his office altogether'. It was also arranged that John Bell in Newcastle would supply the secret agent with funds as and when they were needed.

Harley's instructions to his new man in Scotland were concise but sensible.

1. You are to use the utmost caution that it may not be supposed you are employed by any person in England; but that you come here upon your own business and out of love to the country.

2. You are to write constantly the true state how you find things, at least once a week.

3. You may confidently assure those you converse with, that the Queen and all those who have credit with her, are sincere and hearty for the Union.

Harley added that the occasional politely worded threat to the Scots might not go amiss. 'You must shew them, this is such an opportunity, that being once lost or neglected is not again to be recovered. England never was before in so good a disposition to make such large concessions, or so heartily unite with Scotland, and should their kindness now be slighted . . .'

Daniel Defoe rode wearily into Edinburgh in October 1706 at the end of a wet, two-week-long journey. He is believed to have found lodgings in what is now Moubray House on the north side of the High Street, a few hundred yards from the High Kirk of St Giles. He is said to have lived in rooms on the top floor of the five-storey building. The interior is a small, low-ceilinged, barrel-vaulted apartment that offers a view of the High Street, which was then Edinburgh's main thoroughfare. Moubray House is intact. It sits adjacent to the little museum dedicated to John Knox, and is perched above one of those shops that sells wool and cashmere sweaters to tourists.

Defoe found Edinburgh in a state of tension. 'I had not been long there but I heard a great noise,' he wrote on 24 October 1706, 'and looking out I saw a terrible multitude coming up the High Street with a drum at the head of them shouting and swearing and crying out all Scotland will stand together, no union, no union, English dogs and the like . . . I cannot say to you I had no apprehensions . . . particularly when part of this mob fell upon a gentleman who had discretion little enough to say something that displeased them just under my window.' He went on: 'a Scots rabble is the worst of its kind . . . I was warned that night that I should take care of myself . . .'.

That early experience of the Edinburgh mob seemed to haunt Defoe. For the remainder of his stay in Scotland he lived in some dread of falling victim to it. He may have been over-anxious. While there was plenty of noisy street protest against the union in Edinburgh (and even more in Glasgow) there was very little real violence, and that little was easily put down by Edinburgh's town guard and the castle garrison.

Nervous Defoe may have been, but he worked assiduously. As a Protestant dissenter he knew his stock among Presbyterians would be fairly high, so he set about cultivating the ministers of the Church of Scotland (to find them 'the wisest weak men, the falsest honest men, and the steadiest unsettled people ever I met with'). The presence of Highlanders in unusual numbers in Edinburgh worried him – they preferred the exiled Stuarts to Queen Anne – and on 13 November 1706 he wrote to Harley urging the wisdom of sending 'two or three [English] regiments of horse or dragoons . . . as silently as might be' towards the border: 'All the force this [Scottish] government has to make a stand is not 2,000 effective men and of them I question whether 1,500 could be drawn together.' (Around this time some English units were moved to the north of Newcastle, though whether they were deployed on Daniel Defoe's advice is not clear.)

By the end of 1706 Defoe was well enough connected to dine regularly with the men who were steering the union treaty through the Scots parliament. 'I am perfectly unsuspected as corresponding with anybody in England,' he assured Harley. 'To the merchants I am about to settle here in trade, building ships etc. With the lawyers I want to purchase a house and land to bring my family to live upon it . . . Today I am going into a partnership with a member of parliament in a glass house, tomorrow with another in a salt work. With the Glasgow mutineers I am to be a fish merchant, with the

Aberdeen men a woollen and with the Perth and Western men a linen manufacturer . . .' This cover as an enterprising businessman anxious to settle in Scotland was so convincing that Defoe wormed his way into the heart of the negotiations. Through his contacts he was able to sit in on most of the crucial debates in the Parliament, becoming at one stage an 'advisor' and virtual secretary to one of the Parliament's key economic committees (the one deciding how much 'equivalent' Scotland should be paid for its share of settling England's national debt). He even managed to infiltrate a clandestine meeting of Jacobites who were planning armed resistance. 'Some force was proposed,' he told Harley, 'but they found themselves too weak for the attempt.' He was particularly pleased with that venture. 'In this little scheme of their affairs I have acted a true spy to you, for by an unexpected success I have obtained a converse with some gentlemen belonging to the Duke of Gordon who are very frank.'

Defoe was confident to the point of complacency. In his letters to London he was scathing about the Scots. 'I act the old part of Cardinal Richelieu,' he informed Harley in March 1707. 'I have my spies and my pensioners in every place, and I confess 'tis the easiest thing in the world to hire people here to betray their friends.' A few weeks later he wrote of the Scots clergy: 'I have some engine at work among the ministers. In short, money will do anything here.'

By then the great Whig project was almost in place. Despite the determined delaying tactics of its Parliamentary opponents and the noisy opposition of the Edinburgh mob, the Act of Union trundled its way through the Scots parliament, article by article. It was finally passed on 16 January 1707. The event prompted Defoe to write: 'I am now with joy to acquaint you that the treaty of union received the touch of the sceptre this day and a universal joy of the friends of both nations runs through the city.'

Not that Defoe's work was done. The Act did not take effect until 1 May 1707 and there was still a great deal of bitterness, particularly among the supporters of the exiled James Stuart.

Jacobite agitators were already trying to stir up the Scots against the Union. 'The mob are a machine,' Defoe wrote to Harley. 'The Jacobites have wound them up to a pitch and nothing but time, management, temper and success can reduce them to the proper medium. They must be let run down gradually or they precipitate at once into all manner of confusion.'

Defoe was right to worry about the Jacobites. In the summer of 1707 Jacobite emissaries from France had landed in Scotland and were trying to provoke the Scots to insurrection. Two of them were captured, which prompted Defoe to sound a warning to Harley. On 18 September 1707 he wrote: 'Should the K(ing) of France support them, not with men for they need them not, but should he send about 200 officers, arms and ammunition, artillery etc. to furnish them and about 100,000 crowns in money he might soon get together 12 or 15,000 stout fellows and do a great deal of mischief.'

Within a year the first of the Jacobite insurgencies was under way. In March 1708 a flotilla of French ships tried – and failed – to land troops led by James Stuart (the Old Pretender) in Fife. The ships were chased away by the Royal Navy and a few Jacobite lairds were rounded up, tried and acquitted, to the fury of the Whig regime. Defoe's warnings about the potential menace of the Jacobites were sound. Much more serious Jacobite risings were to follow in 1715, 1719 and 1745.

With his career as a spy coming to an end, Defoe resumed his campaign to acquire an official post. He certainly felt he deserved one. He had been a good and faithful spy. In September 1707 he wrote yet another begging letter to Harley claiming that 'I faithfully served, I baulked no cases, I appeared in print when others dared not to open their mouths, and without boasting I ran as much risk of my life as a grenadier in storming a counterscarp.'

Defoe never lost his interest in Scottish affairs. He continued to lob the occasional letter of advice to the government about its policies in Scotland. One such letter is dated 13 July 1711 and in an argument that is curiously modern he urges the abolition of the post of 'Third Secretary' (Scottish Secretary). In Defoe's opinion having a Secretary of State for Scotland only kept alive the Scots' sense of difference from the rest of Britain. It also represented a centre of political power outside London . 'As to the power they want by the office,' he wrote, 'the very reason why they desire it is a strong argument against Her Majesty's bestowing it.'

In 1719, he published the first volume of *Robinson Crusoe – The Life and Strange Surprising Adventures of Robinson Crusoe of York, Mariner* – which was inspired by the story of a marooned Scottish seafarer, Alexander Selkirk of Largo in Fife.

AS OTHERS SEE US:
JONATHAN SWIFT

IT WAS ROBERT BURNS WHO in his poem 'To A Louse' wrote the famous plea: *'Oh wad some Power the giftie gie us/To see oursels as ithers see us!/ It wad frae monie a blunder free us,/An' foolish notion.'* However, what used to be called 'the Scotch character' has never lacked the well-publicized critique of others. There have been many observers (most of them English) who were happy to point out Scottish shortcomings. Among them was Jonathan Swift, whose hatred of Scotland and the Scots was visceral.

Swift was an ardent royalist who never forgave the Scots for handing Charles I over to the English Parliament. He was also an Anglican who hated Scots Presbyterians more than he disliked Roman Catholics. He seemed to see the whole tragic episode of the mid-seventeenth-century regicide and the British Civil Wars as the fault of the 'cursed, hellish, villainy, treachery, treasons of the Scots'.

In his copy of *Lord Clarendon's History of the Rebellion* (published in 1707) Swift's anti-Scottish bile spilled out in notes pencilled in the margins. Every time Clarendon mentions the word Scot or Scotland, Swift writes 'Scotch dogs' or 'cursed Scotch' or 'cursed

Scottish hell hounds'. Most of Swift's scribblings were in response to Clarendon's more measured judgements.

When, for example, Clarendon ruminates on the nature of the 'declaration' that the Scots army made when it marched into England, Swift adds: 'Abominable, damnable, Scotch hellish dogs for ever. Let them wait for Cromwell to plague them and enslave their scabby nation.' When Clarendon declares that the king's general, the Marquis of Montrose, killed 1,500 men of the Clan Campbell in one battle (Inverlochy), Swift notes: 'Not half enough of that execrable breed.' In Swift's opinion Montrose was 'the only man in Scotland who had ever one grain of virtue; and was therefore abhorred and murdered publicly by his hellish countrymen'.

When Clarendon describes the execution of Montrose in Edinburgh in 1650, Swift reaches an ecstasy of loathing. 'Oh! If the whole nation, to a man, were just so treated! Begin with Argyle, and next with the fanatic dogs who teased him with their kirk scurrilities . . . Most treacherous, damnable, infernal Scots for ever!'

THE ADVENTURES OF
DUDLEY BRADSTREET

ONE OF THE ODDEST CHARACTERS to emerge from the Jacobite insurrection of 1745–6 was a certain Captain Dudley Bradstreet. The escapades of this Irish adventurer were, it is believed, the basis for the exploits of Thackeray's fictional hero Barry Lyndon, a story that film director Stanley Kubrick made into a handsome (and I think underrated) movie. According to Bradstreet – admittedly not the most unimpeachable source – it was he, Bradstreet, who persuaded the Jacobite leadership to turn at Derby and march back to Scotland, where the rebellion collapsed on Culloden Moor in April 1746. If Bradstreet's account is accurate then he single-handedly shaped the course of British history in the middle of the eighteenth century.

This is how he tells the story in his book *The Life and Uncommon Adventures of Captain Dudley Bradstreet*, which was published in the 1750s. When the Jacobite army marched into England, the enterprising Irishman offered his services as a spy to the Duke of Newcastle. The minister took up Bradstreet's offer and assigned him to mix with his fellow Irishmen in London (in Highgate,

Hackney and Hampstead) and try to gauge their Jacobite sympathies. 'I sounded many of them,' he wrote, 'and found none who had any regard for the Pretender's cause.'

Then Newcastle organized a quick show trial and had Bradstreet dumped into a London prison to spy on the criminals and the disaffected. According to Bradstreet, this short spell in jail was fruitful. Not only did he meet the girl with whom he'd had his 'first amour' but he gained the confidence of the Jacobites there and made a string of useful contacts. He supposedly learned that 1,500 French and Spanish prisoners in Portsmouth Castle were planning to break out and join Bonnie Prince Charlie's army, 'which Danger was afterwards confirmed, but prevented in time by my Intelligence'.

So pleased (Bradstreet said) were the Hanoverian authorities with his efforts that they dispatched him north to infiltrate the Jacobite army and do what mischief he could. He was given £100, told to get himself a decent set of clothes, call himself Oliver Williams and pass himself off as an English squireling with Jacobite sympathies. Bradstreet's first stop was Lichfield where he offered military advice to the Duke of Cumberland, who was so impressed that he kitted the Irishman out with 'a fine Gelding, Arms and Furniture' as well as a guide.

On the evening of 5 December 1745, Dudley Bradsteet trotted into Derby to offer his many talents to the Young Pretender. When stopped by a Jacobite officer, he wrote that: 'I told the fellow that I was a Man of Quality come to serve the Prince Regent, and would be followed by all my Friends if my Usage was good, and desired to be brought to the Prince's Quarters directly. I heard them whisper that an *English* Lord was come to join them.'

When he was quizzed by the Jacobite leadership, the spy told them that their position was hopeless. The Duke of Cumberland was at nearby Lichfield with cavalry and nine thousand infantry. The Duke of Richmond was on the right flank with another army, while a force led by Generals Hawley and Ligonier was waiting north of London with another 'eight or nine thousand'. In other words, the forces arrayed against the Jacobites were overwhelming. If they set out for London they would be cut off and then cut to pieces.

When Bradstreet was asked to repeat this depressing but vital information to the entire Jacobite high command in Exeter House, he claimed that Charles Edward Stuart stepped out of a closet, pointed to him and said: 'That fellow will do me more Harm than all the Elector's Army.' Then he turned to the Jacobite leaders and said: 'You ruin, abandon and betray me if you don't march on.' Then he stamped out of the room in high dudgeon.

There is certainly some truth in Bradstreet's account. It is known that Charles and his military advisers fell out at Derby. The Prince believed that the Jacobite army should press on to London. His generals argued that, as they had virtually no support in England and as there was no sign of French reinforcements, they should retreat to Scotland and consolidate north of the border. It is not impossible that the Jacobite leaders used Bradstreet's information to press their argument with the Prince.

'I was afterwards informed the Rebel Prince wept that Night on Account of the Retreat resolved on in Council,' Bradstreet wrote. 'I had them all of my Side the Question, except Cameron of Lochiel (a Man of the greatest Abilities for the Field or Cabinet among them), and Colonel Sullivan, both which were for marching to London. Soon after I withdrew, and the Council broke up, several of them saying . . . if his Highness has a mind to throw away our Lives and his own, we have not.'

When the Jacobite army began its retreat, Captain Dudley Bradstreet was in the ranks. As Mr Oliver Williams he trudged north with the demoralized Jacobites as far as Wigan where he abandoned them and joined the Hanoverian troops who were pursuing the retreating Scots and Irish. He was then dispatched to London for a 'debriefing' about the state of the Jacobite forces.

Bradstreet was in no doubt about his own importance. If, he

claimed, he had not persuaded the Jacobites of the futility of their position: 'I am of Opinion, they might easily have avoided the Duke (of Cumberland) and his Army; nor was there, to my knowledge, four thousand disciplined Men to oppose this Army, flushed with Victory, till they entered our rich and renowned Capital, where the Mob and those of desperate Fortunes would join them, for the Sake of Plunder and Change.'

But if Bradstreet thought that the Hanoverian regime would be grateful for his efforts, he was soon disabused. He spent the next five years trying to squeeze some reward out of the Duke of Cumberland and the Duke of Newcastle. When that failed he began petitioning King George II himself. Nothing worked. Abandoned by his spymasters and paymasters, Captain Dudley Bradstreet embarked on a new career as a playwright, actor and conjuror. He specialized in outrageous sketches, one of which advocated 'a licensed Bawd and Pimp in every Parish, to take only the same Care of the Human Race that is taken of the Brutal'. When his stage career petered out he returned to Ireland and took up business brewing ale. Predictably, perhaps, Bradstreet ended up being pursued across Ireland by officers of His Majesty's Excise.

King George's unlikely secret agent died in his native Ireland sometime in 1763.

CARLUCCIO AND THE
QUEEN OF HEARTS

ON THE SOUTH BANK OF THE River Arno in Florence, on the corner of the Via Mazetta and the Piazza Santo Spirito, there stands a rather run-down mansion known as the Palazzo Guadagni. The sixteenth-century building is handsome enough, but unremarkable in a city of dazzling Renaissance architecture. It serves as a library-cum-community centre. Few tourists pay it any attention.

They should – particularly, perhaps, if they are Scottish. It was behind the Palazzo Guadagni's thick walls and huge wooden doors that the Jacobite dream finally guttered and died. It was in the Palazzo Guadagni that the exiled Charles Edward Stuart, 'Bonnie Prince Charlie', fought his final battles to be recognized as the King of England, Scotland, Ireland and France. It was here that he waged a squalid and ultimately violent war with his young wife, Louise de Stolberg, a woman known to the intelligentsia of Europe as the 'Queen of Hearts' (more than 200 years before Diana Spencer accorded herself the same title). It was in the Palazzo Guadagni that the 'noble cause' of the Stuarts – for which so many people had died – ended in a miasma of bitterness, alcohol and adultery.

What I find most haunting about the Palazzo Guadagni is that it is unchanged. It looks much as it did in the late eighteenth century. It is not hard to imagine the large, florid, overweight figure of Charles Edward Stuart wheezing his way from room to room, or sitting in the shaded gallery overlooking the Piazza Santo Spirito with his bored young wife, squabbling over whom they should or should not invite to dinner, or whether they should avoid the opera because the Duke of Tuscany had forbidden them to set up the coat of arms of the King of England over their box. The atmosphere inside that baroque, florid interior must have been poisonous.

The marriage of Charles Stuart and Louise de Stolberg was a calamity from the beginning. She married him for a throne that he could not deliver: he married her for a male heir whom she failed to produce. He was autocratic and arrogant, with an unshakeable belief in his right to rule from the British throne: she was restless, ambitious and sociable. It proved to be a marriage crafted in Hell. Demoralized by failure, exile and constant diplomatic and social snubs Charles sank ever deeper into drink, illness and self-pity. Louise's response was to learn to despise him and then punish him by taking a string of lovers. With one of them – the poet Vittorio Alfieri – she ran away.

For six years, between 1774 and 1780, against the faded Renaissance interiors of the Palazzo Guadagni, Charles and Louise mauled one another with breathtaking viciousness. Florentine society sniggered and waited for the marriage to fall apart in disgrace, while every twist and turn of their disastrous relationship was charted by spies working for the British government's envoy in Florence, the waspish Sir Horace Mann. Mann's letters to his friend Horace Walpole are the best available record of the turbulent relationship of Louise de Stolberg and Charles Stuart.

Horace Mann had been keeping an eye on the exiled Stuarts ever since he had been made the British government's representative in Italy. He was good at his job. In 1744, the year before Charles

Edward Stuart set foot in Scotland, Mann was warning London that 'The Boy' (as he called Charles) was about to 'make a visit to Miss North and Grey' (his code name for Scotland). But he added prophetically that 'it must end in nothing, for it is not to be supposed that there is any considerable number of people, either in England or in Scotland, so mad as to espouse so foolish a cause.'

Popular history has defined Charles Edward Stuart by one brief period in his life, his career as 'Bonnie Prince Charlie' that began in July 1745, when he landed on the Hebridean island of Eriskay, and ended in the autumn of 1746 when he was picked up at Loch nan Uamh by the French frigate *L'Heureux* and sailed away to France after the Jacobite defeat at Culloden. In fact, he had another forty-two years to live – forty-two years during which he never stopped plotting, scheming and lobbying the European powers to return the Stuarts to the British throne from which his grandfather, James VII of Scotland and II of England, had been driven in 1688.

Charles's most likely ally was the King of France, who was usually happy to support a cause that might embarrass the British. Charles spent the first few years of his 'exile' in Paris until Louis XV tired of him in 1749 and had him run out of the city, trussed hand and foot in 'silken cord', as far as Avignon, where he fell out with the local archbishop when he began organizing prizefights and boxing matches.

For more than a decade Charles wandered around Europe: in and out of Paris; making a secret (and possibly mythical) visit to London, where he ostensibly abandoned Roman Catholicism and converted to Anglicanism in the belief that it would secure the Stuart cause; becoming a father when his loyal mistress, Clementina Walkinshaw, gave birth to a daughter – Charlotte, his only known child – in October 1753.

Then, at the beginning of January 1766, James Stuart, the Old Pretender and Charles's father, died in Rome. His demise provoked Horace Mann to comment: 'The Romans were vastly impatient to bury him, that their theatres might be opened.' On his father's death Charles began describing himself as 'Charles III' of England, Scotland and Ireland, though the British government acted swiftly to make sure that nobody else in Europe called him that. The power and prestige of Hanoverian Britain was growing fast. The Jacobite cause had few advocates. With the major exceptions of France and Spain, no European country wanted anything to do with the defeated and discredited Stuarts.

Charles was undeterred. He had hopes for recognition from the Vatican where his brother Henry was a cardinal. Charles rushed to Rome to start lobbying the Pope to recognize him as the rightful heir to the British throne. At the prodding of Cardinal Henry and the French and Spanish ambassadors, Pope Clement XIII asked the College of Cardinals if the Vatican should recognize Charles. But, to no one's surprise, the Vatican's red hats gave Charles and the Stuart cause the thumbs-down. Sir Horace Mann was delighted: Charles never forgave the Pope or his cardinals and railed against them for the rest of his life.

Charles did his best to play the King in Exile, but was thwarted at every turn. He was installed in the Palazzo Muti in Rome, and the Pope ordered that the royal coat of arms above the gates should be removed. When some Jacobites from the Scots, Irish and English colleges in Rome began deferring to Charles as their monarch, they were banished from Rome. Roman society insisted on treating him as one more aristocrat, and a minor one at that. It was content to know him as the Count of Albany but never as King Charles III.

'The Pretender is hardly thought of even at Rome,' wrote William Hamilton, the British envoy in Naples. 'The life he leads is now very regular and sober, his chief occupation is shooting in the environs of Rome, and the only people he can see or converse with are his few attendants.' Hamilton goes on to quote an English lady who visited Charles in Rome and described him as having 'all the reason in the world to be melancholy, for there is not a soul goes near him, not knowing what to call him'.

But the neglect never dented Charles's dynastic ambitions, and every dynasty needs heirs. His mistress, Clementina Walkinshaw, was a commoner and therefore not marriageable. In the early 1770s Charles sent one of his aides to scour Europe for a suitable wife. He found one in Louise de Stolberg-Gedern, the nineteen-year-old daughter of a minor North German princeling who had been killed fighting for the Austrians in 1757. There was even a Scottish connection: Louise's mother was a distant relation of the Bruces. It was reported to Charles that the blonde and blue-eyed Louise had 'a good figure, a pretty face, and excellent teeth, with all the qualities which Your Majesty can desire'.

Sentimentalists have painted Louise de Stolberg as a young innocent sacrificed to a raddled, middle-aged drunk. But Louise knew what she was doing. She was worldly, well educated and calculating. Charles Stuart was better off than most of the minor royalty Louise might have expected to marry, and he trailed the prospect – however remote – of a crown. In fact, she was impatient to wed him. They were married in Paris, by proxy, on 28 March 1772, and then again, in the flesh, at the Marefoschi Palace at Macereta on 17 April.

Charles and Louise got off to a grand start. Cardinal Henry organized a triumphal procession into Rome for the 'King of England' and his new queen. Every exiled Jacobite in Italy (and many curious Hanoverians) turned out to see Charles and his bride ride in splendour through the streets of Rome. Ensconced in the Palazzo Muti, the couple tried to live the life of European royals, 'receiving' guests in their court, rarely venturing out to socialize with lesser mortals. So far as the rest of Europe was concerned, however, the couple were play-acting. The new Pope – Clement XIV – refused to recognize Charles as a king. The aristocracy of Rome were happy enough to call on the 'Count and Countess of Albany' but declined to see anything 'majestic' in Charles and his consort. As the diplomatic snubs continued, Charles grew increasingly morose and sought refuge in fortified Cyprus wine. By the end of 1773, Sir Horace Mann was reporting to London that the

Louise de Stolberg-Gedern

Pretender was 'seldom quite sober, and frequently commits the greatest disorders in his family'.

Not surprisingly, Louise began to chafe under Charles's regime. She was plainly an attractive and intelligent young woman who had her admirers. One of them, the Swiss *littérateur* Charles Victor de Bonstetten, gave her the title 'Queen of Hearts'. Another of Louise's devotees was a young Englishman called Thomas Coke, who like many of his sort was doing the Grand Tour of Europe before settling down to his estates in England. Whether or not Louise cuckolded Charles with Bonstetten or Thomas Coke is not clear. Bonstetten hints at it. But they were the first of many young men who paid court to the Queen of Hearts over the next five years.

At the beginning of 1774 Charles decided that he could no longer suffer Rome and its perpetual insults. He decided to decamp with his 'court' to Florence. In some ways it was an odd decision. The Duke of Tuscany was just as hostile to the Stuarts as the Pope and had no intention of risking the wrath of the British by welcoming the Pretender. Charles was also putting himself *exactly* where the British government wanted him: in the same city as their most effective spymaster, Sir Horace Mann. In fact, Mann's residence near the Ponte Santa Trinita overlooking the River Arno was within a few streets of the Palazzo Guadagni.

So began Charles's bizarre, pathetic sojourn in Florence. He never abandoned his claim to the British throne. He never stopped seeing himself as the rightful 'King of England'. He was affronted when the Duke of Tuscany refused to recognize him. He was incensed when the Duke ordered that his royal coat of arms be removed from above his box at the theatre.

Only the local Jacobite exiles and the beggars on the street recognized Charles as the king he believed himself to be. He took pleasure in 'laying hands' on the heads of the poor to cure them of scrofula and assorted ailments. In short, he led a strange, twilight existence in which he grew gradually more demoralized and drunken. According to Horace Mann's spies, he was consuming up to twelve bottles of Cyprus wine every day, though this may have been an exaggeration to feed Mann's spite. Charles's health deteriorated. The splendid physique that had enabled him to undertake those long marches through Britain was failing. His legendary 'flight across the heather' in the autumn of 1746 had taken its toll. He became chronically breathless and suffered from occasional attacks of asthma. His stomach was troubled and his belching and farting were a constant source of embarrassment. Apoplexy was never far away. His legs swelled until he had to be half-carried everywhere he went. Dropsy inflated his already ample stomach.

Sir Horace Mann was convinced that the Pretender was on his last legs. In August 1776 he reported to Viscount Weymouth (the British government official responsible for the Mediterranean area) that the Pretender's 'frequent epileptic fits . . . must end in an apoplexy, and that is not far distant . . . His digestion is quite spoilt. Should his death occur, I will dispatch a notice by a courier.' Weymouth was not over-concerned about the Pretender's possible demise. 'If that event should occur,' he replied to Mann, 'the early notice is not of importance.'

But Charles creaked on despite everything, including the loathing of his young wife. She took to writing him poisonous little letters. One dated 5 June 1775 berates him for expecting her to rise at seven a.m. She writes: 'That must be a joke of Your Majesty's, otherwise one would believe you were in your dotage. You are not yet as old as that, Sir, but it certainly would do you no honour in the world to have people imagining that you . . . had degenerated to the point when you did not want to spend more than a few hours in bed with a young woman who is pretty and who loves you.' Louise went on to threaten to tell the world of his physical and sexual inadequacies.

The world might not have been interested but Sir Horace Mann certainly was. He kept an extraordinarily close eye on the couple's sex life. The last thing the Hanoverian regime in Britain wanted was yet another Stuart to carry the Jacobite cause into the next generation. Mann's agents in the Palazzo Guadagni were assiduous. They even scoured the laundry baskets every month to make sure that Louise was still menstruating. Mann was also paying Charles's physician for regular reports on the Pretender's physical and mental health. English and Scottish visitors to the Palazzo Guadagni (and there were quite a few) were expected to pass on their impressions to the British envoy in Florence.

Mann paints a vivid picture of the Pretender's miserable life there. 'He is very ill in his health from eating and more from excessive drinking,' he wrote in 1776. 'He goes every day to the theatre . . . but is frequently obliged by sickness at his stomach to retire to the common and much-frequented corridor. I have seen him in that condition, assisted by two servants, all the others that attend there fly from such a nuisance.' It is a dismal image: the fat, sickly, ageing Pretender to the British throne retching and vomiting in a public place.

Florentine society was not fleeing from Louise. She was an attractive young woman and very popular. According to Mann's report: 'Visitors, however, to his wife go thither as usual. He is jealous to such a degree that neither there or at home is she ever out of his sight. All the avenues to her room, excepting through his own, are barricaded.'

These sad domestic arrangements were at last interrupted by the strange figure of the Italian 'poet and tragedian' Count Vittorio Alfieri of Piedmont. Some accounts claim that Alfieri first saw Louise in a gallery at the Uffizi where she was studying a portrait of one of her distant ancestors, Charles XII of Sweden; that Alfieri then had made for him an exact copy of the suit of clothes that King Charles was wearing in the portrait; and that he walked about in the clothes under the windows of the Palazzo Guadagni. Whatever the truth of this story, Alfieri in the end created a perfectly good excuse to hang about the Palazzo. He was researching the life of Mary Queen of Scots for a play that he intended to write (and eventually did write). Who better to quiz about Mary than one of her descendants, Charles Edward Stuart? Alfieri became a regular visitor to the Stuart 'court'. While the wine-befuddled Pretender dozed on his throne, Alfieri seduced the Queen of Hearts – if, that is, she needed seducing. Alfieri wrote later that this idyll was marred only by his lover's 'querulous, unreasonable and constantly drunken old husband.'

The more Charles drank, the more isolated he became. The Duke of Tuscany saw him as a hopeless menace. Nor was the Duke pleased by the rumours that were circulating about Louise and Alfieri. The Duke labelled the Palazzo Guadagni 'that house of scandal' and eventually forbade the Florentine aristocracy to frequent it. As Charles's social and political isolation increased, he grew steadily more bitter and rancorous, which led Louise to hate him all the more.

It was a tense and squalid situation and on 30 November 1780 it exploded into violence. From all accounts, Charles had been drinking even more heavily than usual and reminiscing about his escapades in Scotland and England during the Jacobite insurrection. A row developed and escalated from their usual shouting match into a physical attack by Charles on his wife. Some claim that he was trying to rape her. Whatever the truth of that, there is no doubt about the attack. Her frantic screams brought a dozen servants rushing into her bedroom, and all of them saw Charles assault his wife.

It was the end of the marriage. With the connivance of her lover, Louise fled into the Convent of the White Nuns in the Via del Mandorlo. When an outraged Charles tried to gain access to his wife, the abbess refused to let him in and left him screaming abuse on the street. A few weeks later, escorted by an armed guard, Louise left the convent for Rome and the palace of her brother-in-law Cardinal Henry. Henry hoped, somehow, to limit the damage to the Stuart cause by reconciling the couple. A forlorn hope: Charles and Louise never met again. Sir Horace Mann, of course, was delighted.

At the end of December he wrote to London: 'The mould for any more casts of Royal Stuarts has been broken, or what is equivalent to it is now shut up in a convent of nuns . . . Out of reach of any Dabbler who might foister in any spurious copy. Historians may now close the lives of that family.'

Charles tried to restore some respectability to the Palazzo Guadagni by 'legitimizing' his daughter Charlotte by his mistress Clementina Walkinshaw. He made her his heir and invited her to live with him in Florence. Charlotte arrived from Bordeaux (where she was the mistress of the archbishop Ferdinand Rohan) and took up residence at the Palazzo Guadagni at the beginning of October 1784. For a while she brought some life into the Stuart 'court'. To her father's satisfaction she took her 'royal' duties seriously by insisting that servants and visitors address Charles as 'Majesty' and herself as 'Highness'. She also tended to the ailing Pretender with a care and affection that Louise had never shown.

On behalf of his Hanoverian masters, Sir Horace Mann continued to monitor Charles's steady decay. 'Poor Count Albany declines every day visibly,' Mann wrote in December 1784. 'The disorder in his legs increases. His daughter did well to come in time to reap his succession, for which she will not wait long. The faculties of his mind are as weak as his body.' As it happened, Sir Horace died first, though Charles's end was not long in coming. Aged sixty-seven, he died in Rome in the early hours of 30 January 1788. His body was carried to the cathedral at Frascati where he lay in splendour, tricked out in royal robes with a replica of the English crown on his head, the sceptre in one hand and the sword of state in the other. His brother the Cardinal said a requiem Mass over his corpse and then declared himself to be Henry IX, King of England, Scotland and Ireland. Henry struck his own coronation medal, which carried the motto *Non desideris hominum, sed voluntate Dei* – not by the wish of men but by the will of God. Charlotte Stuart, née Walkinshaw, followed her father to the grave the following year, killed by a malignancy in her liver.

The Queen of Hearts lived on. Louise found Rome much more to her taste than Florence. She and Alfieri became one of the city's more fashionable, if somewhat raffish, couples. Cardinal Henry contrived to have Alfieri exiled from Rome, but Louise and he found ways to keep their affair alive. When Charles died in 1788 Louise and Alfieri were in Paris, enjoying the treats of that city. Two years later they toured England where they were introduced to King George's consort, Queen Charlotte. Louise found that she did not much like the land that her husband had longed so desperately to rule. Nor was England much impressed by her. Horace Mann's old friend Horace Walpole wrote waspishly of Louise: 'Well! I have seen Madame D'Albany who has not a ray of royalty about her. She has good eyes and teeth; but I think can have had no more beauty than remains except youth. She is civil and easy, but German and ordinary.'

Louise and Alfieri set up home in Paris but never married, perhaps because Louise feared losing her pension from Charles's estate. When Alfieri died in 1803 Louise fled south again to Tuscany. She lived out her days in Florence holding court in her apartment, receiving visitors while seated on a thronelike chair, eating from plates decorated with the English coat of arms and demanding that her servants should address her as 'Majesty' and that they should walk backwards when leaving her presence. She continued acting the part of Queen of England until she died in 1824.

EXECUTING ARCHIE

THEY HANGED THE LAST Jacobite martyr at Tyburn in London on Thursday, 7 June 1753, half an hour after noon. He was Doctor Archie Cameron and he went out in some style: light-coloured coat, red waistcoat, red breeches and a new, well-powdered wig. His dying declaration was an address to Sir Richard Glyn, the Sheriff of London, who was in charge of the hanging (and who couldn't wait to get it over and done with).

'Sir, you see a fellow subject going to pay his last debt,' Archie told the fretful Sir Richard. 'I the more cheerfully resign my life as it is taken from me for doing my duty according to my conscience. I freely forgive all my enemies and those who are instrumental in taking away my life. I thank God I die in charity with all mankind.'

After proclaiming to the crowd that he would die, as he had lived, a faithful Anglican, Archie announced himself 'done with this world', joined in a few prayers, embraced the clergyman and was duly 'turned off'. His body danced on the hangman's rope for twenty minutes before being cut down, stripped, sliced open and the heart removed and burned. After which, Archie's remains were carted off to be buried.

On the face of it, the hanging of Archie was a piece of wanton cruelty. The Jacobite uprising had been over for nearly eight years. The chances of a Stuart comeback were next to nil. Many other Jacobites had been pardoned. Archie's influential brother Lochiel, the chief of Clan Cameron, was five years dead. Archie himself was no military man, but a physician who had tended the wounded of both sides in the insurrection of 1745–6.

His 'crime' was to have slipped into Scotland from France to spread the news that Charles Edward Stuart had abandoned Catholicism to become an Anglican and to invite the Jacobite clans to steel themselves for yet another rebellion once George II had been assassinated. In the exhausted and demoralized Highlands his message went down like a lead balloon. He had hardly been in Scotland a month before he was betrayed (by another Cameron), picked up and bundled off to London for interrogation and trial.

Archie's mission and Archie's fate say much about Jacobitism. Despite everything that had happened, Charles Stuart was still at odds with reality. He believed that all he had to do was join the Church of England and the British people would 'come out' for the Stuarts. It was lunacy, of course, but since the lunatic had the power of France at his back the British government was obliged to take him seriously. Seriously enough, at least, to hunt down and execute Archie Cameron.

Archie's dismal end underscores two crucial aspects of the Jacobite rebellions that popular history forgets: religious conflict and international power politics. They were always present. Every time the Stuart banner was raised in the glens of Scotland, behind it stood a Catholic power, usually France. Where the Jacobites of Britain saw a crusade to restore their 'rightful' king, the British elites saw the manoeuvrings of Roman Catholic absolutism.

It is not too fanciful to compare the situation in mid-eighteenth-century Europe with the Cold War of 1945 to 1990. The parallels are not exact, but they are striking. Europe – and indeed much of the world – was dominated by two competing power blocs, each with its own persuasive ideology. Military power was almost equally balanced between them. Each had its 'spheres of influence', colonies and client states. Neither hesitated to dabble in the affairs of the other. Just as the CIA backed the Contras of Nicaragua and the KGB propped up the Marxist rebels of Angola, so the French regime financed and armed the Jacobites of Britain. The Stuarts, father and son, were pieces in a wider game of power politics. Not pawns, exactly, more like bishops. Quite useful, occasionally important, but in the end expendable. Archie Cameron was put to death by the British government in 1753 on much the same grounds that the Americans sent Ethel and Julius Rosenberg to the electric chair in 1953. He was a threat to security, a representative of an alien ideology, a member of a 'fifth column'. The Hanoverian regime hoped that his death would be an example to anyone else who might be tempted to flirt with the Stuart cause.

Archie Cameron was one of the Jacobites who fled with Charles Stuart on the French ship *L'Heureux* and then joined his brother Lochiel's regiment of the French Army as a surgeon. Like most of the Jacobite exiles he longed to return to Scotland. Unlike many, he plotted to make it happen. As he stood on the gallows at Tyburn that June day in 1753, he must have wished he'd stayed in France.

There is something peculiarly poignant about Archie's death, even after 250 years. If nothing else, Archie is a reminder that there was more to Jacobitism than red-shanked tribesmen with broadswords and Lochaber axes. He was a physician and a civilized man. He had studied moral philosophy under the great Francis Hutcheson at Glasgow University, and medicine at Edinburgh and Paris. He had gone into The '45 with serious misgivings, but through it all he had been loyal to the Stuart cause. His reward was to be crushed in the gear wheels of European politics.

JACOBITE ECONOMICS

IT HAS LONG SEEMED TO ME that Jacobitism was right-wing, backward-looking, intellectually regressive, morally bankrupt, and financed by foreign tyrants. The much-romanticized Jacobite rebellions (1690, 1708, 1715, 1719, 1745) were essentially attempted right-wing *coups d'état*. The brave, half-starved men (Scots, Irish and French) who died in the rain at Culloden Moor deserved better than the coterie of ambitious and bungling aristocrats who led them to ruin. Nothing I have read, heard or seen has persuaded me otherwise.

But for every rule there is an exception. For me the great Jacobite exception is Sir James Steuart. If ever a man's reputation deserved to be resurrected, dusted down and hauled into the light it is Sir James Steuart's. He was a philosopher, social commentator, political analyst and brilliant economist whose work was so dreaded by Adam Smith that he refused even to mention Steuart's name in *The Wealth of Nations*.

James Steuart was ahead of his time by at least one hundred years. If Adam Smith was the messiah of 'the invisible hand' of the free market, James Steuart was the preacher of the gospel of state intervention. The market alone, he argued, would never make a good society. The 'statesman' (as he called the government) had a duty to moderate the economy in the interests of decency and wider prosperity. It was a call that John Maynard Keynes was to echo many years later.

'I say that whoever can transform the most consumable commodities of a country [i.e. human labour] into the most durable and most beneficial works makes a high improvement,' he declared in his 1767 opus *An Inquiry into the Principles of Political Oeconomy*. 'If therefore meat and drink . . . can be turned into harbours, high roads, canals and public buildings, is not the improvement inexpressible? This is the power of every statesman to accomplish.'

Like other Jacobite intellectuals of the time, Steuart was a product of the Scottish Enlightenment. Born in Edinburgh in 1712, the son of a Lord Advocate, he spent much of his life wandering Europe. He was a gifted linguist and spoke French, German, Italian and Spanish. And he seems to have been gripped by that pathological curiosity which, if it loses focus, turns so many Scots into *idiots savants* (I may include myself). Every human activity was grist to Steuart's mill.

Steuart's years in exile between 1745 and 1763 were productive. He studied education in the Duchy of Wurttemberg, irrigation in rural Spain, the plight of agriculture in Picardy, and the economic consequences of the Seven Years' War. He even examined the state of the kitchen gardens around Padua. It all went into his *Principles*. In many places Steuart's prose is leaden, but his ideas leap off the page. He regarded unemployment as a 'breach of contract and an abuse'. He advocated that public money should be (carefully) spent on new and struggling industries 'and thereby keep that industry alive'.

He saw taxes as a good method by which to 'promote industry . . . in consequences of their being expended by the state: that is by increasing demand and circulation'. And he argued for a taxation strategy that would 'advance the pu.blic good, by drawing from the rich, a fund sufficient to employ both the deserving and the poor, in the service of the state'.

At a time when his Prince was whining about his lack of royal palaces and clinging to the notion of the divine right of kings (such as himself), James Steuart was arguing the case for industrial subsidies, public-sector employment, regional subventions and enlightened tax regimes. In short, all the trappings of a modern mixed economy.

He was particularly scathing about consumerism *vis-à-vis* infrastructure. 'If a thousand pounds are bestowed upon making a fire-work,' he wrote, 'a number of people are thereby employed, and gain a temporary livelihood. If the same sum is bestowed for making a canal for watering the fields of a province, a like number of people may reap the same benefit . . . but the fire-work played off, what remains but the smoke and stink of the powder? Whereas the consequence of the canal is a perpetual fertility to a formerly barren soil.'

James Steuart died in Edinburgh in 1780, having changed his surname to Denham (a condition of inheriting the English estates of his uncle, Sir Archibald Denham). He died a saddened man, believing that his genius had fallen on stony ground and that his work had been overlooked. In that, he seems to have been right.

CHEROKEE JOHN ROSS

I'D NEVER HEARD OF JOHN ROSS until one evening in the bar of the Algonquin Hotel in Manhattan. A short, dark-skinned, black-haired man overheard my accent and came over to introduce himself. He told me that he was an oilman from Oklahoma who had spent time in the North Sea oilfield and knew Scotland well. He said his name was Bill Ross and that he was a Cherokee Indian. When I voiced some surprise that a Cherokee should have a name like Ross he told me that Scots names like Ross, Macdonald, MacIntosh, Shorey and some others were very common among the Cherokee. Bill Ross was particularly proud of the fact that he could track his ancestry back to a Cherokee chief called John Ross whom he described as 'seven parts Scotsman and one part Cherokee'.

As Bill Ross enthused about his early-nineteenth-century ancestor it struck me that all I knew about the people whom we used to call Red Indians and now call Native Americans had been shaped by Hollywood, and Hollywood has always preferred colourful leaders like Crazy Horse of the Oglala Sioux or Geronimo of the Chiricahua Apache. No doubt they were formidable men, these Victorian-era horseback warriors, but if my new acquaintance was to be believed none of them did as much for their people as John Ross did for the Cherokee.

That encounter in the Algonquin fired my curiosity. The following morning, with nothing much to do, I wandered down to the New York Public Library to see what I could find about John Ross of the Cherokee. I found that Bill Ross was right. Only *one* of John Ross's great-grandmothers was a full-blooded Cherokee. The rest of his ancestry was Scots, and Highland Scots at that. His father, Daniel Ross, was a trader from Sutherland. His mother was one Mollie Macdonald, the daughter of a merchant from Inverness. John Ross, star of the Cherokee firmament, had hardly any Cherokee blood in his veins.

I also found a few photographs of Ross. They must have been taken in the 1860s when the old chief was in his seventies. He looked no more Indian than I did. In his frock coat, high-collared shirt and glossy stove-pipe hat he could have been a retired general, a senior senator, or a Presbyterian divine of the sterner sort, the kind of clergyman who walked out of the Church of Scotland in 1843 to form the Free Church. What he did not look like was the principal chief of the once-powerful Cherokee Nation.

Yet John Ross was *the* Native American statesman of the early nineteenth century. He was almost as familiar in Washington as he was in the council forums of the Cherokee. He was known on Capitol Hill as 'the Indian Prince'. He met and argued with every US President from James Madison (in 1816) to Andrew Johnson (in 1866). For more than fifty years, forty of them spent as Principal Chief, he worked tirelessly to keep the Cherokee Nation together in the face of the power of the encroaching whites. 'The great object with me,' he wrote towards the end of his life, 'has been to have the Cherokee people harmonious and united in the full and free exercise and enjoyment of all their rights of person and property. Union is strength; dissension is weakness, misery, ruin.'

That encounter in the Algonquin sparked a fascination with John

Ross that has been with me ever since. There was something about this Scots Cherokee that I found irresistible. He was a creature of strange and interesting times: a frontiersman who tried to graft the ideas of the Enlightenment onto an old culture that had hardly changed over hundreds of years; a modernizer who championed a deeply traditional people. He was idealistic, ambitious, energetic and visionary. He was also a man with a talent for making money and a taste for good living. He incurred the wrath of some of the most powerful people in the USA who saw him as a Scotchman on the make, another shifty white man out to exploit ill-educated Indians.

John Ross's story is long and complex, and set against a backdrop of great, sometimes momentous events. Most of what is now the United States was carved out of the American continent during John Ross's lifetime. The dozens of Native American nations who began the century rooted in the eastern USA were driven inexorably west. The story of John Ross offered to take me into that unexplored area where the histories of Scotland and America dovetail into one another, sometimes in the most extraordinary and unexpected ways.

I began in the region where Ross was born, where the states of Alabama, Georgia, Tennessee and North Carolina run into one another. It is a place of fertile fields and water meadows and thickly wooded hillsides. Through it run rivers that still teem with fish. In the eighteenth and nineteenth centuries it was a landscape that also teemed with game: white-tailed deer, beaver, black bear, turkey. Nowadays, in the summer at least, it is alive with tourists, almost all of them from the USA. I don't think I met another foreigner in the week or so that I spent in the region. The one sizeable city is Chattanooga whose suburbs now sprawl southwards across the Tennessee state line into northern Georgia.

Ross was born near Turkeytown in what is now Alabama in the year 1790. Both his father Daniel Ross and his maternal grandfather John Macdonald were traders, middlemen who bought pelts and furs from the Cherokee in exchange for manufactured goods. John was the third child of Daniel Ross and Mollie Macdonald's brood of three sons and six daughters. The Ross family lived on the slopes of Lookout Mountain until 1808 when they moved in with Mollie's father John Macdonald. The house that John Macdonald built – essentially a large log cabin – still exists in a suburb of Chattanooga called Rossville where it is lovingly tended by one of the local history societies.

To get some idea of John Ross's Cherokee childhood I drove a hundred or so miles east into the Great Smoky Mountains of North Carolina to the Cherokee reservation known as the Quallah Boundary. Its capital is a town called Cherokee and it is an awful place: the worst kind of tourist trap, a collection of fast-food emporia and cheapjack stores with names like 'Fort Tomahawk' and the 'Pow Wow Gift Shop'. For all that, there is much in Cherokee that John Ross would have recognized. The Museum of the Cherokee Indian has a fine collection of genuine artefacts – flint arrowheads, stone axes, clay pottery, basket work, tobacco pipes with clay bowls, dugout canoes – all handsomely displayed. And in the Oconaluftee Indian Village on the edge of the town the Cherokees have recreated an eighteenth-century village of snug, well-built log houses scattered among the trees around a traditional seven-sided 'council' building. There is not a 'wigwam' or 'tepee' to be seen. The Cherokee were settled folk, farmers and herdsmen with a culture that was totally unlike that of the nomads of the Great Plains.

I knew that this was a sanitized version of Cherokee society. Life among the Cherokee was no pastoral idyll. They were an ambitious and aggressive people. Rivalries among the tribes of the south-east – the Cherokee, the Creek, the Choctaw, the Chickasaw, the Seminole – were fierce. Warfare might have been small-scale but it was endemic and very brutal. Torture was common. The Chickasaw in particular were dreaded for their cruelty. The Creek and the Choctaw were continually at one another's throats. The Cherokee waged endless war against the Shawnee, their ancient enemies to the north.

And while it may pain sentimentalists to learn it, the Cherokee (like the other tribes of the south-east) were slave-holders. They owned thousands of black slaves. Slave-holding was a mark of affluence. The Native Americans treated their blacks no better than white slave-owners did. Blacks had no status or rights. Families were broken up, bought and sold. Miscegenation was brutally punished. Runaways were hunted down. Slavery is an aspect of Cherokee history that the guides at the Ocanaluftee village do their best to avoid. But in the middle of the nineteenth century slavery was to enmesh the Cherokee in the tragedy of the American South.

Although most of John Ross's later life is well documented, not much is known about his childhood. What *is* known is that after being tutored at home by one George Davis and then a spell at the Reverend Gideon Blackburn's mission school, John and his brother Lewis were sent to an academy at South West Point (now Kingston) in Tennessee, where after school he worked as a clerk in the burgeoning trading firm of Neilson, King and Smith. But John Ross was never drawn into the world of the frontier whites. His affection and respect for Cherokee culture deepened as he matured.

By the time Ross was in his early twenties relations between the USA and Britain were turning sour. Washington suspected (rightly) that British agents were working to stir up the tribes against the USA. The British had found an ally in the Shawnee demagogue Tecumseh, who was convinced that the Native American nations should strike an alliance with George III to drive the European Americans into the Atlantic, and then rid themselves of the British. When Tecumseh took his crusade down into the forests of the south-east he met a chilly reception from the Choctaws and the Chickasaws and outright hostility from the Cherokee.

However, when Tecumseh argued his case to the Creeks (his mother was a Creek), half the Creek townships voted to join the Shawnees' holy war. The Creek War began in July 1813 when a thousand Creek warriors, led by a Scots mixed-blood called Bill Weatherford or Red Eagle, descended on a stockade in Alabama known as Fort Mims and butchered hundreds of white men, women and children. The massacre sent shock waves along the frontier. The Tennessee legislature immediately raised an army under the command of a frontier lawyer and renowned native-hater called Andrew Jackson.

The Cherokee, the Choctaws, the Chickasaws and the non-belligerent Creeks knew that they were in a very dangerous situation. The butchery at Fort Mims had incensed the whites. In an attempt to divert their fury the Cherokee, the Choctaws, the Chickasaws and the anti-war Creeks voted to join Andrew Jackson in his war against the Red Sticks, the hostile Creek faction. John Ross volunteered to serve as adjutant with Colonel Gideon Morgan's Regiment of Mounted Cherokees.

Ross was at the culmination of the war in March 1814 when Jackson's army trapped a thousand Creek warriors and their families at Horseshoe Bend on the Tallapoosa River in Alabama. The Red Sticks fought fanatically but were no match for Jackson's regulars and militiamen and their Native American allies. More than 900 Creeks died in the day-long battle. In his report Jackson wrote: 'The power of the Creeks is, I think, forever broken.' It was. Horseshoe Bend was to the Native Americans of the south-east what the battle at Aughrim in 1691 was to Gaelic Ireland or what Culloden in 1746 was to Gaelic Scotland. It was more than a defeat. It was the end of a way of life.

Before he left on the Creek campaign John Ross had married Elizabeth Henley Brown, better known by her Cherokee name of Quatie. Little is known about Quatie. Ross hardly mentions her in his letters. But she bore Ross five children: James Macdonald Ross, Jane Ross, Allen Ross, Silas Dinsmore Ross and George Washington Ross. And it may have been through Quatie's family connections that Ross became steadily more influential. In 1816 Ross became aide to old Chief Path Killer and it was in this role that he made the first of his many long journeys to Washington to plead the Cherokee case to the US authorities.

At the heart of the Cherokee tragedy was their struggle to cope with the encroaching whites. Like all the Native Americans east of the Mississippi, the Cherokee were under heavy pressure. As immigrants from Europe flooded into the USA, the white people of the Carolinas, Tennessee and Georgia grew resentful that so much prime land was occupied by the Cherokee, the Creeks, the Choctaws and the Chickasaws. The Georgians were particularly hostile to the tribes and campaigned ceaselessly to have them removed west of the Mississippi River.

Cherokee society began to buckle under the pressure. Already, 1,500 or so Cherokee had moved west to settle on the Arkansas River. Others began to talk about joining them. They argued that the Cherokee could no longer live cheek-by-jowl with whites and must move to 'Native American Territory' west of the 'Great Father of Rivers' (the Mississippi). This 'removal party' was led by a respected Cherokee elder known as The Ridge, his son John, and his nephews Elias Boudinot and Stand Watie. The Ridge faction was encouraged and secretly funded by Georgian and US government agents.

The Removal Party represented a very small minority. Like most Native Americans, the Cherokee had an almost mystical affection for their ancestral lands. Every tree, every stream and every stone on it was sacred to them. In fact, the Cherokee had an unwritten law that anyone who sold land without the nation's permission could be executed. It was not an idle threat. In 1807 a Cherokee chief called Doublehead was killed for selling land to the US government. One of the squad who executed Doublehead was The Ridge.

As John Ross grew increasingly influential, the Cherokee Nation stepped up a gear. In 1824, the ruling council decided to build a new capital for the Cherokee Nation at New Echota near the town of Calhoun, Georgia. A Cherokee genius called Sequoia (or George Guess) devised Native America's only written language. In 1827 the Cherokee launched a newspaper called *The Cherokee Phoenix*. That same year the Cherokee published a national constitution that set up a bicameral system of elected committee and council. Executive power was to be vested in the Principal Chief who would be elected every four years by the General Council. The first Principal Chief to be elected under the new system was John Ross, at the beginning of 1828.

This display of constitutionalism by the Cherokee did not go down well with their white neighbours. The whites preferred their Native Americans 'savage' and therefore inferior. In December 1828 the Georgia legislature passed an act declaring itself sovereign over all Cherokee land lying within its boundaries. As this was a breach of all the treaties signed between the Cherokee and the USA, John Ross demanded redress. He was told by the Secretary of War, John H. Eaton, that nothing could be done and the only solution was 'a removal beyond the Mississippi, where alone can be assured your protection and peace'.

Georgia's campaign against the Cherokee was stark. Cherokee law was null and void. Tribal councils were forbidden. Cherokee courts were banned. No Cherokee could give evidence against a white person in court. All whites living among the Cherokee had to take an oath of allegiance to Georgia. Christian missionaries had to apply to Georgia for a licence or risk going to jail. White settlers were encouraged to move onto Native American land. And when gold was discovered in the north-east corner of the Cherokee Nation in July 1829, some of the most brutal whites on the frontier flooded into the area.

Ross chose to fight Georgia in the Supreme Court where he won a major victory – but a victory that the federal and state authorities simply ignored. Having declared itself sovereign, Georgia began sending teams of surveyors across the Cherokee Nation to map the territory and divide it into thousands of small lots. Lottery tickets were then sold to white Georgians for a few dollars. If Cherokee farms or crops or houses happened to stand on the land that was 'won' that was too bad. Of course, no Cherokee were allowed to buy lottery tickets.

The enthusiasm of the whites for the Cherokee land lottery was unbounded. One popular ditty ran:

All I want in this creation
Is a pretty little wife and a big plantation
Away up yonder in the Cherokee Nation.

Theoretically, the lottery winners were supposed to wait until the Cherokee had opted to move. But as soon as the lucky whites knew which patch they had won they moved in, usually ousting the Cherokee families with some brutality. John Ross returned from a trip to Washington to his estate at the Head of Coosa to find Quatie and his children cowering in one room while armed Georgians rampaged through his property. Ross's home and plantation in Georgia had been 'won' by a certain Stephen Carter because Georgia had decided that Ross 'had forfeited his right of occupancy under the existing laws of this state'.

The Georgians had a powerful ally in Andrew Jackson, the victor of Horseshoe Bend, who had by then risen to be President of the United States. Jackson's distrust and dislike of natives – all natives – was well known. One of his first projects was the Indian Removal Act of 1830 which was designed to drive *all* Native Americans into the so-called Indian Territory west of the Mississippi. Although this piece of nineteenth-century ethnic cleansing was hotly disputed, in Congress and Senate and in the newspapers, it became the law.

To many Cherokee, the Georgia land lottery followed by the Indian Removal Act were the last straws. Nothing the Cherokee could say or do would satisfy the whites. The argument in favour of emigrating west grew stronger by the week. The pro-removal faction inside the Cherokee Nation wanted to strike some kind of removal treaty with the USA. They became known as the Treaty Party. One of their adherents was John Ross's younger brother Andrew.

Ross and the majority of the Cherokee dug in their heels, however. They were determined to find some way of staying on their ancestral lands, though Ross did take the precaution of moving the Cherokee Nation's capital across the border into Tennessee, into a sheltered, well-watered site that became known as the Red Clay Council Grounds. Ross moved his own family into a one-room log cabin a few miles away. It was a far cry from the mansion house with its surrounding slave cabins to which the Ross family was accustomed.

The Red Clay Council Grounds are now a State Park that consists of a collection of timber-built, shingle-roofed buildings standing on greensward and surrounded by high trees. There is a copy of the open-sided council building in which John Ross struggled to find a way of coping with the hostility of the white world. I found myself standing under its roof, trying to imagine how this stocky, very Scottish-looking man argued his case to his Cherokee fellow citizens. Many of his contemporaries noted that Ross was never fluent in the Cherokee language and that he addressed the tribe with a translator at his side.

I also found myself wondering what he wore during these crucial, often bitter debates. Was it the leggings, long hunting shirt and turban of the traditional Cherokee? Or did he declaim at the rostrum like a Victorian clergyman in his dark suit of baggy trousers, frock coat and high collar? Probably the second alternative, I decided, otherwise one of the many East Coast and European visitors who saw Ross in action would have remarked on his 'native' attire.

It was here, on the Tennessee/Georgia border, that Ross struck up an unlikely friendship with an actor-turned-journalist called John Howard Payne, the man who wrote the words to the song 'Home Sweet Home'. Payne was in the process of reinventing himself as a serious journalist and had taken up the Cherokee cause. He and Ross were poring over some Cherokee papers in Ross's cabin late one evening in November 1835 when the Georgia Guard crashed through the door, hauled them across the border into Georgia and locked them up. They were both released within a few weeks. Payne was badly shaken by the experience but remained a useful friend to Ross and the Cherokee.

The incarceration was a crude but effective ploy to remove John Ross from the scene while US agents negotiated with the Treaty Party. A few weeks later The Ridge and his colleagues signed the agreement which has gone down in Cherokee history as the Treaty of New Echota. In exchange for five million dollars, the Treaty Party agreed to relinquish all Cherokee lands in the east and move to Indian Territory. It was a desperate act, and one that the Cherokee Nation never forgave. As The Ridge knew, it put himself and his family in serious jeopardy. One of the signatories to the Treaty of New Echota was Ross's brother Andrew.

Ross worked frantically to have the treaty overturned, and when that failed, to delay the emigration. But in the spring of 1838 the government moved 7,000 dragoons and infantry into the Cherokee Nation with orders to move the Cherokee west. The officer charged with the work was General Winfield Scott whose ancestry was as Scottish as that of John Ross. (Scott's grandfather William had stood in the Jacobite ranks at Culloden before fleeing to America.) In May 1838 Scott posted an 'address' to the Cherokee. 'Think of this, my Cherokee brethren,' Scott wrote. 'I am an old warrior and have been present at many a scene of slaughter; but spare me, I beseech you, the horror of witnessing the destruction of the Cherokee.'

Scott's fine words were forgotten when his troops began rounding up the Cherokee. 'Men working in the fields were arrested and driven to the stockades,' wrote Private John Burnett of the 2nd Regiment, Mounted Infantry. 'Women were dragged from their homes by soldiers whose language they could not understand. Children were often separated from their parents and driven into the stockades with the sky for a blanket and the earth for a pillow. And often the old and infirm were prodded with bayonets to hasten them to the stockades.'

Conditions inside the stockades at Ross's Landing and Gunter's Landing were appalling. Behind the walls the Cherokee families were crowded like cattle. Sanitation and medicines were nonexistent. Water was in short supply. In the midsummer heat diseases such as typhoid and dysentery spread rapidly. Hundreds of Cherokee – mainly the young, the frail and the old – succumbed. By the time the first Cherokee parties set out in August 1838 hundreds of men, women and children had already died in Winfield Scott's concentration camps.

A few hundred Cherokee – maybe as many as 1,000 – managed to escape Scott's soldiers. They fled deep into the Great Smoky Mountains where they hid out in the forests and caves. Scott's men made a few half-hearted attempts to root them out but after suffering a few casualties left the survivors alone. The descendants of these runaway Cherokee are still there, on the Quallah Boundary, mostly grouped around the dismal little tourist town of Cherokee. They are now federally recognized and known as the Eastern Band of the Cherokee, a tiny remnant of the once-great Cherokee Nation of the South-East.

As the heat of summer gave way to the rains of autumn and the snow and ice of winter, hundreds more left their bones on the trail as the emigration parties trundled slowly west. The Cherokee still know that journey as the 'Trail of Tears' or 'The Trail Where They Wept'. At every stage of the journey the Cherokee were preyed on – by white ferrymen, toll-keepers, merchants, gamblers and thieves. Decent whites were shocked by the predicament of the Native Americans.

If anything, the plight of the Cherokee travelling by river was even worse. The vessels were so crowded that disease ran riot. The boats were often stranded for weeks by low water and then by ice. Rations were scanty and drinking water was often polluted. Among the families travelling by river was that of John Ross. On 1 February 1839, at the town of Little Rock, Arkansas the journey claimed the life of Quatie Ross. She seems to have died of pneumonia. Her grave at Little Rock has only recently been discovered.

By the time the last of the Cherokee parties made their way into Fort Gibson in Indian Territory (now eastern Oklahoma) it is estimated that around 4,000 of them had died on the journey or in the mustering camps. One Georgia soldier who had done escort duty on the Trail of Tears wrote many years later: 'I fought through the Civil War and have seen men shot to pieces and slaughtered by thousands, but the Cherokee removal was the cruellest work I ever knew.'

The Cherokee Nation's modern capital of Tahlequah, Oklahoma took me by surprise. I had half expected a bigger, brasher, cruder version of the tourist horror that is Cherokee, North Carolina. Instead I found a decent, workaday, slightly run-down little city with agreeable tree-lined suburbs. At its centre is Cherokee Square, built around the handsome nineteenth-century courthouse that used to act as the Cherokee Capitol. The north end of the town is now dominated by the ivy-covered buildings of the Northeastern State University which grew out of the 'female seminary' that the Cherokee built to educate their young women.

The Nation is administered from a cluster of modern buildings on the southern edge of Tahlequah. As I was led along the grey-on-grey corridors by a friendly Native American girl it struck me that I could have been in the headquarters of one of Scotland's smaller local authorities: Perth & Kinross, perhaps, or the Comhairle nan Eilean in Stornoway. After I had spent half an hour discussing John Ross with the Cherokee Nation's publicist, Dan Agent, he suggested that I see another John Ross who was currently chief of a Cherokee organization called the United Keetoowah Band.

I traced this John Ross to the band's headquarters, a cluttered room in the basement of a bingo hall. He was a softly spoken, dark-skinned man in an immaculate white shirt and a 'bola' string tie. 'John Ross,' he said, 'was the greatest chief we ever had. Without him the Cherokee would have been scattered to the winds, the way that other tribes were. He fought for the nation longer and harder than anyone. All the Cherokee – and especially the full-bloods – remember Chief Ross. He was our great man. The Cherokee Nation as we know it now is John Ross's creation.'

The portion of Indian Territory that was allocated to the Cherokee now comprises twelve counties of north-eastern Oklahoma, most of it in the foothills of the Ozark mountains. And while it is far from being the desert wilderness that the Cherokee of the 1830s feared, it hardly compares with the beautiful land they left behind. Nor, in 1839, was it welcoming. The 4,000 or so Cherokee who had drifted west since 1811 feared being swamped by the new arrivals. The families of the Treaty Party, who had signed the Treaty of New Echota before moving west, now dreaded retribution from John Ross's followers.

The retribution was not long in coming. In the early hours of 22 June 1839, The Ridge was shot and killed on a country road in Arkansas, while his son John Ridge was dragged from his bed and tomahawked to death in front of his wife and children. Elias Boudinot was ambushed while working in his garden, stabbed to death and his corpse mutilated. The only Treaty Party leader to escape was Boudinot's brother Stand Watie, who was to become Ross's fierce enemy.

Cherokee historians are still arguing over whether or not John Ross planned the killings. The fact that his brother Andrew – who was also a signatory to the Treaty of New Echota – was untouched suggests that Ross may have had a hand in it. Some say that he knew nothing of it and was appalled when he learned of the butchery. Whatever the truth of Ross's involvement, the fact is that for the next six years a low-level civil war racked the Cherokee Nation. Stand Watie's men and John Ross's supporters assassinated one another with depressing frequency and alarming savagery. Dozens, perhaps even hundreds of Cherokee died.

In 1844 Ross married again. His wife, Mary Brian Stapler, a young Quaker from Wilmington, Delaware, was thirty-six years his junior. He'd been courting her on his trips to the east. It was an odd match, and one to which Mary's family were strongly opposed. But eventually John and Mary overcame the family's objections and, after a brief honeymoon in New York, they went back to the house he had built at Park Hill near Tahlequah and which he named 'Rose Cottage'. It was a handsome, white-painted, two-storey mansion stuffed with expensive furniture, silver and chinaware. An orchard of a thousand fruit trees surrounded it on two sides; at the rear there were stables, a blacksmith shop, a kiln, a laundry, a smoke-house, a dairy and the cabins that housed Ross's fifty black slaves. In these surroundings, John Ross entertained army officers, visiting politicians and wealthy Cherokee. Park Hill became known as the 'Athens of the Indian Territory'. Ross and Mary had two children, Annie and John. Ross rode around the nation in a coach with a liveried driver and slave boy in attendance.

This was the Cherokee Nation's new golden age. Within a few years the Cherokee authorities had given Tahlequah a council building, a courtroom, a jail and two schools. They subsidized a printing press that published the *Cherokee Advocate* (which still exists). Cherokee businessmen built five hotels, a post office, livery stables, blacksmith shops, and an assortment of small stores. By 1845 there were eighteen primary schools on the nation's land and at the end of 1846 work began on two Cherokee 'seminaries' – separate high schools for males and females – both of which were opened in May 1851.

Most Cherokee were smallholders but some of the richer ones ranched cattle at the western edge of the nation. In the census of 1859, the federal agent reported a population of more than 21,000 Cherokee and about 1,000 whites. There were 102,000 acres 'under cultivation', 240,000 head of cattle, 20,000 horses and mules, 16,000 hogs and 5,000 sheep. There were also more than 4,000 slaves. Most of the black families who now live in and around the towns of Okmulgee and Muskogee in eastern Oklahoma are descendants of slaves who were owned by the Cherokee and the Creek.

Peace and prosperity did not survive the American Civil War. When it broke out in 1861 John Ross's strategy was to keep the Cherokee Nation neutral. A wise plan, but it took no account of Scottish Freemasonry. In June 1861 a middle-aged white man with long greying hair and a long beard rode into Cherokee territory. He was Albert Pike, an Arkansas lawyer and a 33rd-degree Freemason of the Scottish Rite, who had been asked by Jefferson Davis to win over the Native American nations for the Confederacy. As many of the chiefs – including John Ross – were Freemasons of the Scottish Rite it was thought that they would listen to him.

John Ross refused to hear his arguments but Pike struck a secret deal with John Ross's enemy Stand Watie, and then spent the rest of that summer travelling until he had signed up for the Confederacy the Creeks, the Choctaws, the Chickasaws, the Seminoles and some of the Western Plains tribes. The Cherokee were increasingly isolated, and when the United States pulled all its troops out of Indian Territory the Cherokee position became untenable. On 7 October 1861, under a tree in Park Hill, John Ross shook hands with Albert Pike over a treaty pledging the Cherokee to support the Confederate side.

In many respects the effect of the Civil War on the Cherokee Nation was like a replay of the violence of the early 1840s, but on a much bigger scale. After a few months fighting for the Confederate cause (in which very few of them believed), thousands of Cherokee defected to the Union army, while their families fled across the border into Kansas. Many of these Cherokee refugees starved to death in makeshift camps. All four of John Ross's sons enlisted in the Union army. But Stand Watie and his men remained loyal to the South and fought a savage – and occasionally brilliant – hit-and-run campaign against the North's army.

In April 1862 federal troops returned to the Cherokee Nation in strength, 'captured' John Ross and his family and took them north, along with the Cherokee archive and the Cherokee treasury. Ross spent the rest of the war shuttling between his wife's family home in Philadelphia and government offices in Washington, doing what he could to relieve the suffering of the Cherokee refugees in Kansas. Abraham Lincoln and his cabinet were sympathetic but did almost nothing.

The Cherokee Nation suffered grievously as Stand Watie's men fought it out with Cherokee loyal to the Union. One of the many casualties was Ross's house, Rose Cottage, which was burned to the ground. Ross's son-in-law John Nave was killed, and Ross's oldest son James Macdonald Ross perished in the notorious Confederate prison camp at Andersonville. Even after Robert E. Lee surrendered in May 1865 the killings in the Cherokee Nation went on as General Stand Watie refused to give in. Stand Watie was the last Confederate general to surrender – on 23 June 1865, by which time the Cherokee Nation had been laid waste.

John Ross's personal tragedy deepened in July that year when his young wife Mary, who had been sickening for some time, died in Philadelphia. A few weeks later John Ross went home to find devastation. Cherokee families were huddled in the ruins of their farms and houses. Crops had been destroyed, fences torn down, orchards uprooted, livestock slaughtered. The corpses of cattle, sheep, pigs and goats were lying in the fields. Most of Tahlequah lay in ruins. One historian of the Civil War has calculated that no part of the American population, North or South, suffered as grievously from the conflict as did the Cherokee.

In September 1865, John Ross travelled to Fort Smith in Arkansas where the US government had called tribal representatives to discuss and decide a post-war settlement. He found that the Cherokee had been branded 'rebels' – despite the fact that far more Cherokee had fought for the Union than against it. The US Commissioner, Dennis Cooley, refused to recognize Ross as the Cherokee leader, declaring him an 'enemy of the United States' and, paradoxically, favouring Stand Watie, the one-time Confederate general. And Watie was once again demanding that the Cherokee Nation should be split in two. Ross knew that this would fatally weaken the Cherokee and would leave them even more vulnerable to the whites who were already prospecting in Indian Territory for land, minerals and railroad access.

John Ross fought his last battle when the Fort Smith conference was reconvened in Washington DC at the end of 1865. Cooley's version of events had gone down well with Andrew Johnson, Lincoln's successor as President. Johnson saw the Cherokee as a stubborn and awkward people and tended to favour their division as proposed by Cooley and Watie. Ross was now ill, but from his sickbed in Joy's Hotel in Washington he ran a brilliant propaganda campaign. For six months, and helped by his brother Lewis Ross and a Welsh pastor, Evan Jones, he wrote pamphlet after pamphlet, letter after letter, refuting Cooley's recommendations. In February 1866, Ross mustered enough strength to leave his bed and attend a meeting with President Johnson, his interior secretary James Harlan, and Commissioner Cooley.

Ross's sincerity worked. Johnson warmed to the old chief and his determination to keep the Cherokee Nation together. Harlan and Cooley were instructed to draw up a new treaty with the Cherokee. Johnson had decided that he would *not* deal with the Watie party. On 19 July 1866, Cooley gave in, abandoned the Watie faction and accepted the treaty that Ross had drafted. John Ross had won a major victory over what seemed like impossible odds.

Ross signed the treaty on Friday, 27 July 1866. Five days later, at seven o'clock in the evening of 1 August he died at his hotel. He was seventy-five years old. His body was taken to his brother-in-law's home in Wilmington, Delaware, where it was buried near the grave of his wife Mary in Brandywine Cemetery. Six days later, on Saturday, 11 August, the US Senate ratified the treaty between the Cherokee and the USA. The Cherokee Nation remained intact. John Ross had won his last great battle.

At its next session the Cherokee National Council decided that it wanted its greatest chief buried in the Cherokee Nation. In May 1867, Ross's remains were taken from Wilmington to Tahlequah and reburied not far from the ruin that was once called Rose Cottage.

I found John Ross's grave in a quiet, unkempt Cherokee graveyard on a hillside south of Tahlequah. The place is full of headstones on which are inscribed Scots names such as Macdonald, McIntosh and MacQueen. It reminded me of many little kirkyards I have seen all over Scotland. It could have been anywhere in the Scottish borders or the southern Highlands. John Ross's bones lie under a granite obelisk, the base of which carries his name and dates of birth and death. At the rear of the obelisk there is an iron plaque marking his service in the war of 1812–15, an episode about which Ross never talked and of which he was probably ashamed.

It is official America's only tribute to the Cherokee Nation's greatest chief.

AS OTHERS SEE US:
CHARLES LAMB

'I HAVE BEEN TRYING ALL MY life to like Scotchmen,' the essayist Charles Lamb wrote in the *London Magazine* in 1821, 'and am obliged to desist from the experiment in despair. They cannot like me – and in truth, I never knew one of that nation who attempted to do it.' Lamb's opinion of his fellow Britons is contained in a short squib piece entitled *Imperfect Sympathies*. In it, he ruminates on his feelings towards three groups – the Scots, the Jews and the Quakers. In the Quakers he finds much to admire. In the Jews and the Scots, very little. The fault, he suggests disingenuously, is not theirs but his own 'imperfect sympathies'.

While he dismisses the Jews as a 'piece of stubborn antiquity', he reserves his most waspish disdain for the Scots. His sketch is elegant and amusing but there is enough substance in it to make any honest Scot wince. He describes that blinkered assertiveness, that preoccupation with irrelevant facts that characterizes a certain Scottish type. He writes:

He (the Scotsman) never hints or suggests anything, but unlades his stock of ideas in perfect order and completeness. He brings his total wealth into company, and gravely unpacks it. His riches are always about him. He never stoops to catch a glittering something in your presence, to share it with you, before he quite knows whether it be true touch or not. You cannot cry halves to anything that he finds. He does not find, but bring.

You never witness his first apprehension of a thing. His understanding is always at its meridian – you never see the first dawn, the early streaks. He has no falterings of self-suspicion. Surmises, guesses, illuminations, dim instincts, embryo conceptions, have no place in his brain or vocabulary. The twilight of dubiety never falls upon him. Is he orthodox – he has no doubts. Is he an infidel – he has none either. Between the affirmative and the negative there is no border-land with him.

You cannot hover with him upon the confines of truth or wander in the maze of a probable argument. He always keeps the path. You cannot make excursions with him – for he sets you right. His taste never fluctuates. His morality never abates. He cannot compromise or understand middle actions. There can be but a right and a wrong. His conversation is as a book. His affirmations have the sanctity of an oath. You must speak upon the square with him. He stops a metaphor like a suspected person in an enemy's country.

THE GLASGOW
FRANKENSTEIN

LIKE MOST VENERABLE institutions, the University of Glasgow (founded 1451) has a large and fascinating archive. Some of the contents are on view in the university's Hunterian Museum (which is named for the renowned eighteenth-century surgeon William Hunter). There are skeletons, medical instruments, tissue samples, and body parts galore. But one of the most intriguing artefacts is a rather elegant armchair of the sort that would grace any late-Georgian dining room. On the afternoon of Wednesday, 4 November 1818, this armchair was at the centre of one of the nineteenth century's most extraordinary medical experiments.

In it that afternoon in the university's anatomy room sat the corpse of one Matthew Clydesdale, a convicted murderer who had been hanged an hour or so earlier. The anatomy room was packed to the rafters with an expectant crowd: students, medical men and an excitable journalist called Peter Mackenzie. 'The murderer himself was then lifted and placed in a sitting posture in an easy arm chair directly looking in front of the audience,' Mackenzie wrote, 'as if he, irrespective of his doom, was one of the audience themselves!' (*Reminiscences of Glasgow and the West of Scotland*, John Tweed, 1865.)

According to Mackenzie, when the proceedings got under way, 'His chest immediately heaved! – he drew breath! . . . A few other operations went swiftly on, which really we cannot very well describe; but at last the tongue of the murderer moved out to his lips; his eyes also opened widely – he stared, apparently in astonishment, around him; while his head, arms and legs . . . actually moved; and we declare he made a feeble attempt as if to rise from the chair whereon he was seated. He did positively rise from it in a moment or two afterwards, and stood upright . . .'

Mackenzie goes on: 'At this sudden, startling and most unexpected sight, some of the students screamed out with horror; not a few of them fainted on the spot; others of a sterner class clapped their hands as if in exultation at the triumph of the galvanic battery!' In Peter Mackenzie's account, the resurrection of Matthew Clydesdale came to a halt only when Dr James Jeffray, the university's professor of medicine, stepped forward with his lancet 'and plunged it into the jugular vein of the culprit, who instantly fell down upon the floor like a slaughtered ox on the blow of the butcher!'

Like many a journalist before and since, Mackenzie was not the man to let the facts get in the way of a good story. The notion of a hanged man being brought back to life by scientists and their mysterious apparatus was guaranteed to send shivers up and down the spines of his readers. Mackenzie milked that notion for all it was worth. Still, it was plain that *something* had happened in that armchair in the university's anatomy theatre that dark November afternoon.

Although Peter Mackenzie only mentions him in passing, the man behind the experiments on Matthew Clydesdale was Andrew Ure, then Professor of Natural Philosophy at the Andersonian Institution (now known as the University of Strathclyde). It was Ure who persuaded the legal authorities to hand over Clydesdale's body, not for the usual purposes of dissection but so that he could carry out a series of electrical experiments on the corpse. It was those experiments that Peter Mackenzie witnessed and tried to describe.

Andrew Ure's name has been almost forgotten, but not quite. Halfway down Glasgow's High Street there is a red-brick hall of residence that the University of Strathclyde named after him. Andrew Ure was one of the many practical scientists whom Scotland produced in the first half of the nineteenth century. He was born in 1778, the son of a Glasgow cheesemonger, studied medicine at Glasgow University, and graduated as a doctor in 1801. He was never a great original scientist, but he was an ambitious and determined experimenter, well travelled and well connected. One of his patrons was the Earl of Glasgow, who introduced him to the great Michael Faraday and Humphry Davy.

Beginning in 1805, Ure held a series of public lectures at the Andersonian Institute, which at his bidding was 'regularly illuminated' by twenty-six gas lamps. His lectures were hugely successful. He believed that 'philosophy stripped of its forbidding airs, of its cumbrous and fantastic trappings, should be rendered accessible to either sex and to every rank in society.' Twice a week, on Tuesday and Friday evenings, Ure regaled the intelligentsia of Glasgow with his thoughts on astronomy, hydrodynamics, hydrostatics, hydraulics, acoustics, pneumatics, musical sounds and electricity.

He was a polymath at a time when it was still possible to be one. Just about every aspect of science intrigued him. He was among the Glasgow scientists who established an observatory on Garnet Hill. In 1810 he corresponded with (and fell out with) Josiah Wedgwood. In 1813 he spent the summer at the Belfast Academical Institution, working on ways to improve the linen industry. In 1816 he toured Europe to confer with (among others) the great French chemists Claude Berthollet and Joseph-Louis Guy-Lussac. On his return he opened a factory in Glasgow to manufacture iodine.

He was also something of a paradox. He peered hard into the

future and clung tenaciously to the past. He was a pious Presbyterian and a firm believer in the divine creation of the earth in seven days. He was also politically conservative to the point of eccentricity. He approved of child labour. He believed in the working of a completely free market and detested 'combinations' (trade unions) of workers. He defended the brutal factory system of the early nineteenth century against the 'increasing attacks of the progressive humanitarian conscience'.

Like many Christians of his day he believed that 'a man must expect his chief happiness not in the present, but in the future state of existence.' There was a moralizing streak in Ure that surfaced constantly. 'The man whose Saturday night is spent in rioting and drunkenness,' he wrote, 'will make a bad Christian on the Sabbath . . . an indifferent workman on the Monday and an unhappy husband and father through the week.' Ure's reactionary fulminations in his *Dictionary of Arts, Manufactures and Mines* (published in 1853) brought down on him the ire of Karl Marx who described him as 'an enemy of society'.

Brilliant, pugnacious, ambitious, sanctimonious and conservative, Andrew Ure was constantly at odds with his colleagues and compatriots. He seems to have fallen out with almost every academic in Glasgow. He is described in the Glasgow satirical sheet *Northern Sketches* as 'Doctor Transit' who 'in proud tones of conscious superiority . . . intrudes on every company; he pesters the learned and insults the ignorant with impertinent recitations of his abilities, his merits and his labours'.

Electricity particularly fascinated him. What was in this power? What could it do? Enter the corpse of Matthew Clydesdale.

The eerie tale of Andrew Ure's experiments on Matthew Clydesdale began a few months earlier when Clydesdale was convicted at the High Court of Justiciar in Glasgow for killing a fellow miner with a pickaxe. Clydesdale is described as a fierce, wiry little man who was suspected of having murdered a widow in

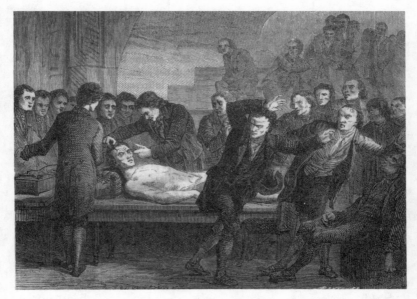

Andrew Ure experimenting on the corpse of Matthew Clydesdale, from Louis Figuier's Vies des savants illustres. *In fact, the corpse was seated.*

Lanarkshire a few years previously. The fifteen-man jury had little hesitation in finding Clydesdale guilty and Lords Succoth and Gillies handed down the grim sentence.

Not only was Clydesdale to be hanged in front of the New Gaol at the bottom of the High Street between two o'clock and four o' clock in the afternoon, but their lordships 'decerned and adjudged that he shall be fed on bread and water only, till the day of his execution, and that his body, after being so executed, shall be delivered up by the Magistrates of Glasgow, or their officers, to Dr James Jeffray, Professor of Anatomy in the University of Glasgow, there to be publicly dissected and anatomised'.

Peter Mackenzie spiced up his story of the Clydesdale affair by claiming that hanging followed by dissection was a rare and (by inference) cruel sentence. It was not. Hanged criminals were almost the only legal source of corpses for the medical profession and its students. The sentence was often handed down in the case of particularly brutal murders, although it has to be said the idea of being cut up *post-mortem* often terrified the convicts more than the idea of being hanged *pre-mortem*.

But even in turbulent nineteenth-century Glasgow corpses that could be legally experimented upon were rare. A few years previously the Glasgow anatomist Granville Sharp Pattison and two of his students had been tried in the High Court in Edinburgh for robbing the city's graveyards. Although the Glasgow anatomists got off, the supply of fresh corpses dried up. The graveyards of Glasgow were carefully watched by the town guard. Relatives of the newly dead had taken to prowling graveyards at night until the corpses of their loved ones had decomposed enough to be no longer of interest to the anatomists and medical men.

So Clydesdale was no sooner in the condemned cell than Andrew Ure began lobbying for his remains. Somehow he managed to persuade both Professor James Jeffray (with whom he'd had many a dispute) and the legal authorities that he should be allowed to carry out a series of 'electrical' experiments on the corpse of Clydesdale. It was agreed that while Ure could direct the experiments they had to be done under Professor Jeffray's supervision. It was also agreed that any cutting of the corpse would be done by Thomas Marshall, one of Jeffray's assistants.

Ure spent the days before the hanging preparing the 'battery' (a new term in 1818) that he intended to use on Clydesdale's body. The device was one that he'd had built in Glasgow to his own design. Inside a mahogany case lay a 'pile' of 270 pairs of zinc and copper discs, each of them four inches in diameter. For the experiments the pile would be charged with a quantity of dilute nitro-sulphuric acid. The weeks of negotiation and preparation almost came to nothing when Clydesdale slashed his throat with a broken beer bottle, but he survived this suicide attempt and science was duly grateful.

The great day arrived. At two o'clock in the afternoon Clydesdale and his fellow condemned (a young man called Simon Ross who was to be hanged for stealing a few items of women's underwear) were marched into the New Gaol's chapel where they were invited to admit to and repent of their sins. Ross did it willingly: Clydesdale was grudging. Then one of the ministers led the singing of the fifty-eighth Psalm, which includes the words: '*The righteous one shall wash his feet/In the blood of wicked men.*' At three o'clock Clydesdale and Ross were led out of the New Gaol, across the street and onto the gallows.

There were rumours that a force of Lanarkshire miners was on their way to Glasgow to rescue Clydesdale from the hangman so the huge crowd was controlled by the 40th Foot (a local militia) and the 1st Dragoon Guards (regular cavalrymen). But there was no attempt to rescue Clydesdale. At five minutes past three Clydesdale and Ross were duly 'turned off' the gallows by the Glasgow hangman Tam Young. Press reports say that Ross 'died after some convulsive struggles' while Clydesdale 'seemed to die almost immediately'.

After hanging for an hour, Clydesdale's body was cut down, coffined and loaded onto a horse-drawn cart, which then trundled at a 'slow and steady march' up the High Street to the university. The macabre little procession was led by ten town officers carrying halberts and wearing red coats, blue breeches, white stockings and black beaver hats. According to Peter Mackenzie, the anatomy theatre was crowded 'not only by the students, but by many grave citizens, up almost to the very ceiling of the institution'.

This is about as far as Mackenzie's version of the events is to be trusted. The most reliable account is Ure's own and can be found in his *Dictionary of Chemistry* (published in 1822) under the entry on 'Galvanism' (so named after Luigi Galvano, the Italian scientist who produced electricity by chemical action in 1792). After a general discussion of the work of various other European 'electricians', Ure goes on to detail the four experiments that he carried out on the body of Clydesdale.

Experiment Number One: an incision was made in the nape of the neck through which one of the vertebrae was removed to reveal the spinal cord. This had the side effect of draining much of the blood from the corpse. A second incision was made in the left hip to bare the sciatic nerve. A third incision was made in one of the heels. When the electrodes were inserted into the incisions the effect was startling. 'Every muscle of the body was immediately agitated with convulsive movements resembling a violent shuddering from cold,' Ure writes. 'The left side was most powerfully convulsed at each renewal of the electric contact. On moving the second rod from the hip to the heel, the knee being previously bent, the leg was thrown out with such violence as nearly to overturn one of the assistants, who in vain attempted to prevent its extension.'

Experiment Number Two: an incision was made above the left shoulder to bare the left phrenic nerve, and another incision made under the seventh rib. The terminals were duly inserted, one onto the phrenic nerve, the other so that it touched 'the great head of the diaphragm'. Once again, the results were remarkable. 'The success of it was truly wonderful,' Ure writes. 'Full, nay, laborious breathing instantly commenced. The chest heaved and fell; the belly was protruded and again collapsed, with the relaxing and retiring of the diaphragm. This process was continued as long as I continued the electric discharges. In the judgement of many scientific gentlemen who witnessed the scene, this respiratory experiment was perhaps the most striking ever made with a philosophical apparatus. Let it also be remembered, that for full half an hour before this period, the body had been well-nigh drained of blood, and the spinal marrow severely lacerated. No pulsation could be perceived meanwhile at the heart or wrist; but it may be supposed that but for the evacuation of the blood . . . this phenomenon might also have occurred.'

Experiment Number Three: an incision was made in the corpse's forehead just above the eyebrow to bare the supraorbital nerve.

Then one of the terminals was inserted into the cut while the other was pushed into the incision on the heel. Yet again, the effect was dramatic. 'Every muscle in his countenance was simultaneously thrown into fearful action; rage, horror, despair, anguish and ghastly smiles united their hideous expression in the murderer's face, surpassing far the wildest [actorly] representations of a Fuseli or a Kean. At this period several of the spectators were forced to leave the apartment from terror or sickness and one gentleman fainted.'

Experiment Number Four: an incision was cut into the elbow to reveal the ulnar nerve. When the terminals were applied – one to the ulnar nerve and the other to the bared spine – once again the dead limbs leapt into action. 'The fingers now moved nimbly, like those of a violin performer; an assistant who tried to close the fist, found the hand to open forcibly, in spite of his efforts. When the one rod was applied to a slight incision in the tip of the forefinger, the fist being previously clenched, that finger extended instantly; and from the convulsive agitation of the arm, he seemed to point to the different spectators, some of whom thought he had come to life.'

Although it was the experiments on the face and arms (numbers three and four) that terrified and disgusted Peter Mackenzie and many of the spectators, Ure himself was in no doubt that the most important experiment was number two, which delivered a charge of electricity through the heart and lungs.

'In deliberating on the above galvanic phenomena,' Ure writes, 'we are almost willing to imagine, that if, without cutting into and wounding the spinal marrow and blood-vessels in the neck, the pulmonary organs had been set a-playing at first . . . by electrifying the phrenic nerve . . . *there is a probability that life might have been restored*.' [My italics.]

Ure goes on to argue that: 'It is probable, when apparent death supervenes from suffocation with noxious gases etc, and where there is no organic lesion, that a judiciously directed galvanic experiment will, if anything will, restore the activity of the vital functions . . . Then indeed fair hopes may be formed of deriving extensive benefit from galvanism; and of raising this wonderful agent to its expected rank among the ministers of health and life to man.'

Two hundred years on, it is easy to see that Ure was experimenting with an early version of a now commonplace technology: the cardiac defibrillator familiar to anyone who watches medical dramas in the scene when the stopped heart and lungs are kick-started by a bolt of electricity and the patient starts to breathe again, to looks of relief from the eyes above the masks.

As Ure points out, this might have worked for Matthew Clydesdale, if his spine had not been mauled and his body almost drained of blood; if he had not been too long dead. It may be, of course, that Clydesdale was not properly dead. It is interesting that both Mackenzie's and Ure's accounts suggest that Clydesdale's neck had not been dislocated by the drop. When they carted the little murderer into the anatomy theatre that November afternoon there might have been more life in him than anyone suspected.

Ure's gruesome experiments on the body of Matthew Clydesdale quickly became a Glasgow legend. Thrilled Glaswegians told one another that the murderer's corpse had walked and talked; that it had pointed to its despoilers and accused them in a hollow voice of doing the devil's work; that the resurrected Clydesdale would have walked out into the High Street had he not been beheaded by James Jeffray with a sword that had been specially blessed by Kirk ministers and kept conveniently to hand.

Andrew Ure abandoned the city a few years later after a messy and acrimonious divorce when his wife Katherine ran off with the anatomist (and grave robber) Granville Sharp Pattison. Ure spent the remainder of his life in London, brilliant, hard-working and cantankerous to the end. Glasgow's own Victor Frankenstein died in 1857 and is buried in Highgate Cemetery in north London – not far from his stern critic Karl Marx.

THE BARD'S OFFSPRING

IT WAS THAT LEGENDARY SONG-and-dance man Gene Kelly who put me on the trail of the sons and daughters of Robert Burns. I was in Hollywood working with Kelly, who was then in his seventies, on a stage musical about Burns (a project that never materialized). One evening, over a pizza in Kelly's house on Rodeo Drive in Beverly Hills, we were discussing the poet and his offspring when Kelly said, 'Didn't I read somewhere that two of the Burns kids became army officers? Colonels or something? In India or someplace?'

The idea startled me. Having been brought up on the pieties about Burns as a hero-martyr of the working and peasant classes, the notion that the great man's sons may have evolved into agents of British imperialism seemed unlikely. On the other hand, the more I read about Robert Burns the less he seemed to fit the role assigned to him by the Sentimental Left. I was learning that Scotland's most famous contribution to the iconography of International Socialism was not what he seemed to be.

Somewhat confused, I told Kelly that I guessed it was possible although it seemed unlikely. I promised to look into it. He just shrugged and said, 'Mebbe I'm wrong.' And the conversation moved on to other things.

But Gene Kelly wasn't wrong. When I began to root around I came across photographs of two portraits from the archives of the East India Company. The portraits are of Colonel William Nicol Burns and his younger brother Lieutenant Colonel James Glencairn Burns. The resemblance between the two is striking: the same dark eyes, the same long nose, the same slightly receding chin. Both are in the dress uniforms of the period: high-collared tunics trimmed with gold braid; two rows of silver buttons down their fronts; epaulettes with gold fringes; pristine white belts with splendid buckles. Both are clutching ceremonial swords in their left hands.

In all their military pomp, they seem to personify mid-Victorian Britain, exuding that determination and disdain that the portrait painters of their day strove to capture. They are imperialism personified. They are the kind of British officers who put down the Indian Mutiny in 1857–8 in the process of creating the biggest empire the world has ever seen.

Plainly, Robert Burns cannot be blamed (or credited) for the lives of his sons, particularly as he had little to do with their upbringing. They were only small boys when Burns died in 1796. But the careers of William and James Burns do tend to deflate the popular myth, which runs something like this: Robert Burns died in poverty and neglect, shunned by the 'unco guid' of Ayrshire, harried by rapacious creditors. Scotland's corrupt aristocratic establishment breathed a collective sigh of relief as the hero-poet and proto-socialist was hurried into a pauper's grave, leaving his wife and bairns to eke out a dismal existence.

The truth is almost the opposite. Hanoverian Britain did Robert Burns proud. Far from being dumped into a pauper's grave, Burns was given a splendid funeral procession. Dressed in the uniform of the Dumfriesshire Militia (which he had helped found) his corpse was drawn through the streets of Dumfries on a gun carriage with a militia guard of honour. One eyewitness wrote: 'In respect to the memory of such a genius as Mr Burns, his funeral was uncommonly splendid.' While Burns was being lowered into the ground his wife Jean Armour was giving birth to his last child, a boy named Maxwell. The little boy died before he was three.

After the poet's death his friends and admirers in the British establishment rallied round to raise money for his widow and family. Aristocrats and rich merchants lobbied the government to secure comfortable careers for his sons. Even his illegitimate children received some modest financial aid (a fairly rare thing in early-nineteenth-century Britain). The offspring of Robert Burns went on to live respectable and, in a few cases, successful and very comfortable lives in Victorian Britain.

The widow Burns was well provided for. Far from being strapped by debt, the Burns estate had bills to the tune of only £14. Robert's brother Gilbert owed him £183, he had £15 in bank drafts, his library was valued at £90. Burns the exciseman had been paying into the 'Excise Incorporation' which qualified Jean for a pension of £8 a year, which was later bumped up to £12. Burns's admirers raised £1,200, which was invested in government stock at three per cent per annum. Another £1,400 was speedily raised from the sale of the poet's collected works. Between them the two funds produced £60 a year for his wife on top of her pension. In 1817, William Maule of Panmure settled another £50 a year on her. One way or another, Jean Armour Burns was better off as a widow than she ever had been when her husband was alive.

It is worth remembering the number of children that Burns fathered. Between 1786 and 1796 he had thirteen children by five different women. Jean Armour, loyal and long-suffering, mothered nine of them: Robert, Jean, unchristened twin girls, Francis, William, Elizabeth, James and Maxwell. Only three of them – Robert, William and James – survived into adulthood.

Burns's oldest son Robert (born 3 March 1786) was a twin whose sister Jean died when she was just over a year old. 'Robert is indeed the mildest, gentlest creature I ever saw,' Burns wrote of his son. 'He has a most surprising memory, and is quite the pride of his schoolmaster.' The quiet, conscientious little boy flourished at Dumfries Academy, studied logic and moral philosophy at Glasgow University and then transferred to Edinburgh University but left without graduating.

In 1804, thanks to the political intervention of Alderman James Shaw (who later became Lord Mayor of London) Robert junior was given a clerkship in the Stamp Office in London. For twenty-seven years he laboured as a minor bureaucrat in Somerset House on The Strand. In 1809 he married Anne Sherwood and in August 1812 the couple had a daughter called Elizabeth. A few years later the little girl was taken by her Uncle James to India where she later married an East India Company physician called Everitt.

Elizabeth Burns may well have been removed from her father's care for her own good. There seems to have been a reckless streak in Robert Burns Jr. He was a hopeless gambler and appears to have run up debts that almost ruined his family. He may also have been a womanizer. Some time in the mid-1820s he abandoned his wife and took up with Emma Bland, the daughter of a London publican. They had two children: Jane Emma (born 1831) and Robert (born 1833).

In 1832 His Majesty's Government gave up on Robert Burns Jr and forced him into early retirement (he was forty-six). But the Treasury was persuaded to give Burns a generous pension of £120 a year; not because he deserved one, but because the British establishment had high regard for 'the great literary talent of his father'. Robert and his English common-law wife moved back to Dumfries where she kept a lodging house and Robert taught mathematics and classics. He also wrote bad poetry and studied Gaelic. A photograph of Robert shows a long-faced, lugubrious-looking old man.

Jean Armour's two younger sons, William Nicol Burns and James

Glencairn Burns, were steadier men. Certainly, they did well for themselves. Both were educated at Dumfries Academy and then at Christ's Hospital in London. Both young men joined the East India Company on 'cadetships' sponsored by Sir John Reid, the Marchioness of Hastings and Sir James Shaw. And both rose through the ranks to become senior officers in 'John Company's' army.

William Nicol Burns was probably the more able of the two. He ended his career as the much-respected Colonel of the 7th Native Infantry and married to one Catherine Adelaide Crone, a young Dubliner and a member of the Anglo-Irish 'ascendancy'. They had no children. After Catherine died in India in 1841 William never remarried. In 1842 he returned to England and settled in the fashionable spa town of Cheltenham in Gloucestershire, a favourite of retired military men.

James Glencairn Burns married Sarah Robinson in 1818 and had three children in rapid order: Jean, Robert and Sarah. But the little family was racked by tragedy. Jean died aged four, Robert died aged eighteen months and their mother died in 1821 while giving birth to her daughter Sarah. Sarah was sent back to Scotland to be raised by Jean Armour, with whom she became a great favourite. When Jean Armour died in 1834, Sarah was taken in by the family of John McDiarmid, editor of the *Dumfries Courier*, until her father returned from India.

In 1828 James Glencairn Burns married for the second time, to one Mary Beckett. They had one daughter, Anne, born in 1831 and known as Annie. When Mary Burns died in 1844, James retired from the East India Company and returned to England with Annie to settle down with brother William in the house in Berkeley Street, Cheltenham. There they were joined by Sarah, James's daughter by his first wife.

Robert Burns's three surviving sons were reunited in the summer of 1844 when William and James made their one and only trip to Scotland to walk in their father's footsteps. They had tea in Edinburgh with Mrs Agnes McElhose, who had been 'Clarinda' to the poet's 'Sylvander' in a famous series of genteel, painfully chaste letters. The three Burns brothers met at Dumfries on the banks of the River Doon. Their reunion was a public affair that attracted a huge crowd of Burns enthusiasts.

The poet's granddaughter Sarah Burns – the little girl who had been raised by Jean Armour – led an interesting life. In 1847 she was married in St Mary's Church, the town of Cheltenham's most fashionable place of worship, to Doctor Berkeley Westropp Hutchinson. Five years later the couple emigrated to Australia but on the long voyage out their three children died, presumably of fever. Sarah Burns Hutchinson then had four more children – Robert, Annie, Violet and Margaret – before returning to England.

Back in Cheltenham, Sarah lived in even greater splendour than her military uncles. She and her husband acquired a house in Pittville Lawn, then (as now) the most fashionable part of Cheltenham. In 1833 Pittville was described by one Scottish lady as 'a scene of gorgeous magnificence' where the houses were 'of every size, shape and character . . . so fresh and clean you would imagine they were all blown out at once like soap bubbles'. Sarah had come a long way from the little house in Dumfries where she had lived with Jean Armour.

Sarah Burns died in July 1907 at the age of eighty-seven. Her obituary was written up in *The Cheltenham Looker-on* ('A Note Book of the Sayings and Doings of Social, Political and Fashionable Life') for Saturday, 7 July 1907. Along with a brief biography there is a photograph of a severe-looking, pale-eyed old lady. Dressed in a lace cap, with a lace shawl round her shoulders, she is sitting in a lace-bedecked armchair, the very essence of late Victorian/Edwardian respectability.

From the expression on her face it comes as no surprise to read that in 1894 she wrote to *The Burns Chronicle* in an attempt to pour cold water on her grandfather's reputation as a wanton drunk. 'My father often said it was disgraceful the statements made out by people who lived in the Poet's time,' she wrote, 'containing, as they did, so much falsehood and exaggeration of the events of his life.'

Burns also had at least four illegitimate children. A daughter (Elizabeth) by Elizabeth Paton, another daughter by May Cameron, a son (Robert) by Jenny Clow and a daughter (Elizabeth) by Anne Park. And some Burns aficionados believe that Mary Campbell, the famous 'Highland Mary' of the song, died in childbirth. Certainly when Mary Campbell's grave in Greenock was exhumed to make way for a shipyard an infant's coffin was found beside her.

Little is known about the lives of the three illegitimate children who survived. The oldest of them, Elizabeth ('Betsy'), his daughter by Elizabeth Paton, was raised by the Burns family until she married John Bishop who became a farm overseer at Polkemmet in West Lothian. She died in 1816 and was buried at Whitburn in West Lothian. Betsy's youngest daughter Jean married James Weir whose family went on to create the west of Scotland engineering conglomerate, the Weir Group. The Weir family have long been supporters of the Scottish Conservative and Unionist Party.

Burns's daughter Elizabeth (Betty) by Anne Park was raised by the long-suffering Jean Armour and later married one John Thomson, a private in the Stirlingshire Militia. After following her husband around for a few years she settled with his family in Glasgow where she supplemented her income by working as a seamstress. Betty Burns, who is said to have resembled her father more than any of his other children, received £200 from the fund raised by Alderman Shaw in the City of London.

Betty's son Robert Burns Thomson was the only one of the poet's descendants with a talent for poetry, albeit a minor one. Thomson penned the words for a song entitled 'My Daddy's Awa' At The War' that was popular during the Crimea conflict. But that was the extent of his literary fame. He went on to manage a textile firm in Glasgow and then set up business as R. B. Thomson & Company of Stockwell Street, Glasgow. The firm manufactured brushes.

Jenny Clow, maidservant to the genteel Agnes McElhose, gave birth to a son, also called Robert. Very little is known about this Robert Burns other than that he became a successful London businessman and was extremely (and probably justifiably) bitter about the way the poet treated his mother. But his son, also called Robert, had an extraordinary career.

Born and raised in London, Robert Burns III was educated at boarding school in Islington. In 1840 he went out to the East Indies to make his fortune. He prospected for minerals in Borneo and then returned to England in 1849 to give evidence to the Parliamentary committee of inquiry that was looking into the harsh regime of Sir James Brooke who became known as the 'white rajah of Sarawak'. Brooke's regime did not survive the investigation.

Robert Burns III returned to Borneo where he married the daughter of a Kayan chief. He lived on Darvel Bay on the north-east coast and made his living as a merchant. In September 1851 the schooner *Dolphin*, which was owned by Burns and his partner, was taken by pirates off Maludu Bay. Robert Burns, his partner and five of their crew were murdered and thrown over the side. A few months later the Royal Navy launched a punitive expedition against the pirates of Borneo. The killers of Burns and his crew were tracked down and executed. Descendants of Robert Burns and Jenny Clow are believed to be still living in and around Darvel Bay in Indonesia.

Gene Kelly, who started me on this genealogical chase, died in February 1996. Had our musical about Burns ever been produced, I doubt that it would have included these facts. Gene's most celebrated excursion into Scottishness remains his star part in *Brigadoon*.

THE DRUG BARONS

ON THE ONE OR TWO occasions when I have entered Stornoway harbour from the sea I have always been impressed by Lewis Castle. It sits on a wooded hillside overlooking the town to the west, and when its turrets, towers and castellated ramparts are floodlit at night it becomes quite the most important-looking building in Stornoway. Of course, it's a fake. A mock-baronial confection run up by a wealthy man, like many other Victorian 'castles' in Scotland. Having served as a military hospital, a further-education college and a school, Lewis Castle was abandoned in 1988. In 2003 it sat empty and boarded up while its owners, the Comhairle nan Eilean (Western Isles Council), decided what to do with it next.

The castle's provenance is interesting. Before it passed into the hands of the local authority it was owned by the Stornoway Trust, a charity set up in 1924 to run the castle, its grounds and all the other land that had been bequeathed to the people of Stornoway by the soap tycoon Lord Leverhulme when he abandoned his schemes to 'develop' the island of Lewis with new fisheries and industries. Leverhulme had acquired Lewis from the family of Sir James

Matheson, the fabulously wealthy Highlander who had bought the island in 1844 from the Mackenzies of Seaforth who had plundered it (as we have seen) from Clan Leod in the early seventeenth century. It was James Matheson who built Lewis Castle as the centre of the Hebridean empire into which he retired.

In other words, it was built on the profits of the drug trade. James Matheson made his vast – and it really was vast – fortune by selling opium to the drug addicts of China. Matheson and his partner William Jardine were the two most powerful *taipans* of the opium trade of the 1820s and 1830s. Largely thanks to their efforts, so that the trade could continue, Britain made war against the feeble Chinese Empire. This, the 'Opium War', is regarded by many Chinese scholars as a defining episode in China's history. 'As a result of the war China's independent power was lost,' wrote the historian Chiang-Chien-fu in 1945. 'The doors were opened, territorial integrity was shattered and authority was compromised, opening the way for invasion by the imperialist powers . . . On the other hand it made for an unprecedented and drastic transformation of Chinese society . . . It placed China . . . onto the contemporary international stage.'

The two men who were to have such a profound effect on Asia were born at opposite ends of Scotland. William Jardine was the son of a border farmer at Lochmaben near Dumfries, James Matheson hailed from Lairg in Sutherland, a sprig of the Highland gentry. Both men studied at Edinburgh University. Jardine graduated as a doctor in 1801 and was made a member of the Royal College of Surgeons of Edinburgh the next year. Matheson graduated in 1805 as a Master of Arts. He was a well-read young man and something of an intellectual, with an enthusiasm for the work of the economist Adam Smith.

Neither man lingered in Scotland. Jardine took a job as a ship's surgeon shortly after he qualified. Matheson, aged nineteen, sailed for Calcutta to join Mackintosh & Company, a trading firm owned by one of his uncles, which then sent him to Canton, one of the two cities in the Celestial Empire (the other was Macao) which were 'open' to European traders. In 1820 the two men met for the first time, although it would be another eight years before they went into business together.

As both Jardine and Matheson quickly found out, the route to serious wealth in China was through opium. With the exception of some textiles, Britain's manufactured products were making no impact on the Chinese market. The balance of trade was very much against the British. The Celestial Empire was remarkably self-contained. If the Europeans wanted to buy Chinese tea, silk, porcelain, lacquered goods and, astonishingly, rhubarb they could, so long as they behaved themselves. Successive emperors had made it known that the European nations had nothing that China needed or wanted. Or nearly nothing.

The exception was opium. Opium was the Chinese plague. Millions of Chinese were habitual users and addicts. Although the drug had been banned throughout China since 1729, the appetite for it continued to grow. And the Honourable East India Company was only too happy to meet China's demand. In India, poppies grown in the fields of the Gangetic Plain were converted into opium paste at East India Company factories and then sold on to favoured merchants who shipped them from Calcutta to Canton. The profits were large, and were normally used to buy Chinese produce – tea, silk, porcelain – which was sent by sailing ship round the Cape of Good Hope to Britain. In this way – with Indian opium – Britain paid for its luxuries from China.

But if opium was illegal in China, how were the British able to export it there? The system that the opium traders put in place was simplicity itself. Their ships would sail up the Pearl River to Lintin Island just south of Canton. At Lintin the opium was transferred into 'scrambling dragons', oar-powered junks operated by Chinese rivermen and pirates, which distributed the 'foreign mud' to the towns and villages in the Pearl River estuary. Then as now the networks of small dealers were run by the Chinese criminal gangs known as Triads.

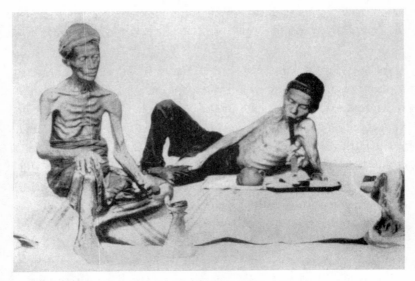

Opium smoking in China

The Lintin System (as it became known) blatantly flouted Chinese law. Its smooth operation depended on thousands of Chinese magistrates, Customs men, soldiers and *cohong*, the Chinese merchants licensed to deal with Europeans, turning a blind eye. The European traders in Canton became adept at bribing and subverting the Emperor's officials. Hundreds of Chinese grew rich on the trade. As the corruption spread, the opium traders grew more and more defiant of the Chinese authorities and began to complain about their 'persecution' by the mandarins who were simply trying to enforce Chinese law.

William Jardine and James Matheson plunged enthusiastically into this swamp of law-breaking, smuggling, addiction and corruption. In 1822, Jardine joined the opium-trading firm of Magniac & Co and quickly became a partner. Matheson was not immediately successful – in the early 1820s he went into partnership with a Spaniard called Xavier Yrissari and was sucked into a few dangerous and unprofitable deals. But the young Highlander was a shrewd and aggressive trader, and quickly came to the conclusion that the opium trade, if it were to expand successfully, had to break out of the Pearl River estuary and set up business in the coastal cities to the north. In 1827, he founded China's first English-language newspaper, the *Canton Register*, which blatantly printed the weekly prices being paid for 'chests' (roughly 140 pounds) of opium. The next year he joined Jardine in Magniac & Co, which became Jardine Matheson & Co, the name under which it still trades, a few years later.

The company had no monopoly. They faced competition from several firms, including Dent & Co (who were English), David Sassoon & Co (who were Jews settled in India), Rustanjee Cowastee (who were Parsis from Bombay), Russell & Co (an American firm headed by one Warren Delano II, the grandfather of President Franklin Delano Roosevelt). It was Jardine and Matheson, however, who effectively doubled the amount of opium entering China when they invested in newer, faster ships that, in a good year, could do three runs between Calcutta and Canton instead of the one that their rivals' older ships could manage. The Scotsmen began to dominate the trade.

In China, the social effects were devastating. Opium addiction spread among the clerks, civil servants and mandarins who ran the country. Even the army had the habit; troops sent to quash rural rebels in 1832 had proved almost useless because so many of the officers and men were addled by opium. What was the Celestial Empire to do? The debate in China at that time has a remarkably modern resonance. One lobby, known as the 'moralists', wanted to use the power of the state to crush the trade and those who depended on it, as users or suppliers. They argued that addicts, dealers, and foreign importers should be rounded up and summarily executed. The 'legalists', on the other hand, argued that such harsh measures would alienate the Chinese people and provoke confrontation with foreign powers. They pressed the Emperor to legalize the drug so that it could be carefully controlled and the money from the trade could go into the public coffers.

The opium traders were well aware of the debate. Writing in the *Canton Register*, Jardine declared: 'It is well known that the Tartar Manchu dynasty floats upon a smooth but dangerous sea, and that its existence depends upon the habit of tranquil obedience to its authority. Sensible of this, the high authorities view with abhorrence anything that savours of perturbation.' By the end of 1838, however, the British opium traders knew that 'perturbation' was on its way and that they would need support in Britain, where opium was hardly a popular cause. At the beginning of 1839, William Jardine (who was retiring in any case) went back to London to lobby for what was euphemistically known as 'the China trade'. Jardine took with him a well-stocked war chest, with the promise of more if it were needed. One of his briefs was 'to secure, at a high price, the services of some leading newspaper to advocate the cause'.

Jardine was no sooner out of the country than the Emperor moved. The legalizers in the Imperial Court lost the argument. The Emperor decided that he would stamp out the trade and delegated the job to one Lin Tse-hsu, who had a reputation as a poet, philosopher, calligrapher and skilled administrator. Lin arrived in Canton at beginning of 1839 and immediately drew up a strategy that would strike against both the demand and the supply. He set up the equivalent of a public health programme, pointing out the dangers of opium-smoking to the people and asking them to report drug dealers to the local magistrates. Village headmen were asked to identify addicts for treatment (not punishment). Schoolmasters were asked to do the same for their pupils. Chinese merchants were warned of the risks they ran by trading with the foreign opium-peddlers. Hundreds of dealers and brokers were arrested and thrown into prison. Many small-time drug dealers were rounded up and strangled or decapitated in public.

At the same time, Lin moved against Jardine Matheson & Co and the other importers, reminding them that they traded in China on sufferance and that the laws of the Celestial Empire applied to everyone inside it, foreigners as well as subjects. Unless they ended opium imports, *all* trade might be stopped. The 'factory' district in Canton where the Europeans lived was half-heartedly blockaded. In March 1839, Lin ordered the opium importers to deliver up all the opium they held to the Chinese authorities.

When the British traders sought help from Canton's British plenipotentiary Charles Elliot they found little sympathy. Elliot's view was that the Chinese had a right to run their own country. Commissioner Lin was startled when the British merchants handed over no fewer than 20,000 chests of opium. The opium was dumped into long trenches, mixed with lime and water and then the slurry drained into the Pearl River. However, even as Lin was chanting a prayer to the River God for forgiveness for polluting the river British opium clippers were racing towards India for fresh stocks. The scarcity caused by Lin's clampdown had sent the price soaring.

At which point Lin made a big mistake. He believed that the confrontation with the British traders had been successful. He thought that British military power was overrated and that the foreign devils could be driven out of China for good. In September 1839, flushed with what he thought was success, he issued an edict to the people of Hong Kong and Kowloon instructing them to cut off all supplies of food and water to the British ships lying at anchor – an edict that sparked the opening shots of what became known as the 'Opium War'.

Acting on Lin's instructions, a flotilla of Chinese junks positioned itself between the British ships and the coastal towns. British pleas for food and water for those aboard, including women and children, were refused. The blockade ended when the twenty-eight-gun frigate HMS *Volage* sailed along the line of Chinese craft, blowing most of them apart. The remains of the Chinese flotilla fled to report to Peking 'a victory over superior forces'.

A few weeks later the *Volage* was in action again, along with the frigate *Hyacinth*. In a forty-minute gunnery engagement in the estuary of the Pearl River they devastated a squadron of junks commanded by the Chinese admiral Kuan. When the British plenipotentiary Charles Elliot ordered the British ships to disengage from a patently defenceless enemy, Admiral Kuan was congratulated by Commissioner Lin on forcing the barbarians to retreat; self-delusion played a leading (and damaging) role in Mandarin psychology. The ability of the Emperor's servants to delude themselves and their Emperor was boundless.

In London, Jardine was lobbying the British government to send an armed force to China. In September 1839, while British warships were reducing Chinese junks to matchwood, Jardine was huddled in a series of meetings with the Whig government's Foreign Secretary, Henry Temple, the Earl of Palmerston. Jardine's view was that the Celestial Empire had to be dragged into the commercial world of the nineteenth century, and that the best way to achieve this was to teach the Emperor and his court a serious military lesson. Palmerston was impressed by Jardine's expertise: here was a man who had long first-hand experience of China – its officials, military strength, smugglers, the hazards of its river navigation. After their first meeting he asked Jardine to write a report on the best way to wage war on the Chinese.

Jardine's subsequent paper (dated 20 October 1839) formed the basis of British military strategy in the war that was to follow, even in the calculation of the naval strength necessary to do the job ('two men of war, two frigates, two river steamers' and transports for 7,000 troops). His report also argued that the Chinese should be forced to open up to European trade the ports at Canton, Amoy, Foochow, Ningpo, and Shanghai, and that the Chinese should compensate merchants (such as Jardine Matheson & Co) for the opium that had been destroyed and for the trade that had been lost. As for the war's timing, Jardine suggested to Palmerston that it might be a good idea to delay until the spring of 1840 when the opium trading season was over.

The Celestial Emperor, meanwhile, sacked Commissioner Lin

and replaced him with a suaver diplomat, Ch'i-shan, who believed that he could negotiate the British into a deal. He too underestimated what the British wanted, or how far they would go to get it. In fact, they wanted far more than he could offer. When Ch'i-shan tried to stall, British warships turned their guns on the Pearl River forts on 7 January 1841 and killed more than 500 Chinese.

Only days later Ch'i-shan and Charles Elliot concluded a deal, known as the Convention of Chuenpi, by which British merchants were to be allowed to resume trading in Canton and to receive £1.5 million for the opium confiscated by Commissioner Lin. Most important of all – the starting point for a long imperial story – the Chinese were to surrender Hong Kong Island to the British Crown. James Matheson himself was there when the British flag was hoisted over the aptly named Possession Point at the end of January 1841. Matheson wrote to Jardine in London, expressing his delight that 'there will be no mandarin interference or control on the island which will be entirely British . . . so independent will Hong Kong be that it will even be allowed to store opium on it as soon as we build warehouses there.'

On the face of it, the Convention of Chuenpi gave the British most of what they wanted. But for Britain it was not enough and for the Emperor it was far too much. Neither side would ratify the treaty. Both Ch'i-shan and Charles Elliot were sacked: the Chinese for giving away too much; the Briton for not demanding enough. Ch'i-shan was stripped of his fortune and sent into exile in Turkestan; Charles Elliot was recalled to Britain and replaced by an aggressive Ulsterman, Sir Henry Pottinger.

Before he set sail for China, Pottinger arranged a discreet dinner. Round the table were William Jardine, his London agent Charles Abel Smith MP, and Matheson's nephew, Alexander. They were joined later by one of Jardine Matheson's ship captains who presented Pottinger with an array of maps, charts and tide tables of the Pearl River and all the other Chinese waterways that had been surveyed by Jardine Matheson. Well briefed by the opium traders, the new plenipotentiary swept into action as soon as he landed in Macao in April 1841.

On Pottinger's orders British warships and paddle steamers prowled the long rivers of southern China in the summer of 1842. They sailed at will, sinking and scattering fleets of junks, demolishing Chinese fortresses, devastating villages and towns. Disciplined, well-equipped British and Indian soldiers gunned down all opposition. There are no figures for the Chinese casualties in the first Opium War, but it was certainly several thousands. British and Indian combat casualties were negligible. Far more died from disease than were killed by the Chinese.

When the Tories moved a motion of censure on the Whig government in April 1840, William Gladstone (then a rising star of the Tory party) condemned the incursion into China in ringing terms: 'A war more unjust in its origin, a war more calculated in its progress to cover this country with disgrace, I do not know and have not read of.' The British flag was being 'hoisted to protect an infamous contraband traffic' that had smeared the name of British civilization: 'we the enlightened and civilized Christians are pursuing objects at variance both with justice and with religion.'

The Chinese were struggling against a technology that they had not known existed. The British ship *Nemesis* proved particularly devastating. With a draught of only five feet and paddles driven by steam engines, the *Nemesis* could operate in the shallowest of waters and against currents and winds, to bring its guns and rockets to bear on any coastal town or village. When sailing ships in the British Fleet were becalmed, the *Nemesis* could tow them into positions where their guns could do the most damage.

The shock to the Celestial Empire was immense. When a British force battered its way up the Yangtse as far as Nanking, the Emperor sent commissioners to talk terms with Pottinger aboard his ship *Cornwallis*. In August 1841, after three days of talks, the Chinese agreed to pay an 'indemnity' of almost £6 million as compensation for loss of opium and loss of trade, and to meet the cost of the entire British military expedition. The Chinese also confirmed the ceding of Hong Kong to Britain 'in perpetuity' and agreed to open the ports of Amoy, Foochow, Ningpo and Shanghai to British merchants. This, known as the Treaty of Nanking, was followed by other treaties that allowed in the USA (in 1844) and France (in 1845). By the end of the nineteenth century almost every European trading power, plus the Japanese, had established a trading presence on the coasts and rivers of China. The Celestial Empire could no longer call parts of China its own.

William Jardine and James Matheson played a crucial role in reducing Cina to helplessness. They did much to start the war, they planned it, and they helped to win it. At the end of 1842 Palmerston (by then out of power) wrote to acknowledge the assistance that the company 'so handsomely afforded us'. He was particularly grateful for Jardine's advice to take the war into the very heart of the Celestial Empire: 'It has turned out that the decisive operation has been in the Yang Tsikiang (Yangtse) which was suggested to our naval commander as far back as February 1840.'

In his account of the company (*Jardine Matheson: Traders of the Far East*, Weidenfeld and Nicolson, 1999) the historian Robert Blake writes of the two Scots that 'for over ten years they advocated through their paper the *Canton Register*, through petitions to the House of Commons, and through private conversations at top level in the Foreign Office precisely the political and strategic policy which Palmerston adopted and which the successor Tory cabinet implemented.' Nor did Jardine Matheson restrict itself to supplying intelligence. Blake goes on: 'During the war they leased well-armed opium ships to the Royal Navy, lent their captains as navigators and their agents as translators, they supplied charts, information and advice.'

After the war, British ships swarmed into Hong Kong and the other newly opened 'treaty' ports and the quantities of opium imported into China soared. The Chinese authorities watched helplessly as more and more of their people became addicted and then destroyed by a drug made in British India. Ten years later, they tried once again to curb the opium trade – and suffered the Second Opium War.

By then William Jardine and James Matheson had retired from the East as very wealthy men. Both had brought in younger relatives (mainly nephews) to run the business. After Jardine returned to Britain in 1839 he never set foot in Asia again. He acquired a house in Belgravia, a Highland estate, Lanrick, on the edge of the Trossachs, membership of Brooks's club, and, in 1841, became Liberal member for the parliamentary seat of Ashburton in Devon. He appears lightly fictionalized in Benjamin Disraeli's novel of 1840s England, *Sybil*. He is the political opponent of the hero, Charles Egremont, who says of him at one point: 'Oh! A dreadful man! A Scotchman, richer than Croesus, one McDruggy, fresh from Canton with a million of opium in each pocket, denouncing corruption and bellowing free trade.' Jardine/McDruggy did not live long to enjoy his fortune. He died in his London house in Upper Belgrave Street in February 1843 at the age of fifty-nine. He is buried near his birthplace at Lochmaben in Dumfriesshire.

But the cause of opium did not go unheard in Parliament. When Jardine died his parliamentary seat was promptly occupied by his old partner James Matheson. 'My political opinions are favourable to every measure of practical and progressive reform,' Matheson declared in his electoral address, 'and I profess myself the zealous and ardent friend of civil, religious and commercial freedom.' He sat as MP for Ashburton until 1847, when he transferred his political allegiance to the Highland constituency of Ross and Cromarty.

In 1844 Matheson paid £500,000 (a huge sum at that time) for the entire Island of Lewis in the Outer Hebrides. He spent the rest of his life acting the enlightened laird, though 'enlightened' perhaps only in the sense that he paid the passage to North America for the many tenants he cleared off Lewis following the potato famine of the late 1840s when they fell behind with their rents. In 1851

Queen Victoria made him a baronet. Like his late partner, he kept a large house in London and belonged to Brooks's. For more than thirty years he lived the life of a wealthy Victorian, shuttling between London and his Lewis estate. Not unusually for rich men of that era, he died on the Côte d'Azur, at Mentone, in 1878. He was eighty-two. Like Jardine, he had no children. His baronetcy died with him.

Today the great trading firm of Jardine Matheson – which still sports a Scottish thistle in its livery – marches on. Through a network of subsidiaries and partly owned companies (among them Jardine Pacific, Jardine International Motors, Jardine Lloyd Thompson, Jardine Strategic, Mandarin Oriental) it employs 200,000 people across Asia, more than 50,000 of them in Hong Kong and China. In 1984, after Margaret Thatcher agreed to hand back the Crown colony to the Chinese when the lease ran out, the company moved its registered headquarters from Hong Kong to Bermuda and its Stock Exchange listing to Singapore. According to the then chairman Henry Keswick (a distant relative of William Jardine) the move was made to ensure 'freedom from politically influenced regulation'.

As for Lewis Castle and the island of Lewis, they were inherited by James Matheson's nephew, Donald, on his uncle's death. Donald had quit Jardine Matheson long before, sickened by the squalid realities of the family business. In 1892 he became chairman of the Executive Committee for the Suppression of the Opium Trade. Whatever the truth is in the saying about the sins of the fathers, it does not apply here to the sins of the uncles.

ALLAN OCTAVIAN HUME

For me – and, I suspect, for most of us – the words 'Indian Congress' conjure up two powerful images. One is of Mahatma Gandhi dressed in his loincloth and carrying his walking staff. The other is of Jawaharlal Nehru in his collarless jacket and white Congress cap. Both men were icons of India's struggle for independence and of anti-imperialist politics in the twentieth century, Gandhi as the popular inspiration for Indian nationalism, Nehru as India's first prime minister. The Congress Party to which Britain handed over India in 1947 is usually seen as their creation. In fact, it was the brainchild of a Victorian Anglo-Scot whose family hailed from the east-coast seaport of Montrose. His name was Allan Octavian Hume, and the portrait photograph that adorns his only biography shows a fair-haired, pale-eyed man with a spectacular moustache and dressed in a high-collared shirt and neat Edwardian suit. Anyone less like the popular image of Mahatma Gandhi it is hard to imagine.

I could find no modern biography of Hume, and plainly he was a man worth learning about. I started my research in Montrose, to see what traces of the Hume family remained. Of Allan Hume himself there was nothing. His father Joseph, however, stands on a sandstone plinth in the High Street, opposite a short thoroughfare called Hume Street that runs down to the Tesco supermarket. In Montrose's little museum, it was possible to glean a little about the Hume dynasty; a story, not untypical of Scotland in the nineteenth century, of the transforming power of education and imperial opportunity.

Allan Hume's grandfather James was the skipper of a coastal schooner that sailed out of Montrose. He died young, leaving his widow Mary (*née* Allan) to support six children, one of whom was Allan's father, Joseph, always known as Joe. The widow Hume scraped a living by selling crockery from a stall in the town's market place. There is an amiable local tradition that young Joe Hume's education was paid for by a local gentryman – Maule of Panmure – after he and Mary Hume conspired to pull off a stunt to impress his associates. Maule, it seems, was much taken with the fashion for mesmerism, the theory that one person's thoughts could influence another person's actions. Sitting in a market-place tavern Maule told his sceptical companions that he could 'mesmerize' Mrs Hume into breaking every piece of crockery on her stall. Maule duly – by advance arrangement – went into a 'trance' and Mrs Hume duly smashed every plate, cup, saucer and jug she had. As a reward Maule offered to educate Mrs Hume's brightest boy, Joseph.

Maule's money (if the story is true) was well spent. Joe Hume left school to study medicine at the universities of Edinburgh, Aberdeen, and London, and then found his way to India where he served in the Bengal Army and later as an interpreter – Hindi or Urdu to English – in some high-level negotiations with the Indian princes. India at that time, the early years of the nineteenth century, also offered British officers plenty of chances to make money unofficially, and when Joe Hume returned to Britain in 1808 he had a small fortune of £40,000. Hume spent the next few years travelling and studying and then, in 1812, began a career as a kind of wandering parliamentarian, representing first the people of Weymouth, and then the constituents of the Border Burghs, Aberdeen Burghs, Middlesex, Kilkenny in Ireland, and finally, until he died in 1855, the electorate of his home town of Montrose.

As an MP, Joe Hume was radical and tireless. He helped abolish flogging in the army and press gangs in the navy. He worked to repeal the Combination Laws that inhibited the free movement of labour, also the Test Acts that discriminated against anyone who was not an Anglican. He advocated the emancipation of Roman Catholics and railed against the corruption inside the East India Company (of which he was a shareholder). When he died in 1855 *The Times* described him as 'the unrelenting persecutor of sinecurists, drones and old men pretending to the work of the young in the state'.

His son, Allan Octavian Hume, was born into this radical, questioning milieu in St Marylebone, London, in 1829. According to Sir William Wedderburn, his biographer (*Alexander Octavian Hume*, T. Fisher Unwin, 1913), he inherited from his father 'not only a political connection with India, but also his love of science, and his uncompromising faith in democracy'. At the age of thirteen Allan Hume enlisted in the Royal Navy as a junior midshipman, from where, after a brief (and probably unhappy) spell on the frigate *Vanguard*, he was sent to Haileybury College, the public school that had been founded to groom young Britons for the East India Company's civil service and the task of administering British rule in India. In 1849, aged twenty-nine, he joined the Bengal Civil Service and was appointed district officer at Etawah, a town about 150 miles south-east of Delhi. The town and its surrounding territories covered 1,700 square miles and contained more than 700,000 people, most of them Hindus.

It was Allan Hume's job to administer this area – as district officer he stood at the apex of Etawah's civil life and a system that encompassed the police, the law courts, rents and taxes. His record there suggests zeal and energy. He did what he could to reform the police and tried to stamp out liquor peddling. Within five years he had established 181 village schools that were educating more than 5,000 children, many of them girls. With money from his own pocket, he built the high school in Etawah that bore his name. He started a local newspaper in Hindi called *The People's Friend*, and created a commercial district in Etawah which is still known as *Humeganj*, or Humetown.

A sympathy and curiosity for Indian life and culture, however, did not mean that Hume was in any sense opposed to the idea of British rule. When the insurrection that British historians call the Great Mutiny and Indian nationalists call the Revolution erupted in 1857, he distinguished himself by his bravery. According to his biographer, when a party of mutineers from the 3rd Bengal Cavalry occupied a Hindu temple near Etawah, Hume and his assistant tried to storm the building, armed with a shotgun and one revolver. Hume's assistant was shot in the face but Hume killed two of the mutineers and drove the rest away. Then, after the troops at Etawah joined the insurrection, Hume and his wife and daughter sought refuge in the British fort at Agra.

Several months later, after Hume had retaken Etawah, he raised a small force of 200 infantrymen and 150 horsemen and spent the next eighteen months clearing his district of mutineers. Most of the time he led from the front. In his report to the Governor-General, the British commander-in-chief asked if he might 'bring to the special notice of His Lordship the extremely gallant conduct of Mister Hume'.

For his part in saving the Raj, Hume was made a Commander of the Bath (CB) in 1860, though he was privately concerned by the vengeful ferocity that characterized British treatment of the rebels. He thought it was likely to prove counter-productive. 'No district [other than his own] in the North-West Province has, I believe, been more completely restored to order,' Hume wrote later. 'None in which so few severe punishments have been inflicted. Mercy and forbearance have, I think I may justly say, characterized my administration.'

Hume's career in India prospered for many years. After Etawah, he was made Commissioner of Customs for the North-West Provinces and in that role dismantled the Customs barrier that stretched 2,500 miles across the north of India, originally set up to exclude cheap salt from the Rajputana states and which had proved a source of delay and corruption. Agriculture became his great enthusiasm. He believed that the way forward for Indian peasant farmers was to build on their own ways of doing things rather than to imitate European methods. He was impressed by their knowledge of their native soils, crops and weather cycles. The condition of their wheat fields, he said, would 'shame ninety-nine hundredths of those in Europe'.

Most of Hume's ideas are contained in his pamphlet *Agricultural Reform in India*, which he published in 1879. As Hume saw it, the greatest need of Indian farmers was for fertilizer. They should spread cow dung on the fields rather than drying it and using it as fuel for heating and cooking. What would Indian peasants use for fuel instead? Hume advocated 'fuelwood plantations', small, local forests of fast-growing trees that could be coppiced for firewood. Such plantations, he wrote, would be 'entirely in accord with the traditions of the country – a thing that the people would understand, appreciate and, with a little judicious pressure, cooperate in'. These ideas prefigured the arguments of twentieth-century environmentalism, and even some aspects of Gandhianism.

In 1869, Lord Mayo became Viceroy of India. Mayo's priority was to reinvigorate farming. 'Agriculture, on which everyone here depends, is almost entirely neglected by the government,' Mayo declared. 'We believe it to be susceptible of almost indefinite improvement.' Mayo's plan was to make Allan Hume head of a new Department of Agriculture, but his project ran into high-level hostility (from his civil service and from London) and Hume had to settle for being secretary to the combined departments of Revenue and Agriculture – a big job, which meant that every year Hume had to shuttle between Calcutta and the government's summer quarters in Simla in the cool foothills of the Himalayas. There Hume spent around £15,000 building a mansion called Rothney Castle, its size partly dictated by his need to accommodate his large and growing collection of stuffed birds and birds' eggs; ornithology was his private passion. (Rothney Castle still stands, now semi-ruinous, having defeated various efforts by modern owners to turn it into a luxury hotel.)

Some of Hume's agricultural ideas were more overtly political. He was appalled at how many Indian smallholders got into debt, lost their land and led lives of grinding poverty. He argued for government-owned banks and cooperatively owned banks that would fund small-scale local enterprises at low rates of interest. And he was critical of what he called 'the cruel blunders into which our narrow-minded, though wholly benevolent, desire to reproduce England in India has led us.'

This kind of thinking did not always go down well in the upper reaches of India's British administration. When Hume's supporter Lord Mayo was assassinated by an Afghan convict in the Andaman Islands in 1872, his star began to wane. The appointment of the poet and romantic imperialist Lord Lytton as Viceroy in 1875 made things worse. When Hume's name was put forward in 1876 as a candidate for the ruling Council of India, it was blocked by Lord Salisbury, who wrote that 'his papers give me the impression of a man more effusive than solid, and the stories I hear of him represent him as little better than a charlatan.' No doubt some of these stories emanated from Lord Lytton, who described Hume in 1878 as a man 'full of crotchets, and, with great intellectual arrogance, he has no knowledge of human nature and tact in his dealing with others'. A year later Lytton complained that 'his insolence and his improprieties are really becoming insufferable.' In the summer of that year, 1879, Hume was ousted from central government and posted as a minor official to Allahabad, in the Gangetic plain. The Indian press saw Hume's fall as an act of political spite.

'A great wrong,' was the opinion of the *Indian Daily News*. 'Undoubtedly he has been treated shamefully and cruelly,' said the *Statesman*. The analysis of *The Englishman* probably came closest to the truth. The paper wrote: 'If he believed a particular policy to be wrong, he opposed it without hesitation, using plain language for the expression of his views. We cannot find that any other charge has been brought against him.'

Hume did not accept his exile gracefully. He continued to bombard his superiors with complaints and suggestions, and further alienated himself from officialdom by steeping himself in the newfangled belief of Theosophy, that Victorian version of Eastern mysticism dreamt up by Madame Helena Petrovna Blavatsky and her American acolyte Colonel Henry Olcott. Hume met Blavatsky in 1879 and was impressed, and though he became less impressed as time wore on (by 1883, she had 'drifted away into a maze of falsehoods') he never lost his interest in Indian mysticism and went on to develop his own brand of Theosophy.

In 1882, aged fifty-three, Allan Hume resigned from the Indian Civil Service and retired to his home in Simla. There, among the stuffed birds, he fretted about the condition of India and the increasing disaffection of Indians, fearing the possibility of a rerun of the bloody insurrection of 1857–8. His biographer William Wedderburn claimed that before Hume retired he had seen seven volumes of intelligence reports from all over India which showed that Indians were, once again, growing resentful of their British masters. The racism of British rule was a standing offence to Indians. Many resented having the British monarch crowned Empress of India in 1877, and resented even more that Indian taxes footed the bill for the lavish celebrations that accompanied Victoria's imperial coronation. The wars in Afghanistan, fought by Indian as well as British troops, were unpopular. The value of the silver rupee against the pound had declined by almost forty per cent. Western education had created a vocal and ambitious middle class. And there had been a genuine renaissance of Indian culture and of the Hindu religion. Hume believed that unless Indians were given free access to political power, then India would once again erupt into violence and the Raj would end in bloody ruin.

In March 1883 Hume published what he called *A Circular Letter to the Graduates of Calcutta University*, which exhorted young Indians to organize into a political body which would act in a peaceful and determined way. No one else, he declared, could do it for them. Of foreigners such as himself he wrote: 'They may place their experience, abilities and knowledge at the disposal of the workers, but they lack the essential of nationality, and the real work must be done by the people of the country themselves . . . If only fifty men, good and true, can be found to join as founders, the thing can be established, and the further developments will be comparatively easy.' Then he went on to warn: 'And if amongst even you, the elite, fifty men cannot be found with sufficient power of self-sacrifice, sufficient love for and pride in their country, sufficient genuine and unselfish heartfelt patriotism to take the initiative, and if needs be, devote the rest of their lives to the cause – then there is no hope for India. Her sons must and will remain mere humble and helpless instruments in the hands of foreign rulers.'

Hume's plea struck chords among the Indian elites. An Indian National Union began to emerge. Local committees were organized in Bombay, Poona, Karachi, Madras, Calcutta, Benares, Allahabad, Lucknow, Agra and Lahore. In 1885, Hume made a trip to Britain to drum up support among the reform-minded groups. He was appalled by the scant coverage of Indian affairs in the British press, so he set up a news agency, the Indian Telegraph Union, to supply British newspapers with copy. Most of the newspapers with which he struck deals were in the north: the *Manchester Guardian*, the *Scotsman*, the *Leeds Mercury*, the *Glasgow Daily Mail*, the *Dundee Advertiser*, the *Bradford Observer*.

Late that same year, on 28 December 1885, in the Great Hall of the Gokul Das Tejpal Sanskrit College in Bombay, the Indian National Congress met for the first time. The Congress delegate from Simla – and the only European – was Allan Hume. Almost all delegates were drawn from the educated, English-speaking elite: lawyers, newspaper editors, merchants, doctors, civil servants, and a few rural landowners. They were overwhelmingly Hindu – a fact that did not go unnoticed by the Muslim press – and not particularly anti-British. According to the *Indian Mirror* the proceedings opened with three cheers for Queen Victoria, which were then followed by three cheers for Allan Octavian Hume. Womesh Chandra Bannerjee was elected the Congress's first president and Allan Hume its first secretary.

This moderate body made moderate demands (for example, that local legislative councils should include 'a considerable proportion of elected members') and to start with the Viceroy, the Marquess of Dufferin, had no problem with Congress and its ambitions. (It might even be that Dufferin and Hume had put their heads together in 1884 to come up with a system that might move India forward without tearing the country apart.) Dufferin regarded the Congress as a useful safety valve, a body that would allow him to keep in touch with Indian opinion while undermining the more radical nationalists. When the second Congress met in Calcutta in 1886, Dufferin invited the 'distinguished visitors' to a garden party at Government House.

But as Congress grew in confidence its propaganda became more strident. The British establishment began to worry about the organization and its advocates. As its secretary, Allan Hume attracted a great deal of odium. He was warned that Congress was providing a platform for those who were not interested in reform but whose 'real quarrel was with British rule in any form'. He was also in danger of 'fostering race hatred and arousing passions which would pass beyond his control'.

By the time Dufferin came to leave India, he had turned completely against Congress. At his farewell dinner on St Andrew's Day 1888, he described Congress as the creation of a 'microscopic minority' who were leading the great mass of Indians badly astray.

As for Hume and his prognosis of violence, Dufferin said, 'Nor is the silly threat of one of the chief officers – the Principal Secretary, I believe – of the Congress that he and his Congress friends hold in their hands the keys, not only of a popular insurrection, but of a military revolt, calculated to restore our confidence.'

But Hume accepted these attacks with equanimity and continued to work tirelessly for the organization that he had done so much to create. By the time he returned to Britain in 1894, the Indian National Congress was thriving. 'Let nothing discourage you,' he told his last audience in India. 'Hold fast to that conviction which all the best and wisest share; that right must, and even does, triumph in the end . . . the spirit of the age is behind you, and win you must before the end comes.'

Allan Hume retired to a modest house, 'The Chalet', in Kingswood Road in the London suburb of Upper Norwood, not far from the Crystal Palace. He died on 31 July 1912 and was buried at Brookwood Cemetery. Indian newspapers carried glowing obituaries. The *Indian Mirror* credited him with 'awakening what is known as the national life of India'. The Muslim newspaper *Comrade* described him as 'one of the few high-souled Indian Civil Service men who devoted their life to selfless service for the people of this country.' The *Mahratta* of Poona said that Hume's great achievement lay with 'the work that he did after retirement in rearing a national Indian institution – the Congress. No one else could be said to have done so much as he did to foster that nursling in these days.'

Nowhere in the town of Montrose is there any mention of Joe Hume's great son, Allan; nor, so far as I can tell, does he have any monuments elsewhere in Britain. Or not, at least, to Allan the politician. Hume the ornithologist is a different matter.

Hume began collecting birds' eggs and birds' 'skins' (for stuffing) almost from the day he set foot in India in 1849. From 1872 to 1899 he wrote and published a bird magazine called *Avian Feathers*. His mansion at Simla housed no fewer than 60,000 stuffed birds and more than 20,000 eggs. Hume's ambition had been to write the definitive study of Indian bird life. Then, in the winter of 1885, his house in Simla was broken into and his notes were stolen. A disaffected servant was the likely culprit. The notes were never recovered. Broken-hearted, Hume offered his entire collection to the British Museum of Natural History which was happy to accept – so happy, in fact, that they sent the head of the museum's ornithology department out to Simla to supervise the packing and shipping.

Allan Hume's collection of birds and eggs can still be seen at the Museum of Natural History in London.

As Others See Us:
T. W. H. Crosland

T. W. H. CROSLAND'S BOOK *The Unspeakable Scot* was in its day
a renowned exercise in Scotophobia. When it was published in 1902
it induced much ire north of the border and some serious head-
scratching among the literati. Was Crosland serious? Or was he writing
with tongue firmly in cheek? Did he loathe the Scots as much as
Jonathan Swift had? Or was his rant just a satire intended to tweak the
noses of the Scots, particularly those in London? Whatever Crosland's
intention, the effect is memorable. A sample from his first chapter:

> Your proper child of Caledonia believes in his rickety bones that
> he is the salt of the earth. Prompted by a glozing pride, not to say
> a black and consuming avarice, he has proclaimed his saltiness
> from the house-tops in and out of season, unblushingly,
> assiduously, and with results which have no doubt been most
> satisfactory from his own point of view. There is nothing
> creditable to the race of men, from filial piety to a pretty taste in
> claret, which he has not sedulously advertised as a virtue peculiar
> to himself. This arrogation has served him passing well. It has
> brought him into unrivalled esteem.

He is the one species of human animal that is taken by all the world to be fifty per cent cleverer and pluckier and honester than the facts warrant. He is the daw with a peacock's tail of his own painting. He is the ass who has been at pains to cultivate the convincing roar of a lion. He is the fine gentleman whose father toils with a muck fork. And, to have done with the parable, he is the bandy-legged lout from Tullietudlescleugh, who, after a childhood of intimacy with the cesspool and the crablouse, and twelve months at 'the college' on moneys wrung from the diet of his family, drops his threadbare kilt, and comes south in a slop suit to instruct the English in the arts of civilization and in the English language.

And because he is Scotch and the Scotch superstition is heavy on our Southern lands, England will forthwith give him a chance, for an English chance is his birthright. Soon, forby, shall he be living in 'chambers' and writing idiot books. Or he shall swell and hector and fume in the sub-editor's room of a halfpenny paper. Or a pompous and gravel-blind city house shall grapple him to its soul in the capacity of confidential clerk. Or he shall be cashier in a jam factory, or 'boo and boo' behind a mercer's counter, or 'wait on' in a coffee tavern, or, for that matter, soak away his chapped spirit in the four-ale bars off Fleet Street.

That was written a hundred years before Scottish influence in London became so dominant in politics and the broadcast media, best illustrated when BBC interviewer A (say James Naughtie) seeks the view of BBC political editor B (say Andrew Marr) about the prospects for Cabinet Minister C (say Gordon Brown), so that today an English reader of Crosland might see his book not so much as satire as prediction. In 1902, it was such a wild success that the publishers rushed out what might be called an uncompanion volume the next year: *The Egregious English* by a Scotsman, Angus McNeill. This was not a success, perhaps because (it must be said) his book was not nearly as funny.

THE McKLANSMEN

THE TOWN OF OKMULGEE in the flat lands of eastern Oklahoma has nothing much to recommend it. It is the kind of dusty, partly run-down place that bakes in the summer heat and raises the question: what is it for? Its only purchase on significance is that it houses the administrative headquarters of the Creek Nation. The Creeks settled around Okmulgee after being driven west of the Mississippi by the US government in the 1830s and many of them are still there. My only reason for being in the town a few years ago was to have a look around the Creek courthouse in the town centre and find something to eat and something cool to drink.

Not far from the courthouse I found a small bar. It was grubby and it was dark, but it was cool and the bartender and his handful of customers seemed friendly enough. While I waited for the bartender to rustle up a chicken salad (which proved surprisingly good) I passed the time studying the flyers and posters plastered on the wall. Most were the usual small-town stuff: barbecues, Little League baseball games, garage sales. One undersized poster caught my eye. It was badly drawn, garishly coloured and cheaply printed. It exhorted 'all patriotic Americans' who were concerned about the 'future of our great country' to enlist in the ranks of the 'Knights of the Ku Klux Klan'. What drew my interest in particular were the crude drawings of the kind of Celtic crosses to be seen in any graveyard in Scotland or Ireland. The border of the poster was a valiant attempt at the elaborately intertwined Celtic design now standard on tourist literature handed out in Edinburgh or Dublin.

One of the blue-collar customers must have noticed me taking notes. He left the bar and sauntered up to me, swigging on his bottle of Budweiser as he came. He was slightly under middling height, but tanned and wiry and dressed in faded denim jeans and a sleeveless denim shirt. I braced myself for trouble, though I knew that if push came to shove I wouldn't stand much of a chance. But I need not have worried. He was merely curious about a stranger taking notes. In fact, he was amiability itself, particularly when he learned that I came from Scotland.

'Hell, fella,' he said gesturing with his Budweiser at the KKK poster, 'Scotland's where the Klan comes from. Any Klansman that's worth buyin' a drink for, he's got family in Scotland. You Scotch guys invented the whole business. But mebbe you don't want to hear that.'

He was right about that. It certainly wasn't the kind of thing a liberal-minded Scotsman wanted to hear. As I was on my way up to Tulsa and had a day to kill when I got there I decided to check out the history of the Klan in the library of the Oklahoma Historical Society. And I discovered that there was a great deal of truth in what the man in the Okmulgee bar had told me. The Ku Klux Klan is indeed a very Scottish creation.

The modern Klan owes its existence to a novel written by one Thomas Dixon, a Baptist clergyman from North Carolina, that was published in 1905 and which is entitled *The Clansman: an historical romance of the Ku Klux Klan*. The Reverend Dixon went on to write a couple of dozen other fictions, but none of them met with anything like the success of *The Clansman*, which is a very Scottish book.

Born in Shelby, North Carolina in 1864, Dixon was the son of the Reverend Thomas Dixon and Amanda Elizabeth McAfee. His uncle (to whom the novel is dedicated) was a Confederate colonel and a 'Grand Titan' of the original Ku Klux Klan. After qualifying as a lawyer, Dixon became a member of the North Carolina legislature from which he resigned to become a Baptist minister. He returned to the law in 1938 to become clerk to a US District Court in North Carolina. Dixon died in 1946 at the age of eighty-two.

The Clansman is set in that peculiarly brutal period of American history, the 'reconstruction' of the southern states following the Civil War. Dixon summarizes the story as the reaction of the white South to the 'bold attempt of Thaddeus Stevens to Africanize ten great states of the American Union'. And how the 'young South' formed the Ku Klux Klan and 'led by the reincarnated sons of the Clansmen of Old Scotland, went forth under that cover . . . and saved the life of a people, [to form] one of the most dramatic chapters in the history of the Aryan race'.

The Scottishness of Dixon's fable is startling. The heroes of the tale are the Cameron family: Doctor and Mrs Richard Cameron, their son Ben and their daughter Margaret. The villains are the newly emancipated Negroes, particularly a grotesque black called Gus. All the blacks are dancing to the tune of a club-footed Yankee called Austin Stoneman (who is plainly Thaddeus Stevens). The Northern politician is described as a calculating monster with 'cold, colourless eyes, with the frosts of his native Vermont sparkling in their depths'.

This undertow of Celtic South versus Anglo-Saxon North runs through the story. Describing Ben Cameron's antecedents, Dixon writes: 'His race had defied the Crown of Great Britain a hundred years from the caves and wilds of Scotland and Ireland, taught the English people how to slay a King and build a Commonwealth, and, driven into exile into the wilderness of America, led our revolution, peopled the hills of the South and conquered the West.' Bad history, and syntax, of course, but the kind of stuff that is still widely believed south of the Mason-Dixon line.

Interestingly, Dixon scoffs at the notion (held by Mark Twain among others) that the South was an aristocratic, 'cavalier' society created by the overblown romances of Walter Scott. 'Cavalier fiddlesticks!' his hero Richard Cameron declares at one point. 'There are no Cavaliers in my country. We are all Covenanter and Huguenot folks.' Which, historically, is true enough. Most of the British immigrants who flooded into the South in the eighteenth and nineteenth centuries were Scots and Ulster Presbyterians, the folk whom the Americans call Scots-Irish.

The formation of the Ku Klux Klan predates Dixon's novel by about forty years, but it was the novel that gave the Klan its most potent piece of symbolism: the Gaelic *crann tara*, the fiery cross. Dixon has his Doctor Cameron declaim: 'In olden times when the chieftain of our people summoned the clan on an errand of life and death, the fiery cross . . . was sent by swift courier from village to village. This call was never made in vain, nor will it be tonight in the New World.' This 'old Scottish rite', he promises, 'will send a thrill of inspiration to every clansman in the hills'.

It certainly sent a thrill of inspiration to D. W. Griffith, the Kentucky-born film director whose father Jacob had been a Confederate colonel. In 1914 Griffith bought the film rights to *The Clansman*, and in February 1915 released America's first epic movie, *The Birth of A Nation* (which, when it was premiered in Los Angeles, had the title *The Clansman*). Between them, Griffith and Dixon restored the Klan's fortunes. In the summer of 1915, on Stone Mountain near Atlanta, Georgia, the first 'Klavicle' of the modern Klan assembled in secret under a fiery cross of the kind that Dixon had imagined in his novel and Griffith in his film. Within a few weeks the new Klan had taken its first victim – a young Jew called Leo Frank who had been accused of murdering a fourteen-year-old girl. Frank was lynched by hooded Klansmen near the town of Marietta, Georgia on 16 August 1915.

The *crann tara* raised on Stone Mountain in 1915 succeeded beyond the dreams of the men who lit its flames. Under the

Klansmen in D. W. Griffith's Birth of a Nation

direction of two talented publicists, Edward Clarke and Elizabeth Tyler, membership of the Ku Klux Klan soared all over the United States. In 1922, the Klan was confident enough to stage a huge march down Pennsylvania Avenue in Washington DC. In 1928, the train carrying Al Smith, the unsuccessful Democratic candidate in that year's presidential campaign, was met by hooded figures in white, many of them carrying fiery crosses, whenever it stopped at an Oklahoma railroad station. As the first Roman Catholic to stand for the presidency, Smith had incurred the wrath of the Klan, which by then had about four million members and was no longer confined to the rural states of the South and the Midwest. In fact, the Klan was at its strongest in America's growing industrial cities where dispossessed whites competed for work with immigrant blacks. Most sizeable towns had their 'Klavicles' manned by white Protestants pledged to defend America against Roman Catholics, Jews, foreigners and, of course, blacks.

By the end of the Second World War its membership had shrunk into insignificance, but its appeal revived during the civil-rights agitation of the 1960s. Today it calls itself the Knights of the Ku Klux Klan and its language is distinctly more circumspect and apparently reasonable than that of its nineteenth- and twentieth-century predecessors, though it is still ardently pro-white and Protestant and deeply suspicious of Catholics and blacks.

The Klan is also increasingly obsessed by its 'Celtic' and particularly its Scottish roots. Many a Southern Baptist now takes a scholarly interest in Scottish Jacobitism, apparently unaware that this profoundly Catholic cause represents everything that he should despise. The Gaelic *crann tara* conjured up by Thomas Dixon is still flickering across the United States. It is one of Scotland's less wholesome contributions to American life.

BLOOD AND WHISKY

ONE OF LONDON'S MORE sedate thoroughfares is St James's Street, just off Piccadilly. I can never walk down it without thinking of American gangsters. On the east side, just opposite the Carlton Club, that shrine to High Toryism, sit the premises of Berry Brothers & Rudd, purveyors of wine and spirits. The discreet shopfront is the essence of gentlemanly retailing. Odd to consider, then, that one day in 1920 the American hoodlum Jack 'Legs' Diamond sauntered into Berry Brothers and ordered several hundred cases of their 'best' Scotch; and that Berry Brothers were most happy to oblige, even though they knew that the whisky would end up in the USA, where alcoholic liquor had just been prohibited by Congress.

Jack Diamond's order set the firm thinking. Francis Berry, the firm's junior partner, reasoned that if a semi-literate lowlife like Diamond could contrive to get Scotch into the USA then so could he. Within a few weeks Berry found himself in Nassau in the Bahamas, doing a deal with a Scots-American seaman from Florida called Bill McCoy.

The Berry/McCoy deal was simple. Berry Brothers would ship their whisky into the British colonial government's warehouses in the Bahamas, from where it would be uplifted by McCoy's schooner and sailed north to international waters off the New York/New Jersey coast. Using his ship as a floating warehouse, McCoy would sell the drink on to the gangsters who were paying fancy prices for Scotch to peddle in their illegal speakeasies. The gangsters would take the whisky ashore in high-powered launches that could outrun the US Coast Guard's fleet of ageing cutters.

The arrangement worked well. The gangsters could not get enough of the product. Within months the Berry Brothers' quality whiskies were the most sought-after Scotch on the USA's eastern seaboard. As a result, Bill McCoy added to his already substantial bank balance, the Berry Brothers' distilleries in Scotland did brisk business, and the firm carved itself a niche in the American market from which they were able to expand when Prohibition ended in 1933. Everybody – Bill McCoy, Berry Brothers, Legs Diamond and his fellow gangsters, the American drinking public – was happy – everybody, that is, except those Americans who regarded Prohibition as a 'noble experiment' (in the words of President Herbert Hoover) and were happy to see it as the eighteenth amendment to the constitution of the United States.

The Scottish whisky industry regarded this as an inconvenient legality. By the early 1920s, Berry Brothers had been joined by familiar names such as John Dewar, the Chivas Brothers, John Walker, James Buchanan, the Distillers Company Ltd, plus a swarm of smaller companies, all united in their determination to keep alive America's taste for Scotch. If that meant dealing with violent criminals, then they would deal with violent criminals.

The very profitable relationship between respectable Scotch-whisky firms and American mobsters is still a largely unknown story. 'Everybody knows that them guys in Scotland are tight and love money,' the gang boss Charles 'Lucky' Luciano told his biographers. 'So one of our guys – Arnold Rothstein – made legit contracts with them and laid down big deposits so we would be guaranteed delivery.' Legit contracts there may have been, but they can be very hard to discover; even now, eighty years on, the Scotch-whisky industry is reluctant to talk about its dealings with the American underworld.

Scotland's 'war' with the USA lasted almost thirteen years, from the day early in 1920 when Prohibition was introduced until the end of 1933 when it was repealed. Dozens of ships were looted or sunk, an unknown number of lives were lost, fortunes were made and spent. The Scottish whisky industry's iron determination to keep open its most lucrative foreign market also caused endless diplomatic turbulence and severely strained British–American relations. The whisky industry never gave up.

In 1920, Scottish whisky as a branded product and fashionable drink was a relative newcomer to the international stage, at least in countries beyond the British Empire. Until the last quarter of the nineteenth century, French brandy, particularly Cognac, was the tipple of choice for those who could afford it. Then in the 1870s French vineyards were laid waste by the bug *phylloxera vastatrix* and French brandy became scarce and expensive, giving the whisky distillers a marketing opportunity that they were quick to exploit. Having more or less eclipsed their rival whisky-makers in Ireland, the Scotch industry launched a sometimes brilliant advertising campaign, first in England and then in the wider English-speaking world.

The Scotch industry was then in the hands of some remarkably able men, the great whisky 'barons' who ran the 'Big Five' firms that dominated the market: John Dewar, John Walker, White Horse, James Buchanan, and the Distillers Company Ltd. It was apparent to all of them that the USA was by far the most lucrative foreign market and the one with the greatest potential. When, on 16 January 1920, that market was closed to them by the national Prohibition Act (better known as the Volstead Act after its promoter Andrew J. Volstead, the Minnesota congressman) they knew that the legislation would somehow need to be circumnavigated if the whisky trade was to prosper.

And so they evolved a system that any present-day cocaine dealer would recognize. They set up a string of import agents in some of the territories that surrounded the USA: Canada, Cuba, Bermuda, the Bahamas, and the French colonies of St Pierre and Miquelon (two tiny islands off the coast of Nova Scotia). These agents then 'bought' and imported – quite legally – large quantities of Scotch into their respective territories, sometimes directly from the distillers, sometimes via syndicates of, say, London or Glasgow businessmen who bought the whisky and then shipped it at their own cost. Whisky exports to the islands of the Atlantic and the Caribbean leapt to extraordinary proportions. Exports of whisky to the Bahamas, for example, rose from 944 gallons in 1918 to more than 386,000 gallons in 1922. The little islands of St Pierre and Miquelon – which had a population of 6,000 people between them – imported more than 116,000 gallons of Scotch in the same year, more than twenty gallons of whisky for every man, woman and child in the colony. Smaller Scotch depots were established in Havana, the Turks and Caycos islands, and on Grand Cayman.

All of them were, of course, merely staging posts for the whisky's onward journey by sailing schooners and tramp steamers to various points off the American coast – and, vitally, just outside American waters – that were known as 'Rum Rows'. Then the ships would loiter until the 'contact boats' operated by bootleggers came out to relieve them of their cargo. 'Rum Rows' existed off the coasts of Texas, Florida, and California, but the largest of them was off the north-east coast: sometimes more than a hundred whisky-filled vessels lay in a 150-mile arc between Montauk Point, at the east end of Long Island, and Atlantic City in New Jersey. A ship might cruise slowly around there for several weeks until it had offloaded its very last case of whisky.

The system proved to be efficient and enormously profitable. Directly and indirectly, the whisky distillers and blenders of Scotland were tapping into the criminal networks run by American gangsters, mainly the 'Seven Group' confederation that controlled the liquor trade on the eastern seaboard and was coordinated from Manhattan by Charles 'Lucky' Luciano and Johnny Torrio (and also included such luminaries as 'Bugsy' Siegel, Meyer Lansky, Joe Adonis, 'Longy' Zwillman, 'Nig' Rosen, 'Nucky' Johnson and 'Waxey' Gordon). Once the Scotch was brought ashore, the Seven Group distributed it to the other organized gangsters down the line: 'Moe' Dalitz in Cleveland; 'Boss' Tom Prendegast in Kansas City; Alphonse 'Scarface' Capone in Chicago.

The linchpins of the whole operation were the sea captains who ran the whisky (and other spirits) from its island depots to the stations on 'Rum Row'. The most notorious of them was Bill McCoy of Jacksonville, Florida, who came from respectable parentage (his father had been a fishing buddy of Andrew Carnegie) and who, ironically, was a complete teetotaller. McCoy and his brother Ben sold their yacht-building yard in Jacksonville to buy a small fleet of schooners, the most famous of which was the *Arethusa*, a 120-foot long, three-masted schooner built in Gloucester, Massachusetts for Atlantic cod-fishing. As the US navy and the US coastguard had the legal right to stop and search any American ship on the high seas, McCoy registered his fleet in the British-owned Bahamas and operated through a company he called The British Transportation and Trading Company.

The Bahamas were a favourite haunt for the liquor smugglers, particularly the islands' chief town, Nassau, which in the 1920s and 1930s became a rough and prosperous place where smuggling crews spent their wages in bars and whorehouses. The colonial government turned a blind eye. Every case of whisky imported into the Bahamas was stored in government warehouses at a cost of $6 (and later $7) a crate, a rate that did wonders for the Bahamian exchequer. By the early 1920s, the Americans, who were well aware of the British colony's key status as an entrepôt, had established a network of informers throughout the islands. Later, after some high-level diplomacy, the State Department won special privileges for US warships and coastguard cutters to chase bootleggers into

Bahamian territorial waters (which they did time and again, with British permission and without it).

The Bahamas were not Bill McCoy's only source of liquor, however. He also operated out of two tiny remnants of France's empire in North America, the islands of St Pierre and Miquelon. Where the British colonial capital of Nassau was a brawling, almost lawless frontier town, the French islands were well regulated by the local *gendarmerie*. Also, the storage rates charged by the islands' government-owned bonded warehouses were cheaper than in Nassau. By the mid-1920s, the warehouses on St Pierre and Miquelon held a truly astonishing range of wines and spirits. All the best-known brands of Scotch whisky were there – Johnny Walker Red Label, Dewar's Ne Plus Ultra, White Horse, Old Parr, Old Claymore, King George Gold Label – and just about every brand, even the more obscure, could be bought on the quayside for from $8.50 to $22.50 a case. On 'Rum Row' the same cases were sold on to the gangsters for as much as $65 a case.

The profits to the smuggler were enormous, but less so to the bootlegger unless he diluted the whisky with water before selling it on. Usually one bottle of Scotch on 'Rum Row' would produce three bottles of whisky in the speakeasies of New York or Chicago; heavier, darker whiskies might even produce four bottles. There is a plausible theory that modern America acquired its taste for light whiskies (such as the Berry Brothers' blend Cutty Sark) after drinking so much diluted stuff during the Prohibition years.

According to popular legend, Bill McCoy, 'King of the Rum Runners', would have none of this diluting. As smugglers went, McCoy was reputed to be an honest man, one who took pride in the quality of the liquor that he shipped. He tried to guarantee that his whisky was never tampered with. His liquor cargoes became known as 'the Real McCoy', though the phrase probably has its origin earlier in Victorian Scotland (and among Scots in North America) when it was applied to a favoured brand of whisky called McKay.

The US coastguards were not the only hazard that the smugglers

Bootlegger's 'rummy apron', 1920s

and bootleggers faced. More dangerous enemies were the 'go-through' men (so-called because they would 'go through' with anything), who were the pirates of the trade and just as ruthless as any of their eighteenth-century predecessors. Freelance mobsters, they would raid the bootleggers' speedboats for their money on their way out to Rum Row or plunder them on the way back for their cargoes. Gun battles at sea between rival criminal gangs in high-speed launches were not uncommon. Occasionally the go-through guys would swarm over the side of a Rum Row ship and leave it gutted. More than one schooner or steamship was found like the *Marie Celeste* – adrift, stripped of its cargo and without a soul on board.

The British two-masted schooner *Patricia M. Berman* met just such a fate in April 1923. She was found by the US coastguard drifting off Long Island with no one aboard, her superstructure shredded by bullets, shell casings and blood stains all over the deck. The US coastguard concluded that the crew had been killed and dumped over the side. From the ship's papers they learned that the *Patricia M. Berman* had been on Rum Row for almost three months, during which she had peddled 3,918 cases of whisky.

One of the first to give up on the business was Bill McCoy, whose bootlegging career came to an end in November 1923, after his ship *Tomoka* (previously the *Arethusa*) was boarded by US agents. McCoy decided to make a run for it, pursued by the coastguard cutter *Seneca* which eventually stopped the *Tomoka* with a series of well-aimed warning shots. McCoy surrendered, his ship and cargo were confiscated, and he went to jail for nine months.

After he came out of jail McCoy never returned to the trade. He had no need to continue the risks that came with law-breaking and with the increasing violence of the trade. In the first few years of Prohibition he had smuggled 170,000 cases of whisky, rum and other spirits into the USA and had made himself a very rich man. He later claimed to have been making $100,000 profit every month. In 1925 he returned to his home state where he made yet another fortune as a real-estate developer in the Florida property boom. He died in December 1948 aboard his yacht *Blue Lagoon* off the town of Stuart, Florida. He was seventy-one.

The task of defending the USA against the liquor pirates and the bootleggers was well beyond the US coastguard's capabilities in the early 1920s. The USA's mainland coastline is more than 6,000 miles long, indented with estuaries, laced with hundreds of little islands and, in the south, edged with swamps and bayous. Blockading such a coastline was an impossible task for a force that was equipped with about sixty ageing and underpowered cutters, most of which could do no more than twelve knots an hour and were no match for the high-powered 'contact boats' operated by the bootleggers.

For the first few years of Prohibition the rum-runners ran rings around the US government. The official estimate is that the US coastguard managed to stop only five per cent of the liquor that was flowing into the USA. The coastguard commanders argued that their hands were tied. Not only were their boats inadequate, but they could only intercept suspected vessels that sailed within three miles of the US coast. And there was always the danger of sparking a diplomatic row because of the rum-runners' habit of registering their ships under the British flag.

Like the modern war against drugs, the war against liquor was a hopeless, one-sided battle that the US coastguard was losing. At the end of 1923 the outgoing coastguard commandant William E. Reynolds warned President Calvin Coolidge that the only way to thwart the liquor pirates was with more men and much better equipment. Reynolds told Coolidge that the coastguard needed another twenty cutters, 203 motor boats, ninety-one small inshore boats and another 3,500 men – at a total cost of $19 million. But Coolidge's administration recognized that something had to be done and at the beginning of 1924 Reynolds's successor, the able and aggressive Rear Admiral Frederick C. Billard, was given enough money to re-equip the service along the lines that Reynolds had suggested.

Between 1924 and 1926 the coastguard's manpower jumped from just under 6,000 to just over 10,000. Twenty destroyers capable of speeds of up to thirty knots an hour were transferred from the US Navy to the coastguard's fleet. An emergency ship-building programme was initiated to provide Billard with more than 200 seagoing patrol boats designed to 'picket' the ships on Rum Row, and another one hundred fast inshore patrol boats, stripped down for speed and fast enough to intercept the 'contact boats' of the gangsters. Reconnaissance aircraft were deployed for the first time: five lumbering biplanes, each with a range of four hundred miles.

Under Frederick Billard the US coastguard saw the biggest and most rapid expansion in the service's history. Also, thanks to the so-called Liquor Convention of 1924, it had greater freedom to operate. The convention, to which Britain was a signatory, gave the US authorities the power to stop, search and seize any ships that were within 'an hour's steaming distance' of the American coast. Which meant that any British rum-runner doing business with a contact boat capable of doing thirty knots an hour could be seized if she was up to thirty miles out to sea. The British and Canadian governments did not particularly like this arrangement, but they put up with it after heavy diplomatic pressure from the Americans.

Of course, the bootleggers were well aware of Billard's updated armoury and responded by acquiring a new generation of purpose-built fast boats, some of them armour-plated, and many of them were powered by war-surplus aircraft engines capable of delivering speeds of up to forty and fifty knots. And so the war intensified. Between 1925 and the end of Prohibition in 1933 the US coastguard hunted British ships all round the coast of America and on into the Caribbean. Dozens of steamers, schooners and yachts sailing under the British flag were boarded and sometimes impounded to be sold at auction. Others were driven onto rocks or sunk at sea. Casualty figures are hard to find but it is certain that dozens of people – perhaps even hundreds – died in the war between the liquor pirates and the US authorities.

Among the British ships impounded in 1925 alone were the *Maplefield*, the *Peschawa*, the *Agnes Louise*, the *Panama*, the *Fannie E. Prescott*, the *Aesop*, the *Ocean Maid*, the *Hazel E. Herman*, the *Frances* and the *Louise*. Some were innocent ships going about their legal business. Most were blatant liquor smugglers. A few became causes célèbres in the British and American press. In 1925 the captain of the British steamer *Pennland* was searched and roughed up when he docked quite innocently in New York. In 1927 the US coastguard attacked and shelled the British collier *Tad Jones*, which they suspected of smuggling liquor. The British ship *Isle of June* was forced into harbour in Miami and the captain arrested and charged with smuggling. He committed suicide in jail.

One of the nastiest incidents was the shelling of the British-owned schooner *Eastwood*, a renowned rum-runner. Before she was attacked the *Eastwood* had been loitering off the coast of New England and New York for some months, wholesaling liquor to a steady stream of contact boats and making the occasional foray into Nassau and Havana to restock her hold with whisky, rum and wine. She was well outside American territorial waters.

Tired of seeing the *Eastwood* flouting American law, Eugene Blake, the skipper of the US coastguard cutter *Seneca*, steamed close to the *Eastwood*, set out his ranging target alongside the schooner and proceeded to 'practise' his gunnery. The *Eastwood* was hit by no fewer than seventy shells and heavy-machine-gun bullets. One shell went straight through the crowded crew quarters without hitting anyone. Another crashed into the engine room. The schooner's rigging and spars were shot to pieces. It was a miracle that no one was killed. The *Eastwood* was forced to abandon business and limp to Newfoundland for extensive repairs.

There were howls of outrage and official 'marine complaints' from the captain and crew of the *Eastwood* and from British shipping interests. The ship might have been up to no good but she was in international waters. The gung-ho Eugene Blake (who is still one of the US coastguard's heroes) had no right to harass the *Eastwood*, let alone open fire on her. Protests flew between the Foreign Office in London and the State Department in Washington.

But the State Department was in no mood to listen to British complaints. In June 1926 it issued an official statement denying that the *Seneca* had deliberately fired at the *Eastwood*. They also claimed that the British ship had been hanging about the coast of the USA for more than a year 'with the obvious intention of landing liquor in the United States'. The US government was therefore 'unable to consider as credible testimony given by such flagrant violators of our laws as the crews of such vessels'.

The *Eastwood* affair generated a good deal of high-level aggravation. The British Foreign Secretary Austen Chamberlain circulated a paper to the British Cabinet saying that the ship's history as a booze pirate was 'not germane to the issue' and that the US coastguard's heavy-handed tactics 'were precisely the sort of reckless conduct which in this matter makes so much difficulty for both governments'. It was, Chamberlain warned, a threat to the future of the Liquor Convention of 1924. One Foreign Office official wrote to Chamberlain with an analysis of the American position: 'provided a ship is a recognized and hardened smuggler, nothing is too bad for her.' This was vividly confirmed three years later by the sinking of the British schooner *I'm Alone*.

The sinking of the *I'm Alone* was the kind of incident which, in other circumstances, might have started a war. On 22 March 1929 the US coastguard cutter *Dexter* overhauled the British schooner about 200 miles out in the Gulf of Mexico and ordered her to heave to. The schooner's skipper Jack Bardell – a veteran of the Boer War – refused on the grounds that the American cutter 'had no jurisdiction' over a ship flying the British flag on the high seas. At which point the *Dexter* opened fire with her four-pound cannon and heavy machine guns, riddling the schooner from stem to stern and holing her below the waterline.

'She went down with the British flag flying,' the schooner's skipper wrote later. She also went down like a stone, leaving Bardell and his eight-man crew of Newfoundlanders, Canadians and French colonials thrashing about in the water without lifebelts. The bo'sun, from the French island of Saint Pierre, drowned. The rest were hauled aboard the *Dexter*, clapped in irons and shipped to New Orleans where they were thrown into jail. There they remained until the United States succumbed to pressure from the British, French and Canadian governments and released them. Irate diplomatic notes flew between governments. An international commission eventually ruled that the US coastguard skipper had acted wrongly and ordered $100,000 dollars in compensation to be shared between the schooner's owners and crew and the proprietors of the cargo.

One of the most determined of the blockade-busters was a Scotsman called Joseph Hobbs who had been an agent for the Distillers Company Ltd in Canada. When Prohibition arrived Hobbs bought a steamship called *Littlehorn* and began running whisky (mainly Teacher's Highland Cream) through the Panama Canal to the coast of California, where it was shuttled ashore by Pacific Coast bootleggers into Los Angeles, San Francisco and San Diego. Hobbs moved hundreds of thousands of cases of Teacher's whisky into the USA and made himself a fortune in the process.

By 1931 Hobbs reckoned that Prohibition's days were numbered and that a 'legitimate' boom was coming. He struck a deal with National Distillers of America and on their behalf returned to Scotland. Through the Glasgow firm of Train & McIntyre, he bought seven distilleries all over Scotland: Bruichladdich, Glenury Royal, Glenesk, Fettercairn, Glenlochy, Benromach and Strathdee. Hobbs and his American backers ran the distilleries for more than twenty years until 1954, when most of them were sold on to the Distillers Company Ltd.

Another enterprising Scot who kept the criminal gangs of America supplied with decent Scotch was James ('Jimmy') Barclay, who became director of a string of whisky houses such as James and George Stodart Ltd, T. & A. McLelland Ltd and the famous

Aberdeen firm of Chivas Brothers, makers of the now famous upmarket blend Chivas Regal. In fact, Chivas Brothers were so heavily involved in Rum Row that they took to prepacking much of their product in buoyant waterproof containers that could be dropped overboard for collection by the contact boats.

By the end of the 1920s it was plain that running Scotch into the USA via the Rum Row route had become too risky and unprofitable. The violence was increasing, the 'go-through' men were attacking the Rum Row ships more and more frequently, and the US coastguard patrols were becoming ever more difficult to avoid. The smuggling of Scotch into the USA was therefore switched landward, across the long and largely unguarded border between the USA and Canada. Imports of Scotch into the Bahamas and St Pierre and Miquelon dwindled as imports into Canada shot up by millions of gallons. The city of Detroit near the Canadian border became the USA's new liquor gateway.

Prohibition agents admitted later that there was almost nothing they could have done to stop this Niagara of whisky from flooding into the northern states. Every kind of craft was used to shift whisky across the narrow waters between Windsor, Ontario and Detroit, Michigan. Boats, rafts, submarine and semi-submersible containers were all used to fox the Americans. Naturally, the US government protested to the Canadians, only to be told to put their own house in order. In May 1929 William Euler, Canada's Minister of National Revenue, told the Canadian House of Commons that twelve boats were regularly plying between Canada and Buffalo, New York with loads of 1,000 cases at a time. But no effort was being made by the American Customs men to stop the traffic. 'If the officers on the American side wished to stop this business they could do it,' Euler said firmly. The US Customs men were in the pocket of the bootleggers.

One of the most effective conduits for Scotch whisky from Canada into the USA was run by Samuel Bronfman. In 1928 Bronfman acquired the firm of Joseph Seagram & Sons and through it bought up a number of Scotch distillers – Milton, Glen Keith,

Keith Maltings, Keith Bonds and those seasoned rum-runners, Chivas Brothers of Aberdeen. The purchases gave Bronfman access to large quantities of high-grade Scotch of the kind favoured by the criminals. According to 'Lucky' Luciano, the enterprising Sam Bronfman was 'bootleggin' enough whisky across the Canadian border to double the size of Lake Erie'.

One way or another the combined efforts of men such as Joseph Hobbs, Francis Berry, Bill McCoy, 'Waxey' Gordon, 'Lucky' Luciano and Samuel Bronfman kept alive America's taste for Scotch whisky. That was to prove decisive in the years that followed the abolition of Prohibition in 1933, when Americans scrambled to set up exclusive agencies for the better-known brands of Scotch.

Some of the commercial arrangements were direct. The gangsters Frank Costello and 'Dandy Phil' Kastel, for example, bought the controlling interest in J. G. Turney & Sons, the holding company that controlled William Whitely of Leith, makers of the whiskies known as King's Ransom and House of Lords. These were favourite tipples among the mobsters – heavy, smoky whiskies that could be profitably diluted so that one bottle of King's Ransom could make four or five bottles of the stuff sold in the speakeasies.

The whisky distillers and blenders of Scotland liked to keep quiet about their war on Prohibition, but it was no secret. When the Labour MP Tom Johnston (later to be Secretary of State for Scotland) waxed indignant in the House of Commons about the iniquities of the Bahamas-based liquor-runners, he was reminded that almost all the whisky handled in the Bahamas was shipped out from the Clyde, and that the whisky makers, bottlers, transport firms and dock workers of Scotland were doing very well out of the trade into the USA.

For Scotland, it was too important a business to lose. In 1931 the whisky magnate Sir Alexander Walker of John Walker & Co was asked by a Royal Commission if the distillers and blenders of Scotland would ever stop running their product into the USA. His reply was terse: 'Certainly not!'

No Irish Need Apply

IF EVER THERE WAS A SYMBOL of the Church Militant it is the one that stands outside the building that used to be the Barony Church in Glasgow (now owned by the University of Strathclyde). It is a red sandstone cross, maybe ten or twelve feet high, but in the place of a Christ figure there is a large, fierce-looking sword, a claymore perhaps, rather like the ones that are carved on Victorian statues of William Wallace.

Inside the building there is a 'chapel' dedicated to the Reverend John White, who ministered to the Barony's congregation in the first three decades of the twentieth century. A brass plaque on the wall is dedicated *To the Glory of God and in Memory of John White*. The last time I visited the building a little crowd of final-year students was hanging about, waiting to sit their examinations. Some of them had been studying Scots history. None of them had heard of the Reverend John White, or knew anything of the role he had played in trying to 'cleanse' Scotland of its large and growing population of Irish Catholics. And yet for much of the 1920s and well into the 1930s the Reverend White and his colleagues tramped around

Scotland warning people of the 'menace' posed to the country by Irish immigrants and demanding that they be 'repatriated' to Ireland. It was a dark and extraordinary episode in the history of the Church of Scotland and has not been forgotten by many older Catholics.

The key document is a report published by the Church of Scotland in 1923 entitled *Irish Immigration and the Education (Scotland) Act, 1918.* 'Already there is bitter feeling among the Scottish working classes against the Irish intruders,' the report declares. 'As the latter increase and the Scottish people realize the seriousness of the menace to their own racial supremacy in their native land, this bitterness will develop into a race antagonism which will have disastrous consequences for Scotland . . . Even now the Irish population exercise a profound influence on the direction and development of our Scottish civilization. Their gift of speech, their aptitude for public life, their restless ambition to rule have given them a prominent place in political, county, municipal and parochial elections . . . An Irishman never hesitates to seek relief from charity organizations and local authorities.'

The Kirk's report concludes that God himself had 'placed the people of this world in families and history, which is the narrative of His providence, tells us that when kingdoms are divided against themselves they cannot stand. The nations that are homogeneous in faith and ideals, that have maintained the unity of race, have been ever the most prosperous, and to them the Almighty has committed the highest tasks, and has granted the largest measure of success in achieving them.'

Some of these sentiments would have been familiar to the architects of South African apartheid and German National Socialism; others bear a close resemblance to elements of Enoch Powell's 'river of blood' speech in 1968. What is truly extraordinary about them today is that they were not the ramblings of a few moorland bigots or Orange extremists. The paper came from the heart of Scotland's ecclesiastical establishment. It was signed by forty leading churchmen of the day including the Moderator of the Church of Scotland. No fewer than twenty-nine of the signatories were Kirk ministers, four of them professors and eight of them doctors of divinity. Of the eleven laymen who endorsed it, two were MPs (James Brown and John Macleod), four were lawyers, and two were peers of the realm (Lord Salvesen and Lord Sands).

The *Irish Immigration* report was the starting point for a sixteen-year-long campaign against Scotland's population of Irish-descended Roman Catholics. They were a people who, the Kirk warned, 'cannot be assimilated and absorbed into the Scottish race'. It exacerbated decades of bad feeling between working-class Scots of different denominations with an agenda that was nothing if not ambitious: to stop immigration from Ireland; to 'repatriate' Irish paupers, cripples, lunatics and convicts; to scrap the Education Act of 1918 which set up state-funded Roman Catholic schools; to reserve jobs in Scotland for members of the 'Scottish race'. Everything was to be done to 'secure to future generations the traditions, ideals and Faith of a great people, unspoiled and inviolate'.

Just why the Church of Scotland found itself in such a reactionary lather over Irish Roman Catholics between the two World Wars is a matter of some debate. Stewart Brown, Professor of Church History at New College in Edinburgh (and an American) believes that the explanation has many strands. According to Professor Brown, 'Some of it was traditional anti-Catholicism, which had been part of Scottish thinking since the Reformation. Some of it was a reaction to the Irish immigration into Scotland in the late nineteenth century. Some of it was fear. The Roman Church was in better shape than it had been for centuries. Protestants everywhere were worried by the hard-line, Rome-centred Catholicism that came out of the First Vatican Council in 1870.'

The Irish historian Owen Dudley Edwards, who has written extensively on nineteenth-century Scotland, argues that to some extent the Irish had themselves to blame. 'Most just *refused* to assimilate into Scottish society,' he told me. 'And they were ruthless when it came to looking out for their own interests. Their Irish priests did everything they could to cut them off from the wider society, to protect their flock from being contaminated by Scots Presbyterianism.'

There was also a political dimension to the argument. The middle-class and largely conservative (and Conservative) men who ran the Kirk were alarmed by the 1922 General Election that returned twenty-nine Labour MPs from Scotland, some of them Roman Catholics. The Reverend William Main (convener of the committee that produced the *Irish Immigration* report) was in no doubt that these new Labour MPs would bring 'scandal and disgrace into the House of Commons'. Some 'commissioners' (that is, delegates) to the 1923 General Assembly questioned the legitimacy of the 1922 election. One Glasgow elder claimed that the west of Scotland was 'so permeated by foreign nationalities' that the results did not reflect 'the opinion of the Scottish people'.

Professor Brown, however, believes that it was the First World War – in which more than 110,000 Scots were killed – that shaped the psyche of the post-war Kirk. 'The Scots had suffered disproportionately in that war,' Brown told me, 'particularly the clergy families. Many of them saw the Easter Rising in Dublin of 1916 as a stab in the back, and that was made worse by the Roman Catholic church's campaign against conscription in 1918. And there had also been a bit of violence in Glasgow, a spillover from the Irish troubles.'

Two Kirk ministers became the leading lights of the anti-Irish campaign: the Reverend Doctor John White of the Barony, and the Reverend Duncan Cameron, minister to a congregation in the town of Kilsyth, a few miles to the north of Glasgow. Cameron drew loud applause when he warned the General Assembly in 1923 that native Scots were being usurped in their own land 'by a people alien to them in faith, and alien also in blood'.

The General Assembly accepted the *Irish Immigration* report and set up a special sub-committee of the influential Church and Nation Committee to fight the anti-Irish cause. Cameron, meanwhile, carried his crusade into the Scottish Protestant Congress which was held in Edinburgh later the same year, where he spoke on 'The Menace to Protestantism in Scotland' and wrote a lengthy article for the congress's handbook which argued that unless Irish immigration was curtailed or reversed 'the Scottish race, as the world knew it only to admire and honour it, must pass away.'

Of the two men, White was by far the more important, in the view of his hagiographer Augustus Muir 'the greatest ecclesiastical statesman of his time in Scotland' and 'a philosopher in action' whose favourite text (from Isaiah) was 'For Zion's sake I will not hold my peace' (*John White, C.H., D.D, L.L.D*, Hodder and Stoughton, 1958). White was also one of the few men to have twice been elected to the post of Moderator of the Church of Scotland (in 1925 and 1929).

Nobody could doubt White's pugnacity or his patriotism. At the outset of the war with Germany he startled his congregation by asking God to 'damn the Kaiser'. As a chaplain to the Cameronians (the most self-consciously Presbyterian of Scottish regiments) he was physically brave to the point of recklessness and much admired by the troops for the time he spent among them in the trenches of the Western Front. Both of his sons also served in France and one was killed with the Royal Flying Corps (his death is commemorated in stained glass in the Barony Church).

After the war White became the dominant figure in the Church of Scotland. To him, the Kirk *was* Scotland. 'It is the chief symbol of Scottish nationality,' he preached. 'It has been the chief factor in moulding the national character. It is the oldest institution in the land. It is rooted in the history, in the life, in the very soil of Scotland.' In White's view anything that threatened the Kirk threatened Scotland itself. It was a kind of ecclesiastical nationalism – and an echo of that old longing for a Scottish theocracy (modelled on Calvin's Geneva) that is now almost never heard.

White found a staunch ally in Duncan Cameron. Like White, Cameron had been much affected by the war. After the hostilities Cameron wrote two books – *The Muster Roll of the Manse* and *The Kirk's Roll of Honour* – which are simply lists of the sons of the manse who had been killed in the Allied cause. They are simple but genuinely moving documents that demonstrate the carnage that the war wreaked among the clergy families of Scotland.

The sons of parish ministers were expected to set an example to their communities by enlisting. Because these young men were better educated than most, they became junior officers. The attrition rate among junior officers was especially high. As a result there was hardly a manse in Scotland that did not lose a son. The minister of Bellahouston Church in Glasgow, for example, lost all four of his sons between 1916 and 1918. William Paterson, the Professor of Divinity at New College in Edinburgh, had three sons at the front, two of whom never returned. Paterson was one of the signatories of the *Irish Immigration* report.

In the year following the General Assembly's acceptance of the report very little happened. Nor was much done during the term of the short-lived Labour government of 1924–5; White and his colleagues knew that they could expect little from the Socialists. But when the Tory party returned to power the badgering began and in November 1926 a joint committee, which included representation from the United Free Church and the Free Church, met the Secretary of State for Scotland, John Gilmour. When Gilmour argued that the government did not like to meddle in religious matters, White assured him that the issue was not religious but 'racial' and that the Kirk's concern was for the 'unity and homogeneity of the Scottish people'. Gilmour was polite, but non-committal. He promised to look into the matter.

By then, the Kirk had found a new argument. The USA had recently cut back on its immigration 'quotas' from Britain and the Irish Free State so the Catholic Irish were 'bound' to flood into Scotland in even greater numbers. Meanwhile much of the reduced

British quota would be taken up by ambitious young Scots. To the Kirk, the possibility of this Irish-for-Scots exchange was baleful. The USA would 'receive with open arms a virile and competent people while Scotland must be content with the redundant population of Ireland which the United States refuses to receive'.

Duncan Cameron went on the stump across Scotland. The Irish were 'a menace more insidious by far, more formidable too, than the menace of the German Empire and its multitudinous legions', he told a public meeting in Paisley in 1926. John White was hardly less strident. Great nations were created by 'race and soil', he wrote. His intention was to prevent the Scottish race from being 'corrupted by the introduction of a horde of immigrants'. In May 1927 the Kirk's Church and Nation Committee reiterated the anti-Irish line when it reported that the Kirk had 'an obligation to defend Scottish nationality' especially when 'our race and culture are faced with a peril which, though silent and unostentatious, is the gravest with which the Scottish people have ever been confronted.'

As John White and his allies also had support from within the Scottish end of the Tory party, the government saw that it would have to take them seriously. In July 1928 a meeting was arranged in London between White's joint committee and the Home Secretary, Sir William Joynson-Hicks, and the Scottish Secretary, Sir John Gilmour. To the dismay of the churchmen, His Majesty's Ministers were cool. The Irish Free State, they pointed out, was a Dominion of the British Empire. Immigration from the Dominions into the 'mother country' could not be restricted. His Majesty's Government had been doing its own sums and they did not square with the Kirk's. The Kirk claimed that the Irish were entering Scotland at the rate of 9,000 a year; the government said that the true figure was between 1,000 and 3,000. Not only that, but the percentage of Irish-born people on the welfare rolls had declined from 11.9 per cent in 1907 to 7.6 per cent in 1927. And, according to the Ministry of Labour, of the 3,844 men employed on public works in Scotland in 1927 only 282 (or 7.3 per cent) had been born in the Irish Free State. In short, the Irish were not the horde of spongers that the Presbyterian establishment believed or claimed them to be. In effect, the Kirk's case was in tatters. A few days after the meeting the Cabinet decided that there was 'insufficient evidence' to promote the legislation the Kirk was demanding.

In March 1929 the Kirk suffered another blow when the *Glasgow Herald* ran a series of five articles on 'The Irish in Scotland', in which an enterprising reporter slogged his way through primary sources such as the steamship companies' records to find that Irish immigration into Scotland was at a trickle, and that many Irish people (like many Scots) were in the process of abandoning Scotland for the USA, Canada and Australia. The newspaper decided that the demand for immigration curbs on the Irish could 'no longer be effectively pressed'. A few months later, in July 1929, the Reverend Duncan Cameron died.

John White was not the man to abandon a war because of battles lost or allies silenced. In 1929 he was appointed the first Moderator of the newly united Church of Scotland and United Free Church (a union that he himself had done much to construct), and quickly made it plain that the 'Irish problem' remained high on his agenda. 'Rome now menaces Scotland as at no other time since the Reformation,' he announced in Dumbarton in January 1930. A few days later he warned that Rome was 'patiently working to secure a grip on every department of the nation's life. We cannot remain inactive when this attack is being made.'

White found another zealous ally in the Reverend J. Hutchison Cockburn of Dunblane Cathedral. Cockburn was the convener of the Church and Nation Committee and possibly even more anti-Irish than White. In May 1930 he led yet another delegation to the Scottish Office to press William Adamson, the new (Labour) Secretary of State for Scotland, to do something about the Irish. Adamson (a pious Baptist) declined.

Hutchison Cockburn's credibility took a serious knock after he wrote to Adamson complaining that the Irish foremen working on the huge public-works project at Peterhead Harbour were hiring only Irish labour. This seemed a clear abuse. But when Scottish Office officials investigated they discovered that not only were there no Irish foremen on the job but that out of the 370 men employed only two were Irish, and that one of those had lived with his Scottish wife in Peterhead for more than ten years.

But the Kirk refused to give up. In 1931, with the British government holding the line and refusing to take any measures against the Irish, the General Assembly instructed the Church and Nation Committee to 'encourage' Scotland's employers not to give jobs to Irishmen (or women). They were to be reserved for 'those of the Scottish race'. Most employers in Scotland ignored the Kirk's call but some did not. Notices declaring that 'No Irish Need Apply' became fairly common, adding to local and unofficial prejudices that already kept Catholics out of many skilled jobs in shipyards, engineering works and factories. According to the historian Tom Gallagher, the publishing, printing and retail trades were notoriously reluctant to hire them. Even today, Catholics are still said to be relatively few in the banking and finance sectors.

Once again, White found his allies in Parliament. The Kirk's grievance was voiced during the debate on the King's speech in November 1932. Once again, the racism was overt. The Scots, according to Lord Scone, were being usurped by a 'completely separate race of alien origin, practically homogenous, whose presence there is bitterly resented'. In the same debate Sir Robert Horne (a former Chancellor of the Exchequer, the MP for Glasgow Hillhead and a university classmate of John White) warned of the hazard of allowing the Irish to hold the balance of power so that 'Scottish Home Rule turned out to be a form of very insidious Irish domination in our politics.' Horne's 1932 speech was an early airing of a notion that has never gone away: 'Home Rule means Rome Rule,' a slogan that still plays among working-class Protestants, particularly in the west of Scotland.

In 1931 the campaign took a new twist. The anti-Irish crusade was handed over to a newly formed body called the Church Interests Committee (CIC) convened by William Curtis, Professor of Biblical Criticism at New College. One of the CIC's first ploys was to urge the Kirk to join the International League for the Defence and Furtherance of Protestantism (ILDFP), a Nazi-dominated anti-Catholic movement recently formed in Berlin.

The ILDFP was a creature of the 'German Christian' movement ruled over by the Hitlerite *Reichsbischof* Ludwig Muller. The ILDFP's journal *Protestantische Rundschau* (*Protestant Review*) reported approvingly in 1933 that the Church of Scotland had come to recognize that the *Judenfrage* in Germany had parallels to Scotland's *Irischen Frage*.

By the mid-1930s many members of the Kirk were beginning to fret over their connections with the German Christian movement, though at the General Assembly in May 1935 Professor William Paterson could still argue that Hitler's regime had done Europe a great service by checking 'the militant atheism associated with continental Communism'.

The Scottish campaign against the Catholic Irish sputtered on. Brownshirt tactics erupted on the streets of Edinburgh in 1935 with the rise of Councillor John Cormack's Protestant Action movement. Catholic meetings were disrupted, Catholic priests attacked and Catholics forced to keep all-night vigils to prevent their churches and chapel houses being vandalized and/or burned down. When, on 25 June 1935, a Roman Catholic 'eucharistic congress' was held in the grounds of Saint Andrew's priory in Morningside, Edinburgh, an estimated 10,000 demonstrators turned out to harry the participants and throw stones at their buses. The streets of Morningside, the epitome of respectable Edinburgh, had to be cleared by police baton charges. The Kirk's warnings of 'race war' between the Scots and the immigrant Irish seemed about to be fulfilled.

As the 1930s wore on, however, the alarmists began to lose the argument. Even to John White and his colleagues it was becoming plain that the Nazi version of Christianity was subservient to a wicked regime. There were forces darker than labouring gangs from Ulster and Connaught stalking Europe. In 1939, on the eve of the Second World War, the Kirk quietly abandoned its long campaign against Irish Catholics. The hunt, at last, was over. During and after the Second World War the Kirk went into reverse and on most social issues (housing, health, home rule etc.) moved somewhere to the left of the Labour Party it had once feared.

The ghosts of the 1920s and 1930s have never been wholly exorcized. Many older Scots Catholics still smart at the memory of John White and Duncan Cameron and their tirades against the 'inferior race'. The Kirk's campaign also had a powerful political effect that still resonates. It gave Roman Catholics good reason to suspect Scottish nationalism while, paradoxically, it lodged in the Protestant mind the suspicion that 'Home Rule Means Rome Rule'.

There was a cultural impact, too. The stridency of the Kirk's campaign had the effect of discrediting Presbyterianism in the eyes of the Scottish intelligentsia. As Professor Stewart Brown points out, when those stalwarts of the Scottish Renaissance of the 1920s and 1930s – Hugh MacDiarmid, Lewis Grassic Gibbon and Neil Gunn – were struggling to recreate a modern Scottish identity they 'tended to seek a revival of Scottish community based on a Celtic or Jacobite past, rather than look back to Presbyterian and Covenanting traditions'.

Which is something of an irony. The racist anti-Irish rantings of White and his followers may have helped to make a modern hero out of Charles Edward Stuart – Bonnie Prince Charlie – a man whose Roman Catholic and Anglo-Catholic enthusiasms they would have loathed and despised, while at the same time they helped to eclipse the huge intellectual and social achievements of their hero, John Knox.

Well into the 1950s John Cormack and his Protestant Action supporters regaled the people of Edinburgh with dire warnings about the Great Satan that was Rome. Usually this was done on Sunday afternoons at the foot of the Mound (then Edinburgh's equivalent of Speakers' Corner at London's Hyde Park). Once or twice I stood in the crowd and listened to the speaker's predictions that idle, unwashed, superstitious hordes were about to take over Scotland. I never could square that image with the handful of Roman Catholic families who lived in our part of working-class Edinburgh. They always seemed rather more hard-working and respectable than the rest of us.

THE GORDONSTOUN
ROUND-UP

GORDONSTOUN SCHOOL IS known for its healthy rigour and its appeal to the British and European aristocracy, including the House of Windsor. The Duke of Edinburgh is one of Gordonstoun's old boys and began a family tradition. His sons, the princes Charles, Andrew and Edward, were all sent there. The most recent royal attendee is the princes' niece, Zara Phillips, daughter of Princess Anne.

Its virtues were not always above suspicion, however. At the outbreak of the Second World War, Gordonstoun was surrounded by rumour and hostile gossip. Its founder and headmaster, Kurt Hahn, was believed to be an intimate of Hitler. Many local people thought that Gordonstoun had been deliberately set up on the coast of the Moray Firth near the new RAF bases at Kinloss and Lossiemouth for sinister reasons. They told one another that the boys were being taught seamanship and navigation the better to guide in the German submarines that would drop off German agents who would subvert Britain's war effort.

When I met him a few years ago, Gordon Columbus, who lives

near the school in the village of Burghead, remembered the paranoia well. 'It was all nonsense, of course, but a lot of people around here really believed it. Some folk were convinced that the laddies at Gordonstoun had been signalling from the cliffs to German U-boats. And that the German invasion – when it came – would land on the sands at Burghead Bay. They took it seriously.'

Kurt Hahn, a German Jew, founded the school in 1934. It was his second school. The first, at Salem in Germany, was forced to close when Hahn fell foul of the Nazi regime in 1933 (the year Hitler came to power) and he was imprisoned. On his release, he and a handful of masters and a few dozen pupils set up a similar school at Gordonstoun. At the end of 1938, Hahn became a British citizen.

The police were well aware of local misgivings about Gordonstoun. As early as September 1939, the chief constable of the Moray and Nairn Constabulary was reporting to Sir Vernon Kell, head of MI5 in London, that there were thirty-five 'enemy aliens' in and around Gordonstoun and that there was 'a strong feeling against so many Germans being in this area, and no doubt this will be intensified as a result of the war operations, and in my opinion, it would be in the interests of many of these people if they were in some safe custody'.

In fact, the Germans at Gordonstoun were refugees from the Nazis almost to a man and woman. The British government, however, was in no mood to give anyone the benefit of the doubt. Rounding up 'enemy' aliens was high on the agenda. In May 1940 the police and MI5 swooped on Kurt Hahn's establishment and took away the German and Austrian staff and eleven boys. They then went on to collar the Germans among Gordonstoun's old boys. Some were teaching at English public schools, others studying at British universities. Most were sent to the large internment camp on the Isle of Man to join others of German, Austrian and Italian citizenship or ancestry.

There were a number of anti-Hitler zealots among the Gordonstoun internees. One of them, Erich Meissner, was described by Hahn as 'the greatest living menace to Hitler's propaganda, a master of satire, invective and argument'. Meissner's wicked lampoons of Hitler had almost cost him his life. Another detainee, Bernard Zimmerman, specialized in 'the character training of adolescents' and had devised early versions of Gordonstoun's 'outward bound' courses together with Lord Malcolm Douglas-Hamilton. A third, Werner Steiner, was a talented physicist who, in Hahn's view, should have been engaged by the British government 'in national work'.

At the same time as the British government was rounding up Hahn's staff, Hahn himself was writing long papers for Churchill on the psychology of Adolf Hitler. Hahn suggested that His Majesty's Government would do well to try to drive a wedge between Hitler and the German people. 'Even today nothing stands in the way of peace but Hitler and his henchmen,' Hahn wrote. 'He loves his power more than his country.'

After the Gordonstoun round-up Hahn moved his school to Montgomeryshire in Wales from where he bombarded the British government with letters pleading for the release of the German and Austrian masters and boys who had been dumped in internment camps. His campaign was, eventually, successful. Gradually, one by one the Gordonstoun internees were released and seemed to bear little or no hard feelings.

OPERATION VEGETARIAN

ONE OF THE MANY SURPRISES on the coastline of Wester
Ross is Gruinard Bay, which lies halfway between the tourist trap of
Gairloch and the fishing village and ferry terminal of Ullapool
among some of the finest scenery in the Western Highlands. The
east side of the bay is particularly fetching: two or three miles of
clean white sand beside a roadway lined with stands of Scots pine
between which wild goats often graze. Behind the trees, rock faces
rise sheer for hundreds of feet and between them are glimpses of
the jagged peak of Ben Dearg Mhor (the Big Red Hill). When the
sun is out, particularly in the late afternoon, the effect is stunning –
the essence of unspoiled natural beauty.

Just a few hundred yards off the beach is a bleak, treeless little
island that measures about one mile long and half a mile wide and
is completely unexceptional in its similarity to hundreds of other
such outcrops of rock and heather that litter the sea-indented west
coast. However, this island, Gruinard Island, has a sinister
reputation. It is known in Scotland as 'Anthrax Island'.

For almost fifty years, noticeboards placed around it warned

Scientists on Gruinard Island, 1986

civilians to keep off. During that time, too, strangely suited figures could be seen once every few years wandering across the grass and heather, taking samples from the soil.

To a large extent, Gruinard Island deserved its dark reputation. It played a central part in the British government's experiments with germ warfare and was heavily contaminated with *Bacillus anthracis*, anthrax, that ancient bacterium which plagues most mammals and particularly goats, cattle and sheep. Anthrax is an old enemy; it might have been what Moses used to wipe out the cattle herds of the Egyptians as part of his campaign to persuade the Pharaoh to let Moses' people go. (Exodus 9:15 may be history's first recorded instance of biological warfare, although Moses did have God on his side.)

Gruinard Island's association with *Bacillus anthracis* began in the early years of the Second World War when scientists from Porton (now Porton Down) in Wiltshire decided to use the little island as a test bed for their experiments. Presumably they calculated that an island a few hundred yards from the Scottish mainland fufilled their notions of safety in remoteness. It is certainly a long way from Wiltshire. Anthrax may not be as deadly as the nerve gases (Sarin, for example) with which the folk from Porton also experimented, but it is nevertheless an extremely unpleasant killer.

Depending on how the bacillus finds it way into its host (through the skin, through the lungs, or through the mouth) it can also kill quite quickly. If it enters via a lesion on the skin then itchy bumps develop into black-centred necrotic ulcers, lymph glands swell, and death occurs within a few days. If it is inhaled, the symptoms may resemble a common cold until breathing becomes impossible and the victim goes into shock and then dies. If the bacillus finds its way into the digestive tract, nausea is followed by fever, abdominal pain, severe vomiting, diarrhoea and then death in sixty per cent of cases.

Humans are in less danger from anthrax than they used to be. If it is detected in time a stiff dose of antibiotics will (usually) see off the bacillus. A programme of penicillin is the favoured antidote but tetracycline or erythromycin will also do the trick. For reasons that are not clearly understood, anthrax finds it relatively difficult to spread among humans. Animals, however, are another matter. Once *B. anthracis* takes a grip on a herd of cattle or a flock of sheep its spread can be rapid, unstoppable and devastating.

When the anthrax experiments on Gruinard first became public knowledge after the war the official explanation was that they were all about defence. According to the British government, the reason that anthrax spores cultivated in the south of England had been shipped up to – and spread over – a small part of Wester Ross was so that Britain could learn how to cope with the bacterium if the Germans ever deployed it as a weapon. That, however, was only part of the truth. The other reason was rather different and came to light only in the 1990s when papers emerged from the Public Record Office in London. They documented an extraordinary wartime venture that was code-named 'Operation Vegetarian' and was the brainchild of the War Cabinet's sub-committee on bacteriological warfare, chaired by Lord Hankey.

'Operation Vegetarian' was simple enough in essence. The plan was to inject millions of small 'cattle cakes' with the anthrax bacterium and then drop them from bombers over the large beef and dairy herds that grazed the North German Plain. The animals would eat the cattle cake and then begin to die. German farmers would need to kill and burn (or bury) the infected beasts. Germany's dwindling food supply would be dealt a savage blow. And if the anthrax leapt into the human population, that would be Hitler's problem.

The man in charge of 'Operation Vegetarian' was Doctor Paul Fildes, director of Porton's biology department and formerly the man in charge of the Medical Research Council's bacterial chemistry unit at the Institute of Pathology at the Middlesex Hospital. Within a very short time he had bumped up Porton's biology department's scientific staff from twelve to fifty, among whom were a sprinkling of Americans and Canadians, and by the beginning of 1942 he was scouring Britain for suppliers and manufacturers. Most of his letters to potential contractors made the point that 'all possible secrecy is to be maintained'.

A number of practical difficulties needed to be overcome. First, Fildes needed to source linseed-oil cattle feed sufficient to make five million small cakes. Then a firm had to be found with the technology to make the individual cakes. Then equipment had to be designed to inject the anthrax spores into each of the five million cakes, not forgetting that sufficient quantities of the bacillus itself had to be produced. Then special containers to carry the cattle cakes had to be designed and made. Finally, some of the RAF's bombers had to be modified appropriately. And it all had to be done as cheaply as possible.

Fildes quickly found the supplier he needed for the cakes' raw material. Step forward the Olympia Oil & Cake Company, one of

Unilever's subsidiaries in Blackburn. But what company had the technology to turn this mass into so many million little cakes? The biscuit makers Huntly & Palmer were approached, but did not seem too keen. Then the famous confectionery firm of James Pascall Ltd (of Mitcham, Surrey) took up the challenge. In February 1942, Pascall's Mr S. E. Perkins wrote to Fildes saying that 'on looking through some of our old samples I found that I had a few shapes of mint lozenges which, I think, will indicate what can be done by means of a compressing machine . . . These sweets were made concave so as to give a lesser weight of material.'

Having satisfied himself that concave, lozenge-shaped cattle cakes would do the business, S. E. Perkins made a stab at the labour costs. He estimated that it would require 'the labour of 17 girls to produce 1 ton in a 9-hour day. Over a five-day week, 5 tons per week.'

This was enterprising of S. E. Perkins, but in the end Pascall's sweets did not get the job, which went instead to Messrs J. & E. Atkinson of 24 Old Bond Street, London W1, perfumers and toilet-soap manufacturers, suppliers of soaps and unguents to the royal family. Atkinson's calculated that they could produce 180,000 to 250,000 cakes in a forty-four-hour week. Each of the cakes would be one inch in diameter and would weigh ten grammes. The price would be fifteen shillings per thousand, reducing as the contract grew to twelve shillings and sixpence per thousand. Messrs Atkinson promised that they could deliver the necessary 5,273,400 cakes by April 1943 – if Fildes could arrange that their workers were exempted from military service during this period. This Fildes duly did. By the middle of July 1942 Atkinson's were pleased to inform Fildes that: 'We are now producing at the rate of 40,000 per day.'

Fildes then tackled the problem of getting enough anthrax bacilli to inject into 5,273,400 cakes, and of finding the means to inject it. The anthrax itself was brewed up by the Ministry of Agriculture and Food at its veterinary laboratory in Weybridge in Surrey. An Oxford academic named Dr E. Schuster was charged with the task of devising an injection pump.

Then there were the boxes to carry the infected feedstuff. The Porton scientists settled on seven-inch cuboid cardboard boxes, each box to weigh eight pounds, three ounces when filled with its 400 cakes and all boxes to be unmarked. They would be sealed with a two-inch wide strip of specially manufactured adhesive tape fitted with a steel handle 'of a size which enables the operator to grasp it without difficulty when wearing thick leather or moleskin gloves'. The boxes were made by Crescens Robinson & Co of Newington Causeway, London, who quoted a price of sixpence each for the first 12,500 containers.

Thirteen women were then recruited from several soap-making firms, shipped down to Porton, sworn to secrecy, and tasked with the job of injecting the cattle cakes with anthrax spores. Three of them were from Atkinson's, but two came from John Knight & Co ('Knight's Castille' was their famous brand), and eight from a company called Christopher Thomas of the Broadplains Soapworks in Bristol. The women (most of them young) were supervised by Miss F. I. Hazell.

At the same time, Fildes and his team were working with the Royal Air Force on the best way of delivering the spiked cattle feed to the German herds. The RAF's aircraft research unit decided that the cakes could be launched from wooden trays that fitted onto the aircrafts' 'flare chutes', the small hatches in the fuselage through which flares could be dropped or fired. The aircraft chosen for the job were Lancasters, Halifaxes and Stirlings from Bomber Command.

The RAF was not overjoyed at the prospect. Expensively trained aircrew were in short enough supply without any of them keeling over with the deadly symptoms of *B. anthracis*. A memo from the RAF to Fildes in October 1942 stated: 'The air staff want to know whether there is any danger if the bun boxes get spilt in the aircraft and crew crush them with their flying boots or handle crushed buns.'

Fildes was able to assure the RAF that 'trials have shown that a member of an aircrew fully clad in thick leather clothing would have no difficulty in carrying out the sequence of operations.' But he went on to say that 'damaged and/or unused boxes, together with any loose tablets should be collected (gloves to be worn when picking up and handling loose tablets) and burnt in an incinerator. Aircrews should be warned accordingly.'

By the beginning of 1944 'Operation Vegetarian' was almost ready to go. In February of that year Fildes laid out the strategy in a long memorandum to his senior colleagues in Porton's biological department. 'The object of this contemplated operation is to infect and kill the largest number of cattle possible in enemy territory in a single effort by means of small, infected cattle cake dropped from the air.' Seasonal timing was crucial. 'The cattle must be caught in the open grazing fields when lush spring grass is on the wane' – which meant, Fildes said, from June to September. 'Trials have shown that these tablets, when dispersed over pasturage in the small concentration of two per acre, are found and consumed by the cattle in a very short time.'

Fildes and his team had worked out that there were at least thirty-five beasts per square mile on the North German Plain. 'Cattle are concentrated in the northern half of Oldenburg and north-west Hanover,' he wrote. 'Aircraft flying to and from Berlin will fly over sixty miles of grazing land.' This meant, according to his calculation, that a bomber would traverse the area in eighteen minutes. 'If one box of tablets is dispersed every two minutes then each aircraft will be required to carry and disperse nine, or say ten, boxes.'

In other words, a Lancaster returning from a raid on Berlin would be able to scatter 4,000 anthrax cakes as a nice little extra on the way home. A dozen Lancasters could drop 48,000 cakes, a hundred Lancasters 400,000 cakes: the prospects for Germany's cattle population looked bleak (to say nothing of the consequences for humans further up the food chain or for the fresh-water supply).

But by the time Fildes's operation was ready to go in the summer of 1944 the Normandy landings had taken place and Allied armies were crashing through northern France. It was becoming clear that the war against Nazi Germany could and would be won by 'conventional' means. At the end of the year 'Operation Vegetarian' was stood down and in 1945 the five million anthrax-infected cattle cakes were incinerated in one of Porton's high-temperature furnaces.

Gruinard Island, where the tests had been carried out, lay under its burden of anthrax-infested soil for another forty-odd years, viewed from the shore as a place of mystery and dread. When a boat laden with day trippers lost power and drifted onto the island in the late 1970s, the Chemical Defence Establishment (as Porton Down was then called) took pains to reassure them that they were in no real danger, despite what the noticeboards said. The same reassurances were given to an Austrian tourist who was stranded on the island in 1982.

There was a very different reaction from Porton Down in 1981, however, when a group of radical environmentalists calling themselves 'Dark Harvest' claimed to have removed 300 pounds of soil from Gruinard Island and deposited it at the gates of Porton Down and at Blackpool Tower during the Conservative Party's annual conference in the town. Considerable efforts were made by the police to track down the culprits, but they all failed.

Then in 1986 and 1987 squads of scientists and workers from the Chemical Defence Establishment descended on Gruinard Island's three poisoned acres and began to decontaminate them with a mixture of sea water and formaldehyde. By the summer of 1987 the Chemical Defence Establishment announced that Gruinard Island had been given a clean bill of health and was now safe for all comers. In 1990 the island was returned to its original owners, the Gruinard Estate.

THE MIDGE WARS

IN RECENT YEARS, BIOLOGICAL and chemical warfare has had a bad press. Even the prospect of it has been enough to invite invasion and occupation. However, there is one chemical warfare experiment that everyone in Scotland wanted to succeed, the one that the British government carried out against that terror of the Highlands, *Culicoides impunctatus*, the biting midge. In 1944, when Britain was still grappling with Hitler and Hirohito, the Secretary of State for Scotland set up a Midge Control Unit (MCU), which was run from Edinburgh University. The MCU's campaign was coordinated by Doctor Douglas Kettle, one of the world's authorities on midges.

It seems unlikely that with Fascism still unconquered the government should turn its attention to this miniature enemy. But the depredations of *C. impunctatus* have long worried British governments. Battle-hardened commandos and agents of the Special Operations Executive who trained in the Highlands were often forced to give up because of the ferocity of the midges. Scotland, the government concluded, would be a better, more efficient place if some way could be found to defeat the Highland midge.

Kettle and the MCU came up with a two-pronged attack: first find an effective chemical repellent; second, strike at the midges' home base in an attempt to reduce their countless numbers. Much of the anti-midge campaign was based around the village of Achnashellach in Wester Ross, which can lay fair claim to be the midge capital of Europe (although this is disputed by the riverside campsite at Sligachan on Skye).

Kettle and the MCU discovered that the anti-mosquito creams developed for British troops fighting in the jungles of Burma and Malaya were reasonably effective repellents. Their base was a chemical known as dimethyl phthalate (DMP) or the slightly stronger diethyl toluamide (DEET). But they were powerful brews and had to be deployed with care. In industry, DMP and DEET are used to soften and then melt hard plastics.

Unfortunately, the chemical weapon that had proved so effective against the mosquitoes of South-East Asia was of little use against the Highland midge. Although midges were no more immune to the chemicals than were mosquitoes, they proved almost impossible to hit. They could either avoid the droplets or take shelter under vegetation. Even if a patch of ground was cleared of *C. impunctatus*, it would be occupied by a neighbouring swarm within days. The insects are so lightweight that they can drift for miles on the slightest breeze.

The only long-term solution, it seemed, was to remove the midges' habitat. That meant draining the ground of water, an impossible task in the sodden peat desert that forms a large part of the landscape of the western Highlands. The MCU were in the process of discovering what everyone north of the Highland line knew – the midges were unconquerable. Against the hordes of *C. impunctatus* there is no real defence. Their size and numbers make them impossible to swat. They are almost impossible to spray. Their habitat is impossible to drain. After a few years His Majesty's Government retired, baffled and utterly defeated.

And by females, too: it is the female of the species that does the damage. She needs mammal blood to nourish her eggs. *C. impunctatus* does not actually bite, she sucks blood through a proboscis. In the process she injects her victim with an anti-coagulant enzyme. It is the body's reaction to that enzyme that raises the itching lumps. No one is immune to midge attacks, but in some people the reaction can be devastating. Fortunately that is rare, otherwise much of Scotland would be uninhabitable.

Midges are an ancient plague. James Boswell and Samuel Johnson railed about midges on their famous tour of the Hebrides in the 1760s. Midges 'devoured' one of Queen Victoria's picnic parties in Sutherland in 1872. There is a Highland legend that an Irish Christian missionary was tied naked to a stake on an island in Loch Maree where he was 'bitten' to death by them. Some years ago there was concern that midges might carry the AIDS virus in the way that mosquitoes carry malaria, but after some hasty research the insect was given a clean bill of health, so to speak.

THE STONE

WHEN TOURISTS VISITING Edinburgh Castle make their
way past a painted (and to my mind rather naff) version of Scottish
history to the room that holds Scotland's crown jewels, they are
usually surprised by what they find. Lying in the same glass case as
the truly beautiful sixteenth-century regalia of crown, orb, sceptre
and sword of state is a lump of cracked, crudely dressed sandstone
with an iron ring at either end. The block is twenty-six inches long,
sixteen inches wide and ten inches deep, and weighs around 336
pounds. It is, of course, the piece of masonry variously known as the
Stone of Scone, the Coronation Stone, or the Stone of Destiny.

Although it has the look of an artefact that has been at the heart
of the castle for centuries, the Stone is a newcomer to Edinburgh.
It has been a resident only since the end of 1996, after Michael
Forsyth, the Tory Secretary of State for Scotland, decided that there
were political points to be scored by returning the Stone to Scotland
after its 700-year-long stay in England. What Forsyth does not seem
to have known (or, if he did, he failed to mention it) was that he was
simply carrying out the policy of one of his Labour predecessors

who had wanted to return the Stone to Scotland forty-five years before.

The Stone of Scone may be the most famous block of rock in Europe. If we are to believe the legend, it was on this piece of Perthshire sandstone that the Kings of Scots sat to be crowned. Until, that is, it was whisked from under their backsides in 1296 by Edward I of England as part of his campaign to reduce Scotland to the status of an English shire. Edward then had the Stone slotted under the English throne as a symbol of the English crown's sovereignty over Scotland.

Which was where it stayed until Christmas 1950, when four Glasgow University students decided to 'liberate' it from the clutches of the English and smuggled it out of Westminster Abbey. The act outraged the British establishment. The Church of England described the theft – ludicrously – as 'blasphemy'. They could not have been more outraged if the lump of sandstone had been a fragment of the Holy Cross. *The Times* thundered about the 'sacrilege at Westminster'. The newspaper's correspondence columns fulminated about 'rude fanaticism', an 'outrage on Church and King', and 'perverted Scottish nationalists'. King George VI was reported to be unamused, indeed 'very distressed'.

Scotland, however, was much amused. Most of the Scottish press (with the exception of the *Glasgow Herald*) were behind the robbers. So were most of the public. The Scottish National Party pleaded for silver to be melted down to make medals for the Stone-snatching heroes. And although the Scottish police had a very good idea from an early stage who the culprits were they did not press the investigation too hard (to the dismay of their colleagues who'd been sent from London).

In the end, the Glasgow students did not know what to do with the Stone. On 11 April 1951 they deposited it in the ruins of Arbroath Abbey and tipped off the local police. Superintendent James Mackenzie of the Angus Constabulary found it lying in a wheelbarrow and draped in a Saltire flag. According to Mackenzie's report (which is written in classic police-speak) the stone 'answered the description of that reported stolen from Westminster Abbey and circulated in the *Police Gazette* of 27 December 1950, Case No. 24'. After an overnight stop in the cells at Forfar police office, the Stone was shipped straight back to Westminster Abbey.

Students with the Stone of Scone, 1953

No sooner was the Stone back in London than Alan Don, the (Scots-born) Dean of Westminster Abbey, was demanding its return to its old home. The Cabinet was not so sure that it should be sent back there, at least not right away. The Westminster dean was angry at the delay, and also angry (together with others in the Anglican hierarchy) that Hartley Shawcross, the Attorney-General, had recommended that the four Glasgow students should not be prosecuted. Any prosecution, he told the Cabinet, would be 'unwise'.

Larceny and/or sacrilege would be hard to prove, he said, and a prosecution would make either heroes or martyrs of the students.

'I am aware that the Archbishop and the Dean have expressed strong views which one can understand,' Shawcross told his colleagues. 'But my impression is that public opinion in England is bored with the whole matter, and there is certainly no enthusiasm for a prosecution. In Scotland a prosecution would produce a very adverse reaction.' The Cabinet agreed.

Meanwhile Hector McNeil, the Secretary of State for Scotland, was penning his own Cabinet memo. As McNeil saw it there were three options: (1) to return the Stone to its place in Westminster Abbey; (2) to put it on show in various Commonwealth capitals as a symbol of British unity; (3) to return it to Scotland. The third option, he thought, was by far the best.

McNeil recommended the ancient St Margaret's Chapel in Edinburgh Castle as the Stone's new resting place. The little church was, McNeil said, 'probably the oldest ecclesiastical building in Scotland and is in the heart of a castle which is generally regarded as Scottish rather than local . . . the castle already houses the Scottish regalia: and the Coronation Stone could, like the regalia, be made the responsibility of the Great Officers of State'.

McNeil went on to suggest that the transfer should be made in June 1951, when King George VI would be in Edinburgh. 'The return of the Stone to Scotland would, I am sure, be regarded by moderate opinion in Scotland as a generous gesture.'

At the same time the Lord Chancellor (Viscount Jowitt) had been rooting in the archives to decide exactly to whom the Stone belonged. He reported back on 30 April 1951 that the Stone did not belong either to the Church of England or to the Dean and Chapter of Westminster Abbey but to King George VI himself. The King had inherited it from his thirteenth-century predecessor Edward I, who became owner 'by right of capture'. As there was no evidence that the English kings had ever given it up, 'effluxion of time will not alter the nature of the King's title.'

The Cabinet agreed to all this, at least in principle. But when they met on 7 May 1951 to consider the future of the Stone they decided to postpone the transfer to Edinburgh 'for at least a year'. To send it north before then, they decided, 'would be widely regarded as a concession to the recent act of vandalism at Westminster Abbey'. Political pranksters must not be seen to be rewarded. The Church of England had been outraged enough.

Postponement was a fatal decision. The Labour Government was ejected from power in the General Election of October 1951. Winston Churchill and the Tories were back. They had hardly warmed their Cabinet seats when Alan Don, the Dean of Westminster Abbey, was pressing his case again in Number 10 and demanding the return of the Stone 'without delay'. Interestingly, Churchill hesitated. But then King George VI died on 6 February 1952 and a coronation was in the offing. The Stone was needed for its official duties.

In a joint Cabinet memo the Lord Chancellor (Lord Simonds of Sparshot) and the Secretary of State for Scotland (James Stuart) told their colleagues that 'nothing is to be gained by postponing the decision about the disposal of the Stone. On the contrary, we should avoid having any controversy about the Stone at or about the time of the Coronation.' The Cabinet agreed. Clement Attlee, now leader of the Opposition, was duly consulted and made no objection. On 11 February 1953, Churchill was briefed by the Cabinet to 'advise' the new Queen that the Stone would be returned to Westminster Abbey in time for her coronation in June that same year.

Two weeks later Churchill informed the House of Commons that the Stone was to be restored to its spot under the throne of Edward the Confessor where it had lain for more than 650 years. And where it had acquired 'a historic significance for all the countries in the Commonwealth. With the approval of Her Majesty's Government the Stone has been returned to its traditional place.'

And there it remained for another forty-three years, until Michael

Forsyth persuaded his Cabinet colleagues to return the Stone to Scotland as a sop to Scottish sentiment. In the summer of 1996, the Stone of Destiny was trundled up the A1, crossing the border at Coldstream, where it was met with some ceremony by Michael Forsyth who was sporting a kilt. On 30 November 1996 (St Andrew's Day), the Stone was installed with maximum pomp in Edinburgh Castle.

I have often relished the irony of the affair of the Stone. Michael Forsyth, the most Tory of Scotland's Tory secretaries of state, had successfully carried out a policy mooted by one of his Labour predecessors. Not that it did him any good. The Scots were their usual ungrateful selves. In May 1997, six months after the Stone was given its exalted place in the castle, Michael Forsyth lost his seat – along with every other Tory MP in Scotland.

AN A-BOMB ON GLASGOW

GEORGE SQUARE IS THE centre of Glasgow. It is flanked to the east by the municipal grandeur of the City Chambers, to the south by the building that was once the General Post Office and is now a block of expensive flats, to the north by Queen Street Station and its renovated railway hotel, and to the west by the kind of exuberant nineteenth-century office building that distinguishes Glasgow from Edinburgh. The square itself has flower beds, saplings, Victorian statues, and an eighty-foot column to the memory of Sir Walter Scott. It is a genuine civic space, used for concerts, art exhibitions, political rallies, and demonstrations. Edinburgh has nothing quite like it. At Christmas it is transformed by Scotland's finest array of fairy lights, decorations and religious statuary. A December evening sees it filled with small children gaping up at the electric glitter the council has laid on for them. It is an amiable place.

I can never cross George Square without recalling a buff-coloured folder I came across by accident in the Public Record Office in Kew. Official documents are sometimes misleadingly described by journalists as 'chilling' when 'mildly worrying' would be more accurate. But this one was a chiller, without a doubt. Commissioned by the Scottish Office in Edinburgh from the scientists of the Home Office in London, it was an official estimate of what would happen to Glasgow if someone (the Soviets, presumably) detonated an atomic bomb over George Square. It had the feeling of worried people trying to come to terms with a real possibility.

There was, I suppose, a lot to worry about in the years of its authorship, 1951 to 1952. The Soviet Union had developed its own atomic weapons. The Chinese People's Army had flooded into North Korea to pursue the war against American-led UN forces that included British troops. The United States was in the grip of what can only be described as paranoia. Two minor Soviet agents – Julius and Ethel Rosenberg – had been condemned to death in 1951 for passing on atomic secrets to the Soviet Union and were later (1953) executed. Atomic devices were regularly tested in the Nevada desert. In May 1951, the Americans tested, in the Pacific, the first hydrogen bomb. It was a triumph of nuclear physics that the Soviets and then the British were to repeat. The 'atomic age' had arrived in earnest.

It was against that background that His Majesty's Government decided to investigate what would happen if a Hiroshima-type atomic device was exploded over the centre of Glasgow. Their calculations are contained in a document marked 'secret' and wordily entitled *Assessment of the Damage and the Numbers of Casualties and Homeless Likely to Result from an Attack on Glasgow with an Atomic Bomb*. The research was carried out between 1951 and 1952 under the direction of E. C. Allen M.Sc. of the Home Office Scientific Adviser's Branch. The Scottish Home Department and the Department of Health for Scotland (both branches of the Scottish Office) had commissioned it, and the result was approved by the government's Working Party on the Effects of Air Attack. When the document was printed and circulated in January 1953, it carried with it the warning that 'the official in possession of the document will be responsible for its safe custody and when not in use it is to be kept under lock and key.'

It is easy to see why the document was kept secret. It vindicates to a large extent the arguments of CND activists (and the left wing of the Labour Party) a decade or so later. The Home Office research showed that Glasgow was peculiarly vulnerable to nuclear attack. The nature of the buildings and the streets, and the density of the population served to heighten the risks. If the Soviets ever struck against Scotland's biggest city, the casualties would be enormous, certainly beyond the capacity of Scotland to cope.

The Glasgow of fifty years ago is now hard to imagine. The heart of the 'Second City of the Empire' (as Glasgow liked to call itself) was not then given over to consumption – shopping, eating, drinking – but to production. An extraordinary amount of industry –

Demonstrators on Sauchiehall Street, Glasgow, 1959

some of it heavy – flourished in and around the city centre. Within a couple of miles of George Square, Glaswegians manufactured cigarettes, railway engines, carpets, shirts, rubber goods, textile machinery, furniture, marine engines and, of course, ships. In city-centre factories they made semolina, milk jellies, caramel desserts, custard and a dazzling variety of sweets. They baked bread and biscuits. They wrote and printed books, magazines and newspapers. A huge workforce of men and women worked in or near the centre of Glasgow, and most of them lived in three- or four-storey tenements, almost all of them stone-built, some of them decrepit. Inner-city districts such as the Gorbals, Springburn and Cowcaddens teemed with people. The huge peripheral housing estates and new towns into which so many Glaswegians were decanted in the 1960s had yet to be built. The great home-ownership drive that saw so many folk find their way into the suburbs had still to happen.

In the early 1950s Glasgow was probably the most densely populated urban centre in Britain, if not in Europe. This fact was recognized by Mr Allen and the Home Office scientists. They calculated that Glasgow's population (in 1951) numbered 1.1 million, packed into 40,000 acres. 'More than 80% of the population lived within three miles of the city centre at a density of 49 persons per acre.' It was over this heavily peopled conurbation that the Home Office scientists exploded their theoretical nuclear bomb.

What Allen and his colleagues postulated was an explosion at 2,000 feet above ground zero by a 'nominal' nuclear device with the equivalent destructive power of 20,000 tons of TNT (roughly the size of the atomic bomb that destroyed most of Hiroshima in August 1945). Two separate scenarios were explored: one in which the bomb was dropped on Glasgow during the day, the other in which the attack occurred at night. The Home Office men calculated that 932,900 people would be within 2.5 to three miles of ground zero during the day, dropping to 854,200 at night. A daytime explosion during the working week was therefore considered to be the greater of the two evils. Glasgow would be about its business. The factories, shops, warehouses, offices, schools, tramcars and streets would be crowded with people. The Home Office team put the number of daytime casualties at 79,700 dead and 25,900 seriously injured, whereas a night-time bombing would yield 59,700 dead and 19,300 seriously injured. In neither case were there any estimates of the numbers of people expected to be moderately or lightly injured. Nor were there any calculations of the medium-term or long-term effects of radiation.

Mr Allen made it plain that these figures were the best that could be expected, the results of a 'straightforward' nuclear explosion. They took no account of what the casualties might have been if the nuclear bomb on Glasgow had ignited the kind of firestorms that had devastated Hamburg in 1944 or Dresden in 1945, where the intense heat had generated enormous tornado-like winds inside the fire. Once a firestorm starts to rage nothing can be done until it runs out of fuel and exhausts itself, and according to the Home Office report the city of Glasgow was just the kind of place where firestorms would spring up. Glasgow tenements had common roof spaces 'allowing fire to spread readily along the block'; the tenements were 'well provided with windows and because the streets are uniformly wide' secondary fires could be expected 'because of the exceptionally large number of open fires in each tenement block'. The report suggests that 'a ring of fires, one mile wide, would be formed beyond a radius of some 3,000 feet from ground zero and that these might possibly link up into one huge conflagration'. If such a firestorm took a grip, then the number of dead would escalate: 75,000 killed in a night attack, 96,000 killed in a daytime attack.

Blast damage to property was also assessed. Up to 3,000 feet from ground zero the effect on stone-built tenements would be 'complete collapse'. At 4,000 feet there would be seventy-five per cent collapse. At 5,000 feet twenty-five per cent collapse. At 1.25 miles all pitched roofs would be destroyed. At 1.5 miles the roof damage would make the building uninhabitable. Beyond two miles the damage would be 'superficial'.

Anyone trapped in the rubble of a collapsed Glasgow tenement had little hope of rescue. Lying under two storeys of London or Birmingham brick is one thing. Lying under four or five storeys of Scottish sandstone is something else entirely. This report took this into account and pointed out that the sheer weight of the debris would mean that 'only a small proportion of the trapped and injured were likely to be saved.' The Glasgow tenement's only – and literally – saving grace was that its thick stone walls offered greater protection against gamma radiation.

The report conceded that official thinking about the consequences of nuclear attack until then had been distinctly Anglocentric. 'Previous studies of atomic attack on British cities made by the Working Party have been based on the assumption that the bulk of the people live in small terraced or semi-detached brick houses. This assumption clearly could not be applied to either Glasgow or Edinburgh.' Glasgow was extraordinarily vulnerable, with special problems. The report concluded: 'These special problems result mainly from the density of population in Glasgow which is greater than that of any British city, but also because much of the population is housed in very large blocks of tenements, some of which are 100 or more years old.'

In other words, no city in Britain would have suffered more grievously than Glasgow in the event of a nuclear attack. So, with these facts and figures at their fingertips, what did the British government do? Ten years later it gave Holy Loch to the US navy as a forward base for its nuclear-armed and nuclear-powered submarines. Soon after it made two more of the Clyde's sea lochs – Loch Long and the Gare loch – into the base for the Royal Navy's new nuclear submarine fleet. Both bases were prime targets for the Soviet Union's nuclear missiles and bombs. Both lay (and in the Royal Navy's case still lie) fewer than thirty miles from George Square and the heart of Glasgow.

AS OTHERS SEE US

'I AM FOR HAVING IN OUR army as many Scottish soldiers as possible: not that I think them more brave than those of any other country we can recruit from, but because they are generally more hardy and less mutinous.' – Lord Barrington, Secretary-at-War, 1751

'Norway too, has noble wild prospects; and Lapland is remarkable for prodigious noble wild prospects. But, Sir, Let me tell you, the noblest prospect which a Scotchman ever sees, is the high road that leads him to England.' – Samuel Johnson, 1763

'Into our places, states and beds they creep;/They've sense to get what we want sense to keep.' – Charles Churchill, 1763

'No Scot ever exerted himself but for a Scot.' – John Wilkes, 1762

'It requires a surgical operation to get a joke well into a Scotch understanding.' – Sydney Smith, 1855

'That garret of the earth, the knuckle-end of England, that land of Calvin, oat-cakes and sulphur.' – Sydney Smith, 1855

'No McTavish/Was ever lavish.' – Ogden Nash, 1931

'It is never difficult to distinguish between a Scotsman with a grievance and a ray of sunshine.' – P. G. Wodehouse, 1935

'Sour, stingy, depressing beggars who parade around in schoolgirls' skirts with nothing on underneath. Their fumbled attempt at speaking the English language has been a source of amusement for five centuries, and their idiot music has been dreaded by those not blessed with deafness for at least as long.' – P. J. O'Rourke, 1976

'One often yearns/For the land of Burns/ The only snag is/The haggis.' – Lils Emslie, 1983

EDINBURGH'S NARROW ESCAPE

ONE OF THE QUESTIONS THAT I am occasionally asked by visitors and newcomers to Edinburgh is why such a stately, well-preserved and overwhelmingly middle-class city is run by the Labour Party. Why do such archetypical 'leafy suburbs' as Colinton, the Grange and Inverleith hardly ever produce a Tory MP? Why is it that even Conservative grandees and erstwhile Cabinet ministers such as Malcolm Rifkind and Michael Ancram get dumped by the citizenry in favour of none-too-impressive Labour Party apparatchiks? Just what happened to prise loose the iron grip that the old Conservative and Unionist Party once had on political power in the Scottish capital?

They are not easy questions to answer. Usually I shrug and point out that Edinburgh is not Bath or Cheltenham and that it is much less middle-class than it at first appears. That the city is ringed by big housing estates – which are Labour strongholds as they are elsewhere in Britain. But even as I offer the explanation I am aware that it is not very satisfactory. It fails to address what might be called the 'Morningside Question': why have the city's resolutely middle-class New Town and expensive suburbs turned their backs on the Tories?

In my view at least part of the answer lies in the bowels of the City Chambers, that neo-classical edifice in the High Street that began life as a commercial 'exchange' at the end of the eighteenth century. Four floors under street level lies the Edinburgh City Archive, a priceless (and lamentably underfunded) repository of Scottish history. Stored in the archive and its suburban outliers are a series of cardboard boxes stuffed with council minutes, technical reports, press cuttings and campaigning leaflets. They trace the history of a 1960s project that turned bourgeois Edinburgh against the party that had run the city for decades.

'That bloody ring road' was how Brian Meek, the city's longest-serving Tory councillor, described the plan to me. 'That was the watershed in Edinburgh politics. The argument over that road ran for years and years and did us no good at all. We were seen as being behind a project that the whole of Edinburgh absolutely hated.' It was hardly surprising, Mr Meek said, that Labour had taken over in the early 1970s and had been there ever since.

I was aware of the great controversy but knew little of it. I was living in London while it raged. Leafing my way through the documents in the Edinburgh City Archive, I was surprised to find that the story began a long way from Edinburgh – in the Austrian city of Salzburg, where in September 1962 a convocation of European town planners from forty cities met to mull over ideas for handling their growing road-traffic problems.

Two of the attendees were from Edinburgh: the City Engineer, Fred Dinnis and the City Planner, Tom Hewitson. The two returned to Edinburgh convinced (in the words of *The Surveyor and Municipal Engineer*) that 'while each city has its own particular problems, the basic principle of constructing an inner ring road around the central area was generally accepted as being sound.' By 1963 Dinnis and Hewitson had thrashed out their plan for coping with Edinburgh's fast-growing road traffic.

The scheme that Dinnis and Hewitson came up with was brutal but simple. They wanted to build a six-lane highway in a loop –

roughly two miles in diameter – around the centre of Edinburgh. The plan was to drive a tunnel through the west end of the Calton Hill to come out at a large intersection at the top of Leith Walk. From there the road would cut a swathe north, down through the tenements and terraces of the Broughton district to Canonmills, where it would turn west and run along the Water of Leith (Edinburgh's only sizeable river) to the suburb of Comely Bank, just south of Fettes College.

From Comely Bank the highway would have turned south again to tunnel under the Queensferry Road and the grounds of Donaldson's Hospital and crash through the Haymarket district to another large intersection at Tollcross. From Tollcross the highway would climb up on stilts and cut through the centre of the handsome parkland known as the Meadows to yet another mammoth intersection at Saint Leonard's. Then it would have gone north again, tunnelling under the ridge of the medieval High Street, over a bridge across the railway at Waverley Station and then back under the Calton Hill.

At every one of the main intersections a tangle of 'feeder' roads would be built. Existing streets would be widened to feed traffic into the new highway. The cost would be £107 million – about £2 billion in today's money – and would take at least ten years to complete.

Even without the benefit of hindsight it was clear that the inner ring road was a monstrous project. It would have transformed the centre and the inner suburbs of Edinburgh. Some of the world's finest Georgian architecture would have been demolished or forced to live in the shadow of a concrete motorway. Tunnels would have cut through some of the city's hills with potentially disastrous effects on the buildings above. Hundreds – maybe thousands – of mature trees would have been felled to make way for the new highway, its feeder roads and attendant car parks. It was 1960s planning at its most brutal.

The planners, Fred Dinnis and Tom Hewitson, were not alone in their enthusiasm for the ring road, however. They had a formidable political ally in Councillor John Miller, the chairman of the city's planning committee. 'Big John' Miller, as he was usually known, was a builder, developer and enthusiastic 'modernizer', close to the archetype of the 1960s businessman-politician. He was a former president of the Edinburgh branch of the Master Builders' Association, a 'name' at Lloyd's of London, and a leading light in the Scottish branch of the Institute of Directors.

Dinnis and Miller hatched their plan in the climate of municipal secrecy that was normal at the time. It was not a cynical exercise. There was no suggestion of graft or gain from lucrative contracts. They were true believers. In a series of *in camera* meetings politicians and officials were told that unless the ring road was built Edinburgh would choke to death on traffic. Clogged roads, endless delays, shortage of parking – these would discourage motorists from entering Edinburgh and they would spend their money elsewhere. The city's shops, hotels, restaurants and pubs would suffer. Business would flee. Gradually Edinburgh would decline into a handsome museum piece stripped of industry, commerce and enterprise. In the early 1960s those were telling arguments. Edinburgh was not so prosperous then. The city's traditional industries (usually characterized as 'books, beer and biscuits') were in sharp decline. John Miller had little trouble drumming up support for the ring road among the Progressive councillors (and later claimed that many members of the Labour opposition were covert supporters of the scheme).

Dinnis and Miller did their best to keep the lid on their plans, knowing that they needed to put as much gloss as possible on the project before it was presented to the public. But Edinburgh is a small city, secrets are difficult to keep, and by the spring of 1963 rumours about a massive road-building project began to circulate among Edinburgh's well-connected middle class. In May 1963 a local architect, Ian Samuel, wrote to the *Scotsman* – in those days the equivalent of Edinburgh's social noticeboard – denouncing the rumoured project as a potential 'disaster' for the city. It was the start of a long and frequently bitter campaign led by a consortium of academics, lawyers, architects, financiers and art dealers; it was, in Scotland, an unprecedented revolt against civic paternalism and the idea that the people's elected representatives and their officials always knew best.

By 1964 it became clear that the opposition to the scheme would be considerable, even though the scheme's details had yet to be officially announced. In May 1964 the architect Sir Robert Matthew (an Edinburgh man who was then president of the Royal Institute of British Architects) tried to head off calamity by suggesting that the council should wheel in Professor Colin Buchanan, then making his mark in the great traffic-in-cities debate. Matthew's advice was ignored. The city's Lord Provost, Duncan Weatherstone, made it plain that the political-commercial establishment regarded the ring road as the only solution to the traffic problem.

When the scheme in all its modern glory was finally made public in November 1965 the Edinburgh elites were aghast. The opposition was at its most vociferous in the north of the city where the plan was to drive the road through a beautiful neoclassical terrace called Warriston Crescent that had been designed by Augustus Pugin's friend James Gillespie Graham. A North Edinburgh Joint Committee was formed which boasted a formidable array of bourgeois talent: the playwright Robert Kemp, the advocate Kenny John Cameron (now Lord Cameron of Lochbroom), the architectural historian Colin McWilliam. The novelist Compton Mackenzie, who lived in Edinburgh's Georgian New Town, wrote a pamphlet against making provision for 'the plague of motor cars which is sweeping the world like the Black Death of the middle ages'. From London, the influential *Architects' Journal* joined the fray with an article entitled 'Edinburgh: Proposed inner ring road provokes outcry' in which the writer Edwin Johnston described the scheme as 'particularly devastating and utterly out of scale and character with the local environment'.

The *Architects' Journal* pointed out that 'an alarming number of listed buildings' were in the way of the line of the new road. Among them: Edinburgh Academy (1823–36) designed by William Burn; Donaldson's Hospital (1842–54) designed by William Playfair; East Claremont Street (1824–30) designed by Thomas Bonnar; Saxe-Coburg Place (1823) designed by James Milne and Adam Turnbull; St Luke's Church (1907) designed by McGregor Chalmers. The greatest loss would have been what Edwin Johnston described as 'two superb Georgian terraces' at Howard Place and Warriston Crescent (1809–20).

The *Scotsman*'s correspondence columns were dominated for months by letters about the ring road, most of them hostile. Eventually, on 1 December 1966, the newspaper insert came out in opposition with an editorial headed 'The Unwanted Road'. A few Tory councillors joined the swelling refrain. At the end of December Michael Clark Hutchinson, the Tory MP for Edinburgh South, described the plan as a 'piece of vandalism'.

John Miller's planning committee, however, held firm and announced that there were no plans to alter any part of the project. The road would go ahead. The planning committee regarded the City Engineer's scheme as viable, affordable and the best way forward.

A public inquiry (which would be held under the aegis of the Secretary of State for Scotland) was demanded and granted. It opened in Edinburgh on 14 January 1967, under the chairmanship of Mr W. A. Elliot QC. When John Miller stepped up to give his opening statement he was unequivocal. 'I am absolutely convinced,' he said, 'that everything that should have been done has been done. And that the . . . plan is in the best interests of everyone concerned in the capital city.' The City Engineer, Fred Dinnis, was equally robust. The ring road, he told the inquiry 'offers the only satisfactory solution to the needs of central Edinburgh'. Not only that, but it was '*the only way* [my italics] by which the New Town, the Old Town and the other unique properties of the city centre can be protected from complete subjugation to the motor car.'

This near-religious level of faith in his own scheme became less convincing when Dinnis was questioned about the probable effects on Edinburgh people of cars, buses and lorries thundering over their heads on elevated roadways. All he could offer was the idea that things were likely to get better in future – with, for example, the introduction of electric cars.

W. A. Elliot QC listened to forty-one days of evidence and then gave the ring road the thumbs-down. In his report to the Secretary of State, he was scathing. 'In the highest scale of human values,' Elliot wrote, 'the preservation of Edinburgh's environment is more important than the speed of a journey to work.' Ring roads were all very well in new towns such as Cumbernauld, he said, 'but the heart of a living city does not lend itself so readily to such treatment.'

He also pointed out that the project's cost of at least £107 million was three times what the government was prepared to spend on Edinburgh's road budget for the following twenty years. 'The allocation of public moneys on this scale involves policy decisions at a high level,' he wrote, 'and, in my view, cannot rest on decisions taken at local-authority level without a full cost/benefit analysis of other (and possibly) cheaper alternatives.'

As soon as they saw Elliot's report Dinnis and Miller knew that the game was up. There was no way that Willie Ross, then Secretary of State for Scotland, would overturn a report as damning as Elliot's. On 10 January 1968, almost a year after the inquiry opened, Ross announced that the inner ring road would not go ahead. The protesters and their mouthpiece, the *Scotsman*, were delighted. 'Edinburgh Preserved' was the headline over the paper's lead editorial on 11 January.

The ring road was down, but not quite out. Willie Ross did give his approval to what became known as the 'eastern link' or the 'Bridges relief' road – in effect half the east side of the ring road. The plan was to run a six-lane highway across the western flank of Arthur's Seat and the Queen's Park, into a tunnel under the High